DATA PROTECTION AND INFORMATION LIFECYCLE MANAGEMENT

DATA PROTECTION AND INFORMATION LIFECYCLE MANAGEMENT

TOM PETROCELLI

Prentice Hall Professional Technical Reference

Upper Saddle River, NJ • Boston • Indianapolis • San Francisco
New York • Toronto • Montreal • London • Munich • Paris • Madrid
Capetown • Sydney • Tokyo • Singapore • Mexico City

Many of the designations used by manufacturers and sellers to distinguish their products are claimed as trademarks. Where those designations appear in this book, and the publisher was aware of a trademark claim, the designations have been printed with initial capital letters or in all capitals.

The author and publisher have taken care in the preparation of this book, but make no expressed or implied warranty of any kind and assume no responsibility for errors or omissions. No liability is assumed for incidental or consequential damages in connection with or arising out of the use of the information or programs contained herein.

The publisher offers excellent discounts on this book when ordered in quantity for bulk purchases or special sales, which may include electronic versions and/or custom covers and content particular to your business, training goals, marketing focus, and branding interests. For more information, please contact:

U. S. Corporate and Government Sales
(800) 382-3419
corpsales@pearsontechgroup.com

For sales outside the U.S., please contact:

International Sales
International@pearsoned.com

Visit us on the Web: www.phptr.com

Library of Congress Cataloging-in-Publication Data
Petrocelli, Thomas D.
  Data protection and information lifecycle management / Thomas D. Petrocelli.
    p. cm.
  Includes bibliographical references and index.
  ISBN 0-13-192757-4 (pbk. : alk. paper)
  1. Computer security. 2. Data protection. I. Title.
  QA76.9.A25P53 2005
  005.8—dc22   2005018394

ISBN 0-13-192757-4
Text printed in the United States on recycled paper at Courier in Stoughton, Massachusetts.
First printing, September 2005

This book is dedicated to my parents, Tom and Doris.

*Their dedication to education is why I was able
to do this in the first place.*

CONTENTS

ACKNOWLEDGMENTS

Writing a book is not a solitary endeavor. I have had the support of many people throughout the creation of this book. They provided me with their knowledge, opinions, stories, encouragement, and patience. With so many people, I am afraid that I might forget someone. If I do, I'm sorry. You know who you are, and know that I'm thankful for all the assistance you have given me.

The people who deserve my deepest thanks are my family: Maria, my wife, and John and Laura, my children. They have put up with my highs and lows, my exuberance and my panics over the course of a year. Without their support, I never would have begun the book, let alone finished it.

I would like to thank Michael T. Carey at Bingham McCutchen LLP, Paul Stonchus at MidAmerica Bank, Gerhard Fielder of PdMain, and Brent Luckman of Transend Services for sharing their stories with me. The richness of their experiences lends a dimension to the book that could never have been there otherwise. Thanks are also in order to Rick Toomey and Mark Stoller of Quantum, Wayne Adams and Patrick Cooley of EMC, Gil Rapaport of XoSoft, and Peter Dixon and Barbara Nelson of NeoScale for taking a risk and helping me contact people who had interesting stories to tell.

I want to extend special thanks to Marc Farley for his encouragement early in the project. Because of Marc, I was able to go into the project with my eyes open. He has always been a great sounding board for ideas, as well as having written one of the best general references on storage networking technology.

Thanks to Mike Alvarado and Tao Xie. They allowed me to bounce ideas off them. They also provided some much-needed advice that helped get me over some tough parts of the book. Special thanks also go out to Tom Coughlin, Mark Ferrelli, Randy Kerns, and the outside reviewers, whose comments went beyond helpful and made me focus on what was truly important.

Last, but certainly not least, I would like to thank the team at Prentice Hall—especially Bernard Goodwin, Michelle Housley, and Lance Leventhal—for helping guide a new author through the traps and pitfalls of writing a book. Thanks for putting up with me this past year.

—Tom Petrocelli

ABOUT THE AUTHOR

Tom Petrocelli is president of Technology Alignment Partners, Inc., where he is also chief analyst. He is a veteran of more than twenty years in the computer technology marketplace and has worked in IT, marketing, product management, and business development. For the past eight years Tom has been involved in the data storage industry, where he has become an expert in data protection issues, especially data movement and security. He has written articles for major data storage industry magazines and is a frequent speaker at major industry conferences and events, such as Storage Networking World.

PREFACE

Data protection is like buying insurance or executing a will: It's something we all know we should do but often put off. We are forced to think about all the unpleasant scenarios that force us to do it in the first place. The process can be complex, even daunting to most people. We forge ahead because we know it's important. Ultimately, we sleep better knowing that we have a safe haven in the face of disaster.

New storage technology, such as storage networks, has allowed organizations to collect and store massive amounts of information about customers, suppliers, and operations. Along with this ballooning of stored data has come a new threat to the organization: loss of key information assets. IT managers now realize that these enormous storehouses of information are often left inadequately protected. At the same time, the ramifications of data loss are increasing. Shareholder lawsuits, government regulation, and extreme financial losses are driving changes in the way data is stored and managed.

The techniques, methods, and technology available to the IT professional have expanded greatly. In the past, backup to tape was pretty much all that was available. Disk-to-disk and disk-to-disk-to-tape systems have expanded the options for backup. Remote copy and replication have enabled organizations to constantly move data off-site, far from harm. As more storage systems are networked, storage security is becoming an important tool for protecting data from harm.

It's not only technology that now sits in the data protection bag of tricks. Strategic methodologies such as Data Lifecycle Management and Information Lifecycle Management add new dimensions to the data protection landscape. Both are policy-based processes for managing data and information according to a lifecycle. While data lifecycle management deals with data on a time-based cycle, information lifecycle management is used to manage information assets in an event-driven fashion. Both promise to allow for better data protection at a lower cost.

Data and information are now recognized as core assets that need to be valued and secured like other assets. This book is a guide to protecting data assets in the enterprise. It presents the technology, techniques, strategies, and best practices used to safeguard data. It may even help you sleep better at night.

WHO IS THIS BOOK FOR?

This book covers topics useful to many people. The primary audience is the IT professional, especially CIOs, managers, and system architects. System administrators, storage administrators, network administrators, database administrators, systems analysts, and business analysts who are involved in storing and protecting critical business data will also find this book to be a vital resource.

Product managers, consultants, technical marketing specialists, and technicians, as well as engineers at value-added resellers, OEMs, ISVs, and service providers, will also be interested in this book. It provides general knowledge about emerging areas of interest to their customers. Marketing communications specialists, PR agents, venture capitalists, analysts, editors, trainers, professors, and students will also find value in this book. It provides these professionals with a general overview of data protection technology and practice in plain language.

HOW THIS BOOK IS ARRANGED

This book takes a progressive approach to understanding data protection. Starting with the most basic topics, each chapter builds on the previous ones. Some chapters are overviews for those who are not well acquainted with important base technologies and practices. Others are more involved, presenting the major ideas, techniques, processes, and technology associated with data protection. Those chapters also end with a case study about real IT professionals and the techniques they have used to solve data protection problems. Finally, the book ends with several appendixes, a bibliography, and a glossary, all designed to enhance your understanding of other parts of the book.

The chapters of *Data Protection and Information Lifecycle Management* are:

Chapter 1: Introduction to Data Protection. This chapter lays the foundation for understanding data protection, introducing the major drivers and techniques behind data protection. It discusses the reasons that organizations spend time and money on data protection and presents a framework for understanding the ensuing topics.

Chapter 2: An Overview of Storage Technology. Chapter 2 provides the technological underpinnings of most data protection. Written for those who may not have a deep knowledge of storage technology, it contains something for everyone. The chapter discusses the basics of data storage necessary to understanding data protection. Furthermore, the chapter presents some of the new technology and practices that impact data protection strategies today.

Chapter 3: Backup and Restore. The classic data protection strategy just keeps getting better. Chapter 3 outlines the most common techniques, such as tape backup, as well as the more recent additions to the backup bag of tricks. The emphasis is on architecture and practices.

Chapter 4: Remote Copy and Replication: Moving Data to a Safe Location. Chapter 4 kicks it up a notch, exploring remote copy and replication—ways of constantly duplicating data in a network. With data synchronized constantly, hot sites can be used that provide immediate failover in case of disaster.

Chapter 5: Basic Security Concepts. This chapter provides the necessary underpinnings for the next chapter, which deals with storage security. It is a quick reference to basic computer security concepts and strategies.

Chapter 6: Storage System Security. Chapter 6 describes a new area of security: storage security. Until recently, the security of the storage system was ignored, since it was safe behind the server security screen. That's no longer true, and data protection demands a new focus on securing the storage infrastructure.

Chapter 7: Policy-Based Data Protection. This chapter outlines the emerging area of policy-driven data protection, especially Data Lifecycle Management (DLM). These techniques are some of the most powerful in the data protection toolbox.

Chapter 8: Information Lifecycle Management. This chapter explores how Information Lifecycle Management (ILM) can be used to enhance data protection. The book takes a detailed look at ILM and shows how it can be used to further information assurance and data protection.

Appendix A: XML Schemas and Document Type Definitions for Policy Statements. The XML schemas and DTDs for the policy examples in Chapters 7 and 8 are listed here, with some additional thoughts on how XML can be used to describe DLM and ILM policies.

Appendix B: Resources. This appendix lists other resources that are helpful to those entrusted with data protection plans: industry groups, conferences, books, and web sites. They provide additional insights into the technology and regulations that are important to data protection.

Appendix C: Acronyms. This appendix lists the acronyms used in the book. *Data Protection and Information Lifecycle Management* is chock full of acronyms. Acronyms are important shortcuts that save us from having to say the same thing over and over again, but they work only if you know what they are.

Glossary. The glossary lists the major terms used throughout the book, along with their definitions.

Bibliography. The bibliography lists the books that provided references for the author while writing this book.

WHAT YOU WILL TAKE AWAY FROM THIS BOOK

After reading this book, you will have a better understanding of how to protect critical corporate data. The techniques, practices, and technology are a mixture of tried and true and the brand new. There are some new takes on older methods, as well as new ideas for old problems. In the end, you will have not only new information to manage, but also better ways of doing it.

1

INTRODUCTION TO DATA PROTECTION

In This Chapter:

- What Does Data Protection Mean?
- A Model for Information, Data, and Storage
- Why Is Data Protection Important to the Enterprise?
- Data Loss and Business Risk
- Connectivity: The Risk Multiplier
- Business Continuity: The Importance of Data Availability to Business Operations
- The Changing Face of Data Protection
- Key Points

The explosion of corporate data in the 1990s, coupled with new data storage technology such as networked storage, has made the accumulation and management of large amounts of data a corporate priority. Corporations *try* to accumulate terabytes of data on increasingly large storage systems. Gathering customer data, vendor information, minute financial measurements, product data, retail sell-through data, and manufacturing metrics are now corporate goals. Even small to medium-size businesses (SMB) have begun to acquire terabytes of data. Management of storage systems, and the data held within them, is a cause of great concern within IT departments, corporate legal offices, and the executive suite.

With the advent of new regulations and the understanding of how incredibly valuable corporate data is, there is a new focus on protecting and accessing data. As companies received hard-earned lessons on what can happen when data is destroyed, damaged, or unavailable, more focus has been placed on protecting mission-critical information than on simply accumulating it.

Typically, IT departments have tried to protect data by using high availability (HA) devices with redundant systems, backing up data regularly to tape, and data duplication techniques. Increasingly, more sophisticated methods of ensuring the *integrity and availability* of important corporate data are being used, including remote mirroring and remote copy, near-line backup, Data Lifecycle Management (DLM), and Information Lifecycle Management (ILM).

WHAT DOES DATA PROTECTION MEAN?

Data protection is just what it sounds like: protecting important data from damage, alteration, or loss. Although that sounds simple enough, data protection encompasses a host of technology, business processes, and best practices. Different techniques must be used for different aspects of data protection. For example, securing storage infrastructure is necessary to ensure that data is not altered or maliciously destroyed. To protect against inadvertent data loss or permanent corruption, a solid backup strategy with accompanying technology is needed.

The size of an enterprise determines which practices, processes, or technologies are used for data protection. It is not reasonable to assume that a small business can deploy expensive, high-end solutions to protect important data. On the other hand, backing up data to tape or disk is certainly something that any enterprise can do. A large enterprise will have both the resources and the motivation to use more advanced technology.

The goal is the same no matter what the size or makeup of the company. Data protection strives to minimize business losses due to the lack of *verifiable* data integrity and availability.

The practices and techniques to consider when developing a data protection strategy are:

- *Backup and recovery:* the safeguarding of data by making offline copies of the data to be restored in the event of disaster or data corruption.
- *Remote data movement:* the real-time or near-real-time moving of data to a location outside the primary storage system or to another facility to protect against physical damage to systems and buildings. The two most common forms of this technique are remote copy and replication. These techniques duplicate data from one system to another, in a different location.
- *Storage system security:* applying best practices and security technology to the storage system to augment server and network security measures.
- *Data Lifecycle Management (DLM):* the automated movement of critical data to online and offline storage. Important aspects of DLM are placing data con-

sidered to be in a final state into read-only storage, where it cannot be changed, and moving data to different types of storage depending on its age.

- *Information Lifecycle Management (ILM):* a comprehensive strategy for valuing, cataloging, and protecting information assets. It is tied to regulatory compliance as well. ILM, while similar to DLM, operates on information, not raw data. Decisions are driven by the content of the information, requiring policies to take into account the context of the information.

All these methods should be deployed together to form a proper data protection strategy.

A MODEL FOR INFORMATION, DATA, AND STORAGE

Traditionally, storage infrastructure was viewed differently from the data and information that was placed on it. A new, unified model has emerged that ties together hardware, management, applications, data, and information. As Figure 1–1 shows, the entire spectrum from devices through information can be thought of as a series of layers, each building upon the others and providing more advanced services at each layer

The model begins with the traditional world of storage: the hardware. The hardware or *device layer* includes all the hardware components that comprise a

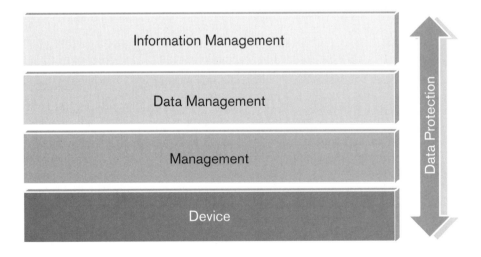

FIGURE 1–1 A MODEL FOR INFORMATION, DATA, AND STORAGE

storage system, including disks and tapes up to entire Storage Area Networks (SAN).

Next is the *management layer.* This layer is comprised of all the tools for managing the hardware resources. Some typical functions of this layer include device and network management, resource management, network analysis, and provisioning.

The *data management layer* consists of tools and techniques to manage data. Some typical functions within this layer are backup and recovery, remote copy, replication, and Data Lifecycle Management practices.

The final piece of the model, and the uppermost layer, is the *information management layer.* This layer addresses the difference between information and data: context. Business practices such as Information Lifecycle Management look at what a collection of data means and manages it accordingly.

Data protection cuts across all levels of the model. A successful data protection strategy will take into account the hardware, especially its security and configuration. The management layer is less pronounced in the data protection strategy, because it mainly serves the hardware. The data management layer is heavily involved, and the information management portion ties many aspects of data protection together while filling in significant gaps.

While reading the rest of this book, keep this model in mind. It will help provide a framework for thinking about data protection.

WHY IS DATA PROTECTION IMPORTANT TO THE ENTERPRISE?

There are several reasons for spending money, time, and effort on data protection. The primary one is minimizing financial loss, followed by compliance with regulatory requirements, maintaining high levels of productivity, and meeting customer expectations. As computers have become more and more integral to business operations, data requirements from regulators such as the U.S. Securities and Exchange Commission (SEC), as well as from customers, have been imposed on businesses. There is a clear expectation that important data be available 24 hours a day, 7 days a week, 365 days a year. Without a working data protection strategy, that isn't possible.

The single most important reason to implement data protection strategies is fear of financial loss. Data is recognized as an important corporate asset that needs to be safeguarded. Loss of information can lead to direct financial losses, such as lost sales, fines, or monetary judgments. It can also cause indirect losses from the effects of a drop in investor confidence or customers fleeing to competitors. Worse yet, stolen or altered data can result in financial effects that are not known to the company until much later. At that point, less can be done about it, magnifying the negative results.

Another important business driver for data protection is the recent spate of regulations. Governments throughout the world have begun imposing new regulations on electronic communications and stored data. Businesses face dire consequences for noncompliance. Some countries hold company executives criminally liable for failure to comply with laws regarding electronic communications and documents. These regulations often define what information must be retained, for how long, and under what conditions. Other laws are designed to ensure the privacy of the information contained in documents, files, and databases. Loss of critical communications can be construed as a violation of these regulations and may subject the corporation to fines and the managers to legal action.

A third driver, which does not get the attention of the press but is important to organizations nonetheless, is productivity. Loss of important data lowers overall productivity, as employees have to deal with time-consuming customer issues without the aid of computer databases. Data loss also results in application failures and similar system problems, making it difficult for people to do their jobs. A poor data protection strategy may leave people waiting for long periods of time for systems to be restored after a failure. During that time, employees may be idle or able to work only in a reduced capacity, further diminishing productivity.

The demands of a 21st-century business are such that customers expect the business to operate at all times. In an increasingly global economy, downtime is not tolerated by customers, who can readily take their business elsewhere. The inability of a business to operate because of a data loss, even a temporary one, is driving many businesses to deploy extensive data protection schemes. It is not only the e-commerce world that experiences this situation. All types of businesses—including health care, financial, manufacturing, and service—operate around the clock, or at least their computer systems do. Even when no humans are around, computers are available to take and place orders, send orders to the warehouse, and manage financial transactions. Data protection strategies need to take into account these 24/7 expectations.

DATA LOSS AND BUSINESS RISK

Risk is a measure of potential economic loss, lack of return on an investment or asset, or material injury. Another way to state this is that risk is a measure of exposure to harm. Some common risks are material loss (for example, damaged equipment, facilities, or products), risk to sales and revenue, lawsuits, project failure, and market risk. Risk is associated not only with hard assets, such as building or machinery, but also with revenue, customer loyalty, and investments in projects.

How risk is measured depends on the assets deemed to be at risk. In computer security circles, risk is usually a measure of threats (the capability and willingness for malicious behavior), vulnerability (the holes in the system that can be exploited), and harm (the damage that could be done by a threat exploiting a vulnerability). No matter how you measure risk, the most important component is harm. Without harm, there is no risk.

Insurance, locked cabinets, background checks, and currency hedges are ways that companies seek to minimize harm to their assets and the profitability of the business. If one thinks of information as being a corporate asset, protecting the underlying data is necessary to ensure the value of the asset and prevent its loss. Ultimately, data protection is about mitigating business risk by reducing the ability of some threat to do harm to mission-critical data.

The Effect of Lost Data on Business Operations

Companies recognize that data loss represents a business risk. Even if a monetary value is not assigned to the data, the negative effects on operations can be significant. In many cases, corporate operations can be so adversely affected that companies feel the need to mention the risk in regulatory filings and shareholder reports.

Three types of damage may occur because of data loss. First, data may be unrecoverable. In this case, important business records may be lost forever or available only in hard-copy form. Any business process that is dependent on that data will now be considerably hindered. This is the worst form of damage that can occur.

Next, data may be recoverable but may require considerable time to restore. This scenario—the most likely—assumes that data is backed up in some other place, separate from the primary source. This is a better situation than irrecoverable loss, but the data will be unavailable while recovery operations take place. In some cases, not all the data may be recovered. This is a common problem with data restored from nightly backups. Any data created during the day when the primary data was lost is not on the backup tapes and is lost forever.

Finally, while data is unavailable, either permanently or temporarily, applications not directly related to lost data may fail. This is especially true of relational databases that reference other databases. Loss of a central database of customer information, for example, may cause problems with the sales system because it references customer information. A loss of this type can result in cascade failures, in which several applications fail because of their dependence on another application's data.

RISK TO SALES   A company may suffer measurable harm when data loss makes it impossible for it to interact with customers. The result is that the company will not realize sales and revenue.

E-mail has become a primary form of corporate communication. Losing an important e-mail or attachment may mean that a customer may not be serviced correctly; thus, sales are lost. This is especially true of companies that sell capital equipment to other companies. A hard drive crash on the e-mail server may cause an important bid to go undelivered. The salesperson may not even know that the bid was not received by the customers (because it is sitting in the Sent folder stored on a local hard drive) until the sale is lost.

As large companies have become more dependent on call centers, they have become equally dependent on the customer relationship management (CRM) systems that help them track customer issues and orders. This represents a risk to sales, revenue, and profitability. If this risk is realized—if the worst-case scenario comes true—the harm done to the business may be severe enough to propel it into bankruptcy.

Even Mother Nature Fears Data Loss

In the quarter ending March 31, 2000, Mothernature.com, an Internet-based retailer of health and beauty products, saw fit to mention the following in its U.S. Securities and Exchange Commission (the U.S. regulatory body for public companies and markets) Form 10-Q filing:

"If our existing technical and operational systems fail, we could experience interruptions or delays in our service or *data loss,* and could be unable to accept and fulfill customer orders."[1]

In the paragraph that followed, the company outlined how the risk of data loss could make it impossible for it to meet customer expectations and fill orders. Clearly, inability to ship an order represents a major risk to a catalog or Internet reseller.

INABILITY TO OPERATE Extreme data loss such as loss of an entire database, even temporarily, has been known to cause organizations to fail. A company may not be able to fulfill orders, update employee records, produce financial reports, manufacture goods, or provide services. It may not even have an operating phone system. Computer technology and the data associated with it are integrated into all aspects of an organization's operations. Because of this dependence on information technology, there is a *clear risk* that data loss can make it impossible for an organization to perform properly.

Even partial data loss can disrupt business operations and produce negative effects. Employees may be idled for long periods of time while data is re-created or recovered, reducing productivity. Applications may fail unexpectedly when referencing data that is no longer available. Essential reporting may be incomplete because component data is not available.

Loss of data also makes it difficult for managers to measure company operations. Most modern businesses rely on financial, market, and manufacturing metrics. Without the ability to gather and report on key business indicators,

---

1. Mothernature.com Inc. Form 10-Q, filing date May 15, 2000.

managers are running blind as to the health of the business. Destroyed, damaged, or altered data skews metrics and disrupts decision-making. The overall effect of this type of disruption is reduced revenue and higher expenses, leading to loss of profitability.

LAWSUITS AND FINES   There is potential for lawsuits and fines when a company experiences data loss. With shareholder lawsuits fairly common, failure to protect data could easily lead to litigation, especially if data loss can be tied to a negative change in the share price of the company's stock. A more likely scenario is that data loss will affect operations and sales, causing the business to underperform. This can then trigger shareholder suits.

Other types of legal action can result in adverse judgments for companies. Companies may be sued for failure to perform duties outlined in contracts or the inability to produce goods and services that have been paid for. A lost order record may result in a customer's suing for direct and collateral damages.

Regulators now have the power to impose data retention requirements on companies. *Data retention requirements* tell a company what data must be kept and for how long. Fines can be levied when these requirements are not met.

It is not enough simply to have good policies; the policies have to be followed up with good practices. In 1997, Prudential Insurance was fined heavily because it did not properly *implement* existing electronic document retention policies. This led to the destruction of electronic documents needed as evidence. There was no indication that employees willfully destroyed evidence—only that the company did not take *sufficient action* to ensure that it was preserved. Though Prudential had a good electronic document retention policy in place, its inability to implement it properly cost the company $1 million in fines.[2]

Damaging legal situations can occur when data loss causes financial information to be released late. Regulators, markets, and shareholders expect certain reporting to occur at previously announced intervals. When a company fails to meet these expectations, that failure often leads to fines, lawsuits, drops in price of the company's stock, or even delisting from financial markets.

All these situations represent financial harm to the business. As such, steps need to be taken to protect the business against the risk of lawsuits and fines.

THEFT OF INFORMATION   Another type of harm that requires data protection is theft of corporate information. This may take the form of theft of secrets or a violation of private data. Theft of secrets happens when a thief is able to access internal company information vital to current and future operations. Some examples of this these secrets are product plans, product designs, and computer source code. The economic impact of theft of secrets is difficult to ascertain, because the harm is indirect and manifests itself over long periods of time.

---

2. *The National Law Journal,* November 3, 2003.

Theft of private information, such as customer information, may have three effects:

- Lawsuits may arise when it is known that this information has been stolen. Customers may sue for damages that result from the use of this confidential information.

- Regulators in some countries may be empowered to take criminal and civil action against a company that suffers such a breach. The European Union, for example, requires that "Member States shall provide that the controller must implement appropriate technical and organizational measures to protect personal data against accidental or unlawful destruction or accidental loss, alteration, unauthorized disclosure or access, in particular where the processing involves the transmission of data over a network, and against all other unlawful forms of processing."[3]

  Other political entities have similar laws that require the safeguarding of information from destruction or breach.

- Customers may refuse to do business with a company that allows such a theft of private information. It is reasonable to assume that a customer would not want to continue to do business with a company that has not taken adequate care to safeguard private information.

Reasons for Data Loss

As one might expect, there are many reasons why a corporation might lose important data. Broadly, they can be broken into the following categories:

- Disasters
- Security breaches
- Accidents or unintended user action
- System failure

Some data protection techniques can be applied to all these causes of data loss; others are better used for specific categories.

DISASTERS Disasters are the classic data-loss scenario. Floods, earthquakes, hurricanes, and terrorists can destroy computer systems (and the data housed on them) while destroying the facilities they are kept in. All disasters are unpredictable and may not behave as forecast. The goal of data protection is to create an

---

3. Directive 95/46/EC of the European Parliament and of the Council of 24 October 1995, Section VIII, Article 17.

environment that shields against all types of disasters. What makes this difficult is that it is hard to predict what type of disaster to guard against, and it is too costly to guard against all of them. Companies guard against the disasters most likely to occur, though that is not always good enough. Until just a few years ago, most U.S. companies did not take into account terrorism when planning for disasters.

There are two classes of disasters: natural and manmade. Natural disasters are often large in scope, affecting entire regions. Earthquakes and hurricanes, with their ability to do widespread damage to infrastructure, are especially worrisome; they rarely provide enough time to develop a plan for data protection if one is not already in place. After the disaster begins, it is too late to try to save data.

Manmade disasters are often more localized and generally create much less damage. Fires are the most common manmade disaster, although many other manmade incidents can cause data loss, too. The worse manmade disaster resulting in widespread loss of data (and life) was the September 11, 2001, terrorist attack on the World Trade Center in New York City. The destruction of key computer systems and the harm that it wrought to the economy of the United States led the U.S. Securities and Exchange Commission and the Comptroller of the Currency to jointly issue policies[4] requiring that data be adequately protected against regional disasters.

SECURITY BREACHES   When an intruder breaches the network, server, or storage defenses of a company, he usually has one of three goals: to look at information he shouldn't look at, to deny the company the use of its data, or to damage and destroy data. Because the harm is intentional, an intruder can do more selective damage aimed at long-term harm.

Intruders come in two types: insiders and outsiders. The press tends to accentuate the problem of outsiders, yet insiders are as big a problem. Insiders can do more damage because they already have access to vital systems (and don't have to work as hard to get at important data) and know what type of damage can do the most harm. Insiders also have the advantage of less scrutiny. Most IT departments have sophisticated methods of detecting outsiders trying to break in. Fewer companies monitor activity inside their network. For this reason, insiders can go undetected until they do damage, whereas outsiders are often stopped at the network perimeter.

Security concerns affect data protection strategies in two ways. First, it is important to keep backups or copies of data, in case a security breach results in damage or destruction of critical data. Second, part of the data protection strategy needs to be securing vital data and information assets against harm. Although network and server security is well formed and understood by IT professionals,

---

4. SEC Policy Statement [Release No. 34-48545; File No. S7-17-03].

storage system security is much less mature, in terms of both technology and best practices.

ACCIDENTAL DATA LOSS Accidental loss represents one of the most common data loss scenarios. End-users are often the culprits; they delete, overwrite, and misplace critical files or e-mails, often without knowing they've done so.

In the 1980s and early 1990s, it was not at all unusual for the help desk to get frantic calls from end-users who had reformatted their hard drives. Fortunately, changes in desktop operating systems have made accidental reformatting of a hard drive much more difficult, and it is now a rare event. Damaged or reformatted floppy or Zip drives are still a common problem, though this usually destroys only archive data. As other forms of mobile media, such as solid state memory devices, are used by more people, the likelihood of loss of data on these devices grows. And yes, people sometimes drop their smart media cards in their coffee.

Though IT personnel may feel frustrated by the silly errors end-users make that result in data loss, they are responsible for quite a few errors themselves. Botched data migrations, hastily performed database reconfigurations, and accidentally deleted system files are everyday occurrences in the IT world. One of the most common and most damaging IT errors occurs when a backup tape is overwritten. Not only is the previous data destroyed, but there is no good way to recover much of it. Also, quite a few backups are damaged due to sloppy storage practices.

The risk that the end-user represents is usually a recoverable one. Although it's a hassle to dig out backups and pull off individual files, it is still something that can be done if the data in question is important enough. Good habits, such as backing up files to file servers or automated backups and volume shadow copying (now part of the Windows operating system), can alleviate many of the effects of end-user data loss.

IT mistakes represent much greater risk. The effects of an IT accident are not limited to individuals; instead, they affect entire applications and systems, many of which are mission critical. Strict policies and controls are necessary to prevent these types of errors.

SYSTEM FAILURE System failures often cause data loss. The most famous type of failure is a hard drive crash. Although hard drives don't fail with the frequency that they used to, failures are still a major problem for many system administrators. This is especially true of drives in high-use servers, in which drive failure is inevitable. Data can also be corrupted or destroyed because of spurious errors with disk array hardware, Fibre Channel and SCSI host bus adapters (HBAs), and network interface cards (NICs). Fluctuations in electricity, sudden power outages, and vibration and shock can damage disks and the data stored on them.

Failures in software are also a source of data loss. Updated drivers and firmware are notorious for having bugs that cause data to be erased or corrupted. The same can happen with new versions of application or database software. The failure of IT to properly back up and *verify the integrity* of a backup before installing new software is an age-old problem leading to irrecoverable data loss.

System failures cannot be completely prevented, but steps can be taken to reduce the likelihood of losing data when they occur. One of the most common steps is to buy high availability (HA) devices for mission-critical applications. HA units offer better protection against shock, flaky electricity, and link failures that can corrupt data. They also have software protection that ensure that I/O is complete and that bad blocks do not get written to disks. Good backup and archive procedures are also important parts of a plan to protect against system failure.

CONNECTIVITY: THE RISK MULTIPLIER

When networking was introduced, the risks associated with it were relatively low. Most networks were small, with only a handful of computers linked. The Internet started as a network of only four mainframes. Local-area networks (LANs) did not become widely deployed until the late 1980s. Access to these networks was very limited, and the number of assets involved was low.

As the networks grew, both in size and complexity, security problems became more prevalent, and the risk involved in using a network became higher. There were more devices of different types, with many more access points. Whereas in the past, disasters or hackers could be contained to one computer, networking allowed problems to spread throughout a large number of machines. There is now network access to more computers than at any time before. Many homes now have several linked computers and network devices, and have become susceptible to the same security and network problems that have plagued the corporate world for years.

Network Attached Storage and Storage Area Network technology have had a similar effect on storage. Data storage devices have traditionally been isolated behind a server. Secure the server, and you secure the storage as well. That is no longer the case, and storage devices are experiencing many of the same problems that other network devices do. Some people would argue that the ability to get unauthorized access to a Fibre Channel SAN is low. However, if a malicious hacker does get through system defenses, he or she now has a greater number of devices to wreak havoc on. *Connectivity increases risk* because it gives more access to more resources that can be damaged.

Because risk is outcome based, the outcome of a successful intrusion or data corruption in a networked storage environment can be much more devastating than with an equal number of isolated, directly connected storage devices.

Even when system security is not the issue, connectivity can magnify other problems. Previously, one server could access only a small number of storage devices. If something went wrong, and the server caused data to become corrupted, it could do so to only a small amount of data held on its local resources. Servers can now potentially access hundreds or even thousands of storage devices and can corrupt data on a scale that was not possible before.

Networked storage also has increased the complexity of the storage system, which can introduce more problems. The complexity of the storage infrastructure has increased dramatically, with switches, hubs, cables, appliances, management software, and very complicated switch-based disk array controllers. The opportunity to introduce errors into the data stream and corrupt or destroy it is much higher with so many devices in the mix.

In the networked storage environment, there are many servers and many storage devices. More servers can damage or provide unauthorized access to data. Even a single server can affect many data storage devices. The potential harm is multiplied by the high degree of connectivity that a modern storage infrastructure allows for.

BUSINESS CONTINUITY: THE IMPORTANCE OF DATA AVAILABILITY TO BUSINESS OPERATIONS

Business continuity is the ability of a business to continue to operate in the face of disaster. All functional departments within a company are involved in business continuity. Facilities management needs to be able to provide alternative buildings for workers. Manufacturing needs to develop ways of shifting work to outsourcers, partners, or other factories to make up for lost capacity. Planning and execution of a business continuity plan is an executive-level function that takes into account all aspects of business operations.

Information technology plays a key role in maintaining operations when disaster strikes. For most modern companies to function properly, communications must be restored quickly. Phone systems and e-mail are especially important, because they are primary communications media and usually are brought online first. After that, different systems are restored, depending on the needs of the business.

Protecting data and the access to it is a primary component of business continuity strategies. Restoring systems whose data has been destroyed is useless. What is the point of restoring the financial system if all the financial data has disappeared? IT, like other departments, needs to ensure that the data entrusted to it survives. In many cases, it is less important that the hardware systems themselves survive, so long as critical data does. If the data is still intact, new hardware can be purchased, applications reloaded, and operations restored. It might be a slow process, and there will be financial ramifications, but at least the business will eventually return to normalcy. Without the data, that will never happen.

THE CHANGING FACE OF DATA PROTECTION

In the past, data protection meant tape backups. Some online protection could be obtained by using RAID (which is explained in Chapter 2) to keep data intact and available in the event of a hard drive failure. Most system administrators relied on copying data to tape and then moving some of those tapes offsite. This is still the most common form of data protection, but only part of a whole suite of techniques available for safeguarding data.

Remote Data Movement and Copy

It was natural to extend the paradigm of duplicating important data on another disk (RAID) to duplicating it to another storage system, perhaps located in a different place. In this process, called remote copy, exact copies of individual blocks of data are made to a remote system. This system might be right next door or hundreds of miles away. Remote copy allows a second storage system to act as a hot backup or to be placed out of harm's way and available for the disaster-recovery site to use. At present, remote-copy systems tend to be expensive. The telecommunications needed to support them present the IT manager with a high recurring expense. The costs involved with remote copy have tended to relegate its use to high-end applications and very large companies.

Disk-Based Backup

Typically, backups consist of copying data from a disk system to a magnetic tape. Tape is, unfortunately, slow to write to, lacks the capacity that modern disks have, can be difficult to manage, and is very slow to recover data from. Because the purpose of a backup, as opposed to an archive, is to produce a copy of the data that can be restored if the primary data source is lost, slow recovery is a problem.

Because of these limitations, disk-based backups are gaining in popularity. Originally positioned as a replacement to tape, this method is seen as being part of a more sophisticated backup strategy. With disk-based backups, similar software and techniques are used as with tape, except that the target is a disk system. This technique has the advantage of being very fast relative to tape, especially for recovery. The disadvantages are that disk drives generally are not removable, and the data cannot be sent off-site the way a tape can.

Networked Storage

The biggest changes in data protection come courtesy of networked storage. In the past, storage was closely tied to individual servers. Now storage is more distributed, with many clients or servers able to access many storage units. This has been both positive and negative for data protection. On the one hand, networked storage makes certain techniques—such as remote copy, disk-based backup, and distributed data stores—much easier to implement and manage. The ability to share certain resources, such as tape libraries, allows for data protection schemes that do not disrupt operations.

However, the networked storage environment is much more complex to manage. There tend to be many more devices and paths to the data. Because one of the key advantages of networked storage is scalability, these systems tend to grow quickly. This growth can be difficult to manage, and the sheer number of devices in the storage system can be as daunting as other types of corporate networks.

Networked storage allows for multiple paths between the server or client and the data storage devices. Multiple paths work to enhance business continuity by making link failures less of a problem. There is less chance that a broken cable will cause applications and backups to fail. Overall, networked storage is more resilient. It produces an environment in which safeguarding data and recovering from failure are performed more quickly and efficiently.

Information Lifecycle Management

The future direction of data protection is in a recent concept called Information Lifecycle Management (ILM). ILM is less concerned about the underlying data than about the upper-level information. Information is data with context; that context is provided by *metadata,* or data about the data. ILM guides data protection by determining what type of protection should be applied to data, based on the value of the information it supports. It makes sense to spend a lot of money on remote copy for very valuable information. Other information may not be worth protecting at all. ILM helps determine which path to take in making those decisions.

KEY POINTS

- Data protection is the safeguarding of important data from destruction, alteration, or loss. It is achieved through a combination of technology, business processes, and best practices. Core components of a data protection strategy are backup and recovery, remote data movement, storage system security, and Information Lifecycle Management.

- Business drivers influencing data-loss strategies are fear of financial loss, the need to comply with regulations, attempts to maintain high productivity, and the need to meet ever-increasing customer demands.

- Risk is potential exposure to harm. An organization can be harmed when data is unrecoverable, applications fail as a result of data loss, or the time to recover data is unacceptable. The risk to a business manifests itself in lost sales, the inability to operate properly for some time, lawsuits and fines, and the effects of theft of critical information.

- Increased connectivity creates a risk multiplier. The more resources that can be affected by an event, the greater the potential harm.
- Business continuity strategies strive to keep businesses operating in the event of disaster. Data protection is a key component of business continuity.
- Data protection is changing. New practices and technologies include disk-based backup, networked storage, ILM, and remote data movement. These practices and technologies are providing system architects more options for protecting data.

2

AN OVERVIEW OF STORAGE TECHNOLOGY

In This Chapter:

- A Quick History of Data Storage
- Storage I/O Basics
- The I/O Stack
- Direct Attach Storage
- Network Attached Storage (NAS)
- Storage Area Networks (SANs)
- Extending SANs over MAN and WAN
- Key Points

Data protection is closely linked to storage architecture and technology. The methods used to protect data depend on the storage infrastructure as much as on the company goals. It does no good to try to implement a strategy that is not supported by the architecture. Nor does it make sense to build a storage architecture that will not support the data protection strategy. They are intertwined.

Storage technology is implemented at the device and management layer (Figure 2–0). The primary focus is on the devices that make up the storage infrastructure, as well as the software that manages and organizes stored data.

This chapter will provide a brief overview of modern data storage technology and architecture. It is by no means meant to be comprehensive. There are many books available that detail different aspects of storage infrastructure. One of the best general books on storage is *Building Storage Networks*, by Marc Farley. It is detailed and comprehensive.

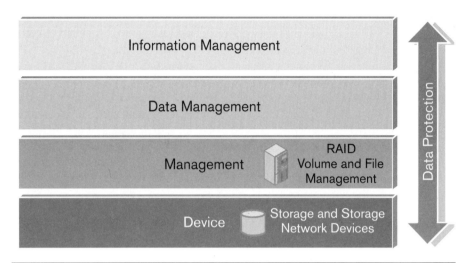

FIGURE 2-0 STORAGE TECHNOLOGY OPERATING AT THE DEVICE AND MANAGEMENT LAYER

A QUICK HISTORY OF DATA STORAGE

Data storage used to come in only one type: Direct Attach Storage (DAS). It wasn't called that at the time. Storage was simply storage. The primary storage media were magnetic tape for backup and archive, floppy drives, and hard disks for primary storage. In the IBM mainframe world, hard disk systems were referred to as DASD (Direct Access Storage Devices). By today's standards, DASD was large, slow, and cumbersome.

In the early 1980s, the first small hard disk drives were developed and became ubiquitous. The hard drive as we know it grew alongside the PC and open enterprise systems that dominate computing today. This led to a close coupling of data storage to the individual computer. Drives were addressed only from the computer they were directly attached to.

The advent of SCSI (Small Computer Systems Interface) and IDE/ATA storage protocols meant that drives were no longer proprietary. They did not have to be tied to a specific computer architecture or operating system. Drives were still held captive behind the server. The introduction of the file server further encouraged this model. Hard disk drives were accessible by anyone in the network, but only by going through the network server's processor and network operating system (NOS). The file server was unique because the NOS allowed many users to connect to the computer simultaneously while maintaining the integrity of the data on the disk.

The landscape changed dramatically in the late 1990s. Products built around the concept of network storage were developed. This changed the way storage architectures were designed. Although it was often argued that Network Attached Storage was just a better form of file server, Storage Area Networks (SANs) were entirely different. With the SAN architecture, disks or RAID groups could be accessed directly, at the block level, from remote machines without the intervention of a network operating system. Raw access to a disk or tape could now be performed over a network. This allowed for distributed storage architectures that could support fast applications, such as relational databases and tape backup.

SANs also led to better utilization of storage resources. By sharing resources, the problem of uneven allocation of disk and tape capacity can be eliminated. Rather than have some resources overburdened while others are underused, networked storage allows for more even usage of storage.

The Roles of Different Storage Devices

The purpose of a data storage system is to provide *persistent* or nonvolatile storage for data. It does not need to be as fast as random access memory, but when the power is turned off, the data has to continue to exist. Without persistent data storage devices, computing devices would need to have an uninterrupted power source, or else data stored on them would be lost. A variety of devices act as persistent data stores, each with its own specific role. Table 2–1 shows a partial list of these devices.

TABLE 2-1 Storage Media (Early 2005)

Device	Role	Capacity
Hard drive	Persistent online storage Near-line backup Temporary swap space	Up to 400 gigabytes
Floppy drives	Small file transport Software and data distribution	1.44 megabytes
Magnetic tape (various styles)	Backup Archive	Up to 1.3 terabytes (with compression)
CD-ROM/RW	Archive Software and data distribution	Up to 740 megabytes
DVD-ROM/RW	Archive Software and data distribution	Up to 9.1 gigabytes
Magneto-optical disk	Archive	Up to 50 gigabytes

(continues)

TABLE 2-1 *(CONTINUED)* Storage Media (Early 2005)

Memory stick	Large file transport	Up to 4 gigabytes
Flash storage	Individual backup	
USB flash drives	Primary storage for small peripherals	

Hard disks are fast devices with high storage capacity. Magnetic tape has the advantage of also offering high-capacity data storage, though it is slower than hard drives. Tape is still the media of choice for backups, because tapes can be removed and moved off site. CD-ROM/RW and DVD-ROM/RW have moderate capacity, but high-quality media can last a very long time and do not degrade quickly with usage, unlike tape. They also are extremely inexpensive, which is why they are used extensively for software distribution as well as long-term storage of archival data. Floppy drives are used almost exclusively for transferring files between computers. The low capacity and relatively slow speed of the floppy drive has placed it on the road to extinction. Many computers today do not even ship with a floppy drive.

Magneto-optical disks, which combine the properties of magnetic and laser-based disks, have high capacity but are expensive and slow. They are sometimes used for long-term archive of large files.

Solid state, nonvolatile storage is a departure from the magnetic and laser media that dominate other data storage products. Utilizing flash RAM, solid state products have become a cheap method of transporting moderate-size files. They are important storage devices for mobile consumer electronic devices such as digital cameras and MP3 music players. USB flash drives are quickly supplanting floppy drives as a way of transporting files between computers.

Arrays, Libraries, and Jukeboxes

Hard drives dominate as primary storage, as tape does for backup. These technologies are supplemented by CD-ROM/RW and DVD-ROM/RW for archive and software distribution. Often, storage devices are aggregated into arrays, libraries, or jukeboxes of drives and media. They are the basic building blocks of the massive storage systems prevalent in large enterprises.

Arrays are large collections of hard drives tied together into a logical whole. A device called a *controller* provides the interface to the computer or network and manages the drive set. Advanced controller technology can provision the drives into a variety of configurations. In many cases, a large number of drives can appear to be one single large drive or many smaller drives.

There are advantages to aggregating drives into arrays. An array allows for larger disk space than is possible with a single drive. When multiple small disks

Controllers

Each disk, tape, and CD-ROM/RW drive has an interface that allows it to connect to a specific type of bus or network. This interface is called a *drive controller,* because it controls the movement of the mechanical parts of the drive.

Arrays, libraries, and jukeboxes are collections of single drives. They need an interface for the *entire collection* to the bus or network. This is usually accomplished through use of a device also called a controller. A controller provides the interface to the individual drive controllers and a common interface to the bus or network. Often, controllers will have processors and memory that allows them to host embedded services specific to storage device.

are combined into a single, large storage device, very large files and databases can be stored on a single *logical* drive. Hard drives also have performance limitations. By streaming data to multiple drives simultaneously, storage systems can read and write data much more quickly than if only one massive drive were present. From a data protection point of view, having data parceled out to many drives is a major advantage. Disk failure won't destroy all the data stored in the array unit. In fact, all data may be recoverable even in the event of single drive failure if copies are made to other disks.

Tape libraries and CD-ROM/RW jukeboxes are better suited to managing multiple access to the individual tape and optical media. Because tapes, CDs, and DVDs are removable, manually placing and changing tapes and CD-ROMs is unproductive, as well as an opportunity for human and computer error. The sophisticated robotics in these systems can automate the movement of media in and out of drives. In the case of tape libraries, allowing multiple backup processes to stream data to multiple tapes makes the best use of a high-speed connection.

As with disk arrays, libraries and jukeboxes often have the advantage of having more than one drive. If one tape or CD-ROM/RW drive fails, the others in the library or jukebox can still be used. At least some servers will be backed up, and the data on the tapes or CD-ROM/RWs will still be accessible.

STORAGE I/O BASICS

Data storage uses a variety of technology to store data. Some devices—such as hard drives, floppy drives, and tape—use magnetism to encode information on the media. Others, such as CD-ROM/RW and DVD-ROM/RW, use lasers to burn information in the substrate of a disk. Still others, such as solid state storage, use a charge in a solid state device to store data. Whatever the media, all data is stored as bits (1s and 0s) on some device that can be read back later.

To be found, stored data must have a structure that can be understood by an operating system. If this structure doesn't exist, data cannot be written to the storage media. Reading back data would be an exercise in futility. At the lowest level, the drive and protocol determine how data is organized and transferred to and from a device. Unfortunately, the high-level structure is imposed by the operating system. This makes file systems unique to the operating environment. It is why a file written to a hard drive by Microsoft Windows cannot be read by any other operating system, such as a Macintosh, without a translation program that understands both file systems.

I/O

I/O stands for *Input/Output*. For most uses of the term, it means data moving to or from some device or software element. Most protocols follow a client-server or master-slave model. To *read* data, a command has to be sent to the storage device to request the data. The storage device then responds with correct blocks of data or error codes. Writing data is done in a similar way. Reading or writing data requires that one or more transactions (I/Os) be completed.

How Data Is Accessed and Stored on Media

With the exception of solid state storage, data is stored by encoding a bit onto a material, called the *media*. The electromechanical devices that are used to read and write data are called the *heads*. The read and write heads are mounted on an arm called the *head assembly* or *actuator assembly*.

Disks and tape write data by positioning the *write heads* over the place on the disk or tape where the data is to be stored. The head then changes the magnetic state at that spot. To read the information stored on the disk, the read head is positioned over the spot where the data is stored. For magnetic media, the head measures the magnetic field at that spot and determines whether a 1 or 0 is encoded there.

For optical media, such as a CD-ROM or DVD-ROM, a laser is used to read and write data. To write, the laser burns a pit in the surface of the media to represent a 1. When reading, the laser shines on the surface and, depending on how it reflects back, determines whether a pit (a 1) is there. If a pit is not there, it is a 0.

Access Time

The amount of time it takes for a controller to find and read data on a media is called *access time*. Access time is an important performance measure because it directly measures the time it takes to retrieve data from the media. With disk drives, access time is a measure of the latency and transfer time of the disk.

LATENCY   Storage devices that are mechanical in nature take time to find the data on the media and place the read or write heads over it. The time it takes to place the heads over the spot where the data is stored or will be stored is called the *latency*.

For hard disks, the read/write heads have to be positioned over the exact spot where the data has been stored or will be stored. The drive controller has to wait for the disk to spin around to the arc of the disk to the desired spot. It then extends the heads over the interior to that spot. All of this movement determines the latency of the disk drive. CD and DVD media works in a similar way, only using a laser instead of magnetic heads.

A similar process takes place for magnetic tape. It is the magnetic tape that is moved, however, not the heads. A tape device's latency is the amount of time it takes to move the tape so that the tape heads are over the spot where data is to be written to or read from.

Solid state media has incredibly low access time because it is made out of RAM. It does not suffer from the effects of slower mechanical components and, hence, has almost no latency.

TRANSFER TIME   *Transfer time* is the amount of time it takes the disk, tape, or other storage media to transfer data off the media and onto the data bus or network. It is a function of a number of variables, including how fast the heads can detect the magnetic field on the disk or tape (in the case of magnetic media), the performance of the drive mechanisms, and the speed of the electronic components. Latency and transfer time together help define the access time for disk- and tape-based media.

Streaming Tape

Tape is different from disks. It *streams,* or moves continuously, from one end of the tape to the other unless told to stop. To find something on a digital tape (which is the prevailing type today), the tape drive controller reads information, encoded at the beginning of the tape, that tells it where the data is stored. It then begins to spool the tape forward until it reaches the desired position. Having previously read the data location information at the beginning of the tape, it can find additional blocks by moving the tape back and forth. This is inefficient, and a tape will wear out quickly if it is searched in a random fashion. Instead, tape software attempts to read and write starting at the beginning and not stopping until the very end of the data. Tape is best used in applications in which the tape can be kept streaming, such as backup and restore.

THE I/O STACK

Data is usually structured in a layered fashion, starting with bits, then bytes, blocks, volumes, and finally files. It is encoded on a media as bits—a series of 1s and 0s. If the drive only placed a stream of bits on a media, it would be very difficult to find anything on the media. This layered storage architecture is known as the *I/O stack* (Figure 2–1). The I/O stack is *the logical representation of the hardware and software* that data must pass through when it is moving back and forth to storage.

The drive itself creates the first level of structure by organizing data as blocks. A *block* consists of some number of bytes held at a specific location on the disk. Blocks are further organized into volumes. *Volumes* (Figure 2–2) are logical, mountable portions of physical storage. A volume may be an entire disk or tape, a portion of a disk, or an aggregated collection of disks or tapes. A volume can be thought of as a virtual set of blocks controlled by software called a *volume*

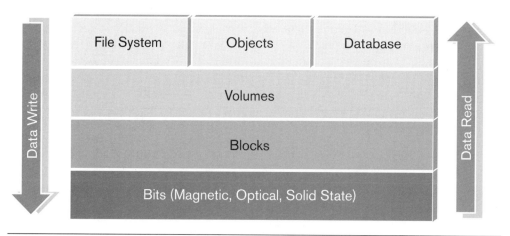

FIGURE 2–1   THE I/O STACK

manager. The operating system and applications access data as blocks, but how those blocks are addressed is up to the volume manager.

File systems then organize data on a volume as files or objects. The manner in which blocks are organized into directories and files is unique to each file system. The file system used by Microsoft Windows NT/2000/XP, for example, is called NTFS (for <u>NT</u> <u>F</u>ile <u>S</u>ystem) and is different from and incompatible with the system used by Linux. Applications access the file system to create and access files and are responsible for their own files' internal structure.

File systems add a lot of overhead to I/O operations. This doesn't affect typical productivity applications, such as word processors. A few extra milliseconds

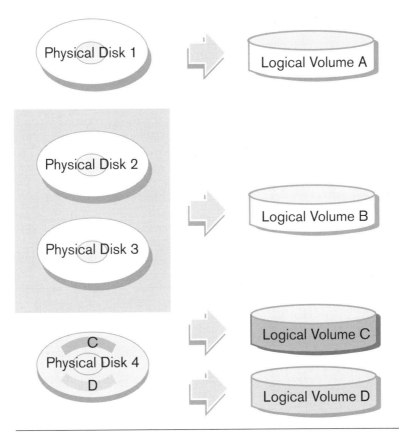

FIGURE 2–2 VOLUMES

opening or writing a file are hardly noticed by the end-user. The overhead is significant, however, for high-performance applications such as databases. Relational Database Management Systems (RDBMS) often bypass the file system and access the volume directly.

There is a serious movement to dispense with the traditional file system in favor of an object-oriented file system (OOFS). Despite the name, data is not organized into files at all. Instead, the OOFS creates and manages data as objects. Objects marry data with application or component behavior. There are advantages to this approach, but it has been feasible only in very specialized circumstances. The theoretical underpinnings of an OOFS were laid down in the early 1970s, though it has proved to be technically difficult to deploy with reasonable performance.

Block I/O

When a protocol accesses data on a disk as blocks, it is referred to as *block I/O*. Certain types of applications prefer to access data directly as blocks. This is especially true of high-performance system applications such as databases. They maintain their performance levels by defining their own structure separate from the operating system's file system. This allows them to use specialized techniques to search through data quickly and write data efficiently. Backup and retrieval applications also prefer to use block I/O. This allows them to restore the original structure of the data without really knowing what it was.

File I/O

Most end-user applications need to have data organized in an easy-to-understand format. The most common form is the file. The operating system imposes the file structure on the data through its file system. Accessing data through a file system is called *file I/O*. It is easier for an application to use the existing mechanisms in a file system for most I/O than to deal with data at a block level.

The general structure of a file is defined by the file system and is unique to it. Applications define the internal structure of the file—Microsoft Word–format documents, for example. Network attached storage and file servers allow for shared file access over the network.

RAID

RAID (Redundant Array of Independent Disks) is a schema for using groups of disks to increase performance, protect data, or both. RAID comes in different *RAID levels* that define its functions (Table 2–2). In all cases, RAID copies data blocks to *multiple disks* to accomplish its goals. RAID can be accomplished in software, in hardware, or both.

TABLE 2-2 IMPORTANT RAID LEVELS

RAID Level	Features
0	Striping
1	Mirroring
5	Striping with parity (parity is written across several disks)
10	Mirroring with striping (blocks are striped across mirrored sets of drives)
0+1	Striping with mirroring (striped sets of mirrored drives)

RAID functions are broadly defined as striping and mirroring. *Striping* occurs when *different data* is written to or read from multiple disks. This allows for the creation of a disk virtual space larger than an individual physical drive would allow. It also increases performance by spreading I/Os across multiple drives at once. Striping aggregates individual disk spaces into a much larger one while increasing performance.

Mirroring is the copying of the *same data block* to different disks to have a copy of the block available in the event of a failure of a disk. It is sometimes referred to as *shadowing*.

RAID levels are referred to by the term RAID plus the level. For example, RAID level 0 (striping) is described as RAID 0. RAID 0, 1, and 5 are the most common forms of RAID. RAID 0 (Figure 2–3) uses only striping to achieve a larger volume space and better overall performance. RAID 1 (Figure 2–4) uses mirroring to protect data by placing redundant copies of data on two or more disks. RAID 5 (Figure 2–5) uses striping to achieve a larger volume space but employs parity to ensure that data can be re-created quickly if there is loss or damage. RAID 5 spreads the parity data through the disk set rather than to a separate disk. By spreading parity data over many disks, RAID 5 guards against performance degradation when a

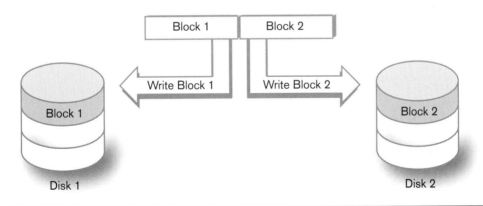

FIGURE 2-3 RAID 0

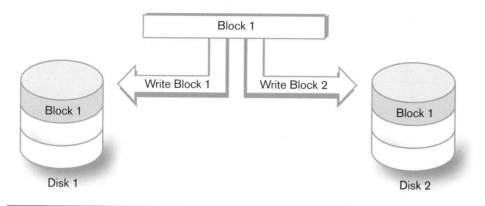

FIGURE 2–4 RAID 1

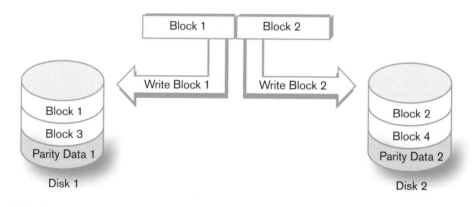

FIGURE 2–5 RAID 5

disk is lost and data must be recovered. Its write performance is less than that of RAID 0 or 1 and is almost always supported with hardware in a RAID controller. RAID 10 provides for high volume space and protection. It is similar to proprietary copy schemes within large disk arrays, so it is less common than RAID 5.

There are other RAID levels, including RAID 2, 3, and 4. These are much less common and are not supported by all products.

RAID CONTROLLERS Although RAID can be performed in software, which is common in small systems with internal disks, the predominant method of providing RAID services for external systems is through the use of a *RAID controller*. This is a specialized version of a disk array controller that marries the disk interface with the RAID software. Often referred to as *hardware-assisted RAID* or *hardware RAID*, RAID controllers perform RAID functions very quickly and are the only reasonable way to perform RAID 5. RAID controllers are available as separate add-on devices or are built into disk arrays.

DIRECT ATTACH STORAGE

The term Direct Attach Storage, or DAS, did not exist before there was networked storage. Then, it was simply storage, and all of it was attached directly to a mainframe or server. Only after Storage Area Networks become popular did the DAS term become common.

DAS refers to any storage that is attached *locally* to a computer. In the case of large arrays of devices, the computer may be connected to a controller. The controller then provides a single interface for many devices. The hard drive in a PC is an example of DAS. A multiterabyte disk array that is connected to a server via a SCSI cable is also DAS. Size does not determine whether storage is DAS—only its architecture.

Most open-system DAS devices use the SCSI or ATA standards to communicate to the storage devices or to a controller. ATA is more commonly used for slower, less reliable storage such as desktop storage, whereas SCSI is used for high-performance, high-reliability systems. That said, SCSI has shown up in desktop computers and ATA in enterprise-class arrays. Mainframes use their own protocols and specifications, most of which are proprietary.

SCSI

The term *SCSI* (pronounced "scuzzy") stands for *Small Computer Systems Interface*. It defines a specification for both hardware and software protocols, used to transfer data between peripheral devices and the peripheral bus in a computer. Although SCSI is not used exclusively for data storage, the most common usage of the technology is for mass storage devices. More expensive and complex than many other methods of storing data, SCSI tends to be deployed in situations where high performance is necessary.

The SCSI standards (Table 2–3) define both a set of hardware specifications and a software protocol. The hardware specifications include how many wires are used to move data and control information, addressing, basic topology, voltage, clock speed, and error correction methods. The software protocol defines how requests for data are made, how devices respond, and how information about devices can be retrieved.

Parallel SCSI is the predominant form of SCSI today. It is called this because it transmits all of its data and control bits at the same time. The SCSI software protocol has also been adapted for use over Fibre Channel interfaces and designated as FCP. Other forms of the SCSI protocol are also available, although they are new and not yet widely deployed. iSCSI is a networked version of SCSI that transmits

TABLE 2-3 COMMON SCSI TYPES

SCSI Type	Bits Transmitted	Maximum Data Transfer Speed (Mbytes/Sec)	Number of Addresses	Maximum Cable Length (Meters)
Ultra SCSI	8	20	8	SE : 1.5 HVD : 25
Ultra Wide SCSI	16	40	16	HVD : 25
Ultra2 SCSI	8	40	8	LVD : 12 HVD : 25
Wide Ultra2 SCSI	16	80	16	LVD : 12 HVD : 25
Ultra3 SCSI/ Ultra160 SCSI	16	160	16	LVD : 12
Ultra320 SCSI	16	320	16	LVD : 12
FCP (SCSI over Fibre Channel)	1	100	> 15 Million	NA
SAS	1	300	128	NA
iSCSI	1	Depends on network speed	IP address limits	NA

data over an IP network. Serial Attached SCSI (SAS) is used for Direct Attach Storage but sends information one bit at a time for faster, more reliable data transfers. The type of SCSI implementation is usually denoted by the width of the data path (normal or Wide) and error correction method (Single Ended or SE, Low Voltage Differential or LVD, or High Voltage Differential or HVD). There are also several types of serial SCSI.

TARGETS AND INITIATORS The SCSI command protocol is based on a client-server architecture. With SCSI, the device that will request data is the initiator, and the device that will return data is the target. Most often, the initiator is a host bus adapter (HBA). An *HBA* is a peripheral board or embedded processor, used to connect a host's peripheral bus to the SCSI bus. The target is the storage device or device controller, such as a RAID controller or tape drive.

In all cases, the initiator is the master, and the target is the slave. The initiator begins all conversations and requests all data. The target provides whatever the initiator requests unless there is an error. It is possible to be both a target and an initiator. This is unlikely in the DAS situation, but there are Fibre Channel and management devices that use this capability.

Targets and Devices

Even knowledgeable people in the storage industry use the terms *device* and *target* as though they were synonyms. Although it is often the case that a storage device is the target, it is not always so. This causes confusion, because initiators are devices as well. The terms should not be used interchangeably.

SCSI ADDRESSING Parallel SCSI allows for either 8 or 16 addresses. Each device has an address with an ID from 0 to 7 or 0 to 15, depending on the SCSI implementation. The number of addresses is related to the number of control lines available, which is the same as the size of the data path. This is not a very large address space.

To expand this limited address space, an additional addressing layer was added to SCSI. Each SCSI address can also be broken down into sub-addresses, called *Logical Unit Numbers* (LUNs). A LUN represents a logical, rather than a physical, address. LUNs can be assigned to portions of a physical device, and multiple LUNs can be assigned to the same device. In Parallel SCSI, there can be 16 LUNs for each SCSI address, for a total of 256 device addresses. Other implementations of SCSI use LUNs to provide a very large address space.

The different Serial SCSI implementations maintain the same overall SCSI addressing scheme by mapping native addresses, such as Fibre Channel or IP addresses, to SCSI addresses and LUNs. Extensions to the SCSI addressing model allow for hierarchical addressing and a much larger address space. This is usually used to accommodate networked SCSI implementations.

Hierarchical Addressing

Even with the use of LUNs, the SCSI address space is very small. To compensate, the range of possible addresses was increased by use of hierarchical addressing. *Hierarchical addressing* adds sub-addresses to existing addresses and LUNs. Getting the Parallel SCSI hardware to cooperate with extended addressing requires LUN extenders. Many users of LUN extenders—those needing a large address space—have moved on to networked storage such as Fibre Channel or Serial Attached SCSI.

PARALLEL SCSI Until there were serial implementations of SCSI, Parallel SCSI was simply SCSI. The "parallel" part was added to differentiate it from the new serial forms of SCSI, especially Fibre Channel SCSI (FCP). The name refers to the fact that data is transferred in parallel, on all wires in the cable at once. For Ultra and Ultra2 types of SCSI, 8 bits are sent at once, with 16 bits sent for Wide versions. Starting with Ultra3 SCSI, all implementations are Wide.

NOTE Parallel SCSI is a *hardware standard*. It is separate from the SCSI software protocol, which operates over several different hardware architectures.

Parallel SCSI varies by three main characteristics. They are

- Data transfer rate
- Data path width
- Hardware error correction method

The data transfer rate indicates how many blocks of data can be transferred in a given time period and is given in megabytes per second. This is a theoretical maximum rate based on the standardized signal speeds, not true access time. What is most confusing about SCSI nomenclature is that most implementations do not actually say what the data transfer rate is numerically. Instead, Parallel SCSI uses the term Ultra SCSI, Ultra2, and Ultra3 SCSI. Only with the advent of Ultra320 was a real data transfer rate mentioned. Many elements can affect the real throughput of a SCSI data transfer. These include software overhead in the SCSI host bus adapter and storage controller, the speed of the media itself (especially tape drives), and the condition and quality of the connector cables used.

The second major characteristic is the data path width. As previously discussed, Parallel SCSI has two different options: an 8-bit path and Wide I (16 bits).

The last characteristic is the error correction method. Originally, SCSI had no hardware error correction. All bits were sent down a single set of wires. This type of SCSI is known as Single Ended, or SE for short. SE hardware does not detect and resend individual bits when they are corrupt. The upper-level protocols have to detect corrupt data. The target then has to resend all the data in the requested block. One corrupted bit could cause an entire block, which might be megabytes in length, to be resent. This reduces the actual throughput of the device.

One of the major causes of lost or corrupted data is noise. The effects of noise become more pronounced as cable lengths increase and signal rates go up. After a certain length and speed, bit errors due to noise will occur frequently. Because of this, SE SCSI requires very short cables. The cables, however, are cheaper, as is the rest of the hardware. Single Ended SCSI can be used in places where the cable lengths are very short and noise well managed, such as inside a server.

It was quickly realized that the short cable lengths were a real hindrance to external system implementations of SCSI. Although SE was fine for attaching a few hard drives inside a file server, it was often impractical for longer external connections to storage devices such as disk arrays. Moreover, as disk arrays and tape libraries became larger, internal cable lengths became a serious issue. The cable length limitations affect the entire data path, including the cabling inside the arrays. The answer was Differential SCSI. With Differential SCSI, two wires are used. The voltage on one wire carries the data, and the voltage on the other is the exact opposite. One is represented as –SIGNAL and the other as +SIGNAL. If you add the two voltages together, you should get 0. If not, something is wrong, and just the most recent byte or two of data needs to be resent. This allows SCSI to operate in much noisier environments without significant loss of throughput. The upshot of it all is that much larger cable can be used. The downside of differential SCSI is that hardware and cables were more expensive.

To make matters more confusing, there are also two versions of Differential SCSI: High Voltage Differential (HVD) and Low Voltage Differential (LVD). The major difference between the two is obvious: the voltage. LVD uses lower voltage differences to make its comparisons and detect lost bits. With the introduction of the Ultra2 standard, SE was supplanted by LVD. LVD is less expensive than HVD, and the cable lengths are somewhat shorter (though much longer than SE) and able to operate at data transfer rates that SE could never achieve. LVD worked well enough that it is the only method used for Ultra3 and Ultra 320.

There has been considerable debate as to which are better: Serial implementations of SCSI (especially Fibre Channel) or the Parallel ones. It is a silly argument, because each is better in some ways and poor in others. Parallel SCSI has the advantage of being very cheap and very fast. It is used extensively for connections inside disk arrays and tape libraries, because it is tried-and-true technology. The best place to use Parallel SCSI is in instances where distances are short, and speed and reliability are important.

SERIAL ATTACHED SCSI (SAS) Serial Attached SCSI, or SAS, is relatively new, but the premise is simple. Use the same SCSI protocol, but rethink the hardware layer. Instead of sending 8 or 16 bits at a time, send only one, like Ethernet. Connectors and cables are kept small, and reliability is kept high. This makes for a very inexpensive, yet very fast way of connecting storage devices within a computer or array.

SAS has been envisioned as an in-the-box technology. A typical way to make use of SAS is inside a disk array that has external Fibre Channel or Ethernet connections. SAS is also likely to become popular as a replacement for internal SCSI drives.

SAS and SATA

SAS hardware, interestingly enough, also supports Serial ATA, an entirely different serial storage protocol. Although this is very good from the

(continues)

system architect's point of view, it is unusual. Even in situations where low-level hardware components are the same, as is the case with Fibre Channel and Gigabit Ethernet, it is rare that two different storage protocols will be able to share the same wire.

This is fine in theory, but it remains to be seen whether all manufacturers will support this capability. Even more important, will system administrators and architects want it, and will this mix-and-match capability actually work?

THE SCSI PROTOCOL   No matter which hardware architecture is used—be it SAS, a flavor of Parallel SCSI, or Fibre Channel SCSI—all architectures use some form of the SCSI protocol. At a software level, they all are very similar, with differences due mostly to addressing. From the perspective of the applications and operating systems that interface with SCSI devices, they are all the same. The same software architecture and commands are used by all types of SCSI devices. This helps to account for the longevity of SCSI as a protocol. It has been adapted to a variety of platforms and architectures without causing major changes in applications and operating system interfaces.

SCSI uses a client–server architecture, though it doesn't use the terms *client* or *server*. The initiator sends commands to the target, which is then expected to respond. All commands follow a standard format called the Command Descriptor Block (CDB), which contains the command plus the target address. The target device responds with what was requested or an error block.

There are a number of phases to the protocol. The first few—Bus Free, Arbitration, Selection, and Reselection—are used to allow initiators to gain control of the SCSI bus so they can send a command. These phases do not necessarily apply to all types of SCSI. Next is the Command phase, where the target requests a command from the initiator. The Data phase occurs when the initiator sends its command and gets a response from the target. The final phases are used by the target to request messages and information from the initiator.

SCSI has a lot of commands. The most common are used to read and write data to block devices, such as tapes and disks. Other commands exist that allow an initiator to request addressing information, error messages, and device configurations. Specialized commands exist for media changers on tape and CD-ROM libraries, and so do a host of other read and write commands.

LUN MASKING   *LUN masking* is a technique that hides LUNs from certain initiators. When a target implements LUN masking, it will respond only to the SCSI Inquiry command from select initiators. Other initiators will believe that no device exists at that LUN address. In this way, only select initiators will know of the existence of a device at certain LUN addresses. There are advantages to this approach. In large disk arrays, which are shared among several different hosts, the array can be partitioned among hosts. It is often used in environments where the hosts have different operating systems and could corrupt other hosts' disks. It is even used as a crude form of security.

LUN masking only hides the LUN from the SCSI Inquiry command. If an initiator continues to send commands to that LUN anyway, the target will respond normally.

SCSI Standards

SCSI standards are developed and governed by the T10 technical committee of the InterNational Committee on Information Technology Standards (INCITS). The rules under which this committee operates are approved by the American National Standards Institute (ANSI), which also publishes the standards. SCSI standards are often referred to as ANSI standards. The process is very rigorous.

The major complaint leveled at SCSI and similar storage standards is that they are "loose." Whereas many network standards, like those that govern Ethernet, begin with statements such as "It MUST," many SCSI standards say, "It MAY." This has led to compatibility problems with "standard" equipment from different vendors. The storage industry is famous for having to run plug-fests to find out which equipment that complies with ANSI standards has interpreted the standards differently.

The T10 committee's web site (www.t10.org) has documents that discuss all aspects of the standards that SCSI is based on, as well as work that is in progress by the committee.

ATA

ATA is the most popular mass storage device interface specification in use today. ATA stands for *AT Attachment,* as in the IBM PC AT, from roughly 1982. It is the interface of choice for desktop hard drives. It is also used extensively for CD-ROM/RWs in desktop and laptop PCs. Currently, ATA is used mostly inside computer and similar devices.

Parallel ATA, like Parallel SCSI, uses a bus architecture with a limited address space. Each ATA channel can only address two devices: a primary and secondary, also called the *master* and *slave.* Most desktop computers have controllers with two parallel ATA channels. It is not uncommon to have an ATA interface with a channel for two hard drives and another channel for the CD-ROM/RW and DVD-ROM/RW drives.

As is the case with Parallel SCSI, Parallel ATA transmits bits in parallel, 16 bits at a time. Data can be transferred to and from only one device at a time.

Whichever device has control of the bus keeps it until it is finished with the transfer. This means that two high-usage devices will often be in contention for the bus, and performance will suffer. It is also why it is common to put the CD-ROM and other slow devices on a separate channel from the hard drives.

ATA also uses a protocol layer that is similar to SCSI, making it independent, in some respects, from the hardware specification. This is one of the reasons that it has been adapted for Serial ATA and that other protocols can run over the ATA hardware. ATAPI, an offshoot of ATA, is used mostly for removable media, such as CD-ROM and tape drives. It employs SCSI commands over the ATA hardware to communicate with these devices.

ATA Limitations Are Not Really Limitations

Much has been made about the so-called limitations of ATA compared with SCSI and Fibre Channel. ATA's hard drive performance, addressing, and reliability are inferior to those of SCSI and Fibre Channel. This is not a function of the drives themselves but of the interface. The drives are usually made with similar components, though the design is simpler.

ATA was meant to be inexpensive, and compromises were inevitable. It is an example of a technology that is good enough. It does the job splendidly, but the job is not to have server-class performance and reliability. Instead, it provides just what a desktop needs at a cost that is reasonable. If computer manufacturers had to rely on SCSI drives, only the highest-end users would have a hard drive bigger than 10 gigabytes. It simply would not be cost effective. Instead, it is common to find $1,000 home computers with 120-gigabyte drives.

ATA is being used successfully to design new types of drive arrays that are much less expensive than SCSI or Fibre Channel arrays, but with performance and reliability that is close to what they offer. By using a reliable, high-performance interface and enclosure, array manufacturers are able to take advantage of the lower cost of ATA drives and components. ATA is able to meet the requirements of a vast number of applications.

Different versions of ATA are usually referred to by their data transfer speed. Common implementations are ATA/33 (33 megabytes per second), ATA/66, ATA/100, and ATA/133.

SERIAL ATA (SATA)   For much the same reasons that Serial Attached SCSI was created, so was Serial ATA. They are, in fact, linked because the hardware layer is the same for both. The difference between SAS and SATA is the protocol that they use. This provides backward compatibility with the maximum number of applications and operating systems while keeping costs low. Like SAS, SATA is viewed best as an in-the-box technology, used to create very inexpensive, yet high-performance, disk arrays.

SATA works well for hot backups, staging data, and snapshots, and as storage for less important data. Performance should approximate that of SAS, and the reliability of SATA disk arrays should be nearly as good as that of a SCSI or Fibre Channel array.

NETWORK ATTACHED STORAGE (NAS)

Network Attached Storage (NAS) provides large amounts of file space as a network resource. In some respects, NAS is little more than a self-contained and highly optimized file server. NAS units support the same network storage protocols as network operating systems do. Many high-performance NAS disk arrays use proprietary operating systems; others use embedded versions of the Windows or Linux network operating system.

NAS has several advantages over a traditional file server. Some characteristics that make NAS attractive to system architects are the use of open protocols for shared file services, ease of installation and management, scalability, and high performance. The ability to install and manage NAS devices easily also translates into lower operating costs. A file server may take hours, or even days, to get up and running in its most basic form. A NAS system might do the same in minutes.

Another important advantage is that a NAS device does only file services. At first this seems like a small thing, but it makes a difference when it comes to maintenance, performance, and uptime. NAS devices are unencumbered by the extra capabilities that a general-purpose operating system has to have. Everything that is not related to efficient file serving can be stripped out. There is also a lower chance that a nonstorage program will crash the system, because none can be installed.

In the early days of networked storage, there was a tendency for storage vendors to argue over which was better: Network Attached Storage or Storage Area Networks. The debate was silly and unproductive. Both are useful for different applications and must be viewed by themselves, not in opposition to each other.

Storage Appliances Have a Distinct Advantage

NAS arrays are appliances: special-purpose systems that perform one function very well. It is easy to think of storage appliances as being similar

(continues)

to a network router. In the early days of networking, routing was accomplished with software running on a general-purpose computer. Most server operating systems, such as UNIX and Linux, can still perform this function. It was just inefficient. Too many things could happen to the general-purpose server that affected availability or performance. The dedicated router or a router embedded in a network switch overcame these limitations, and the server acting as a router all but disappeared.

The same holds true for NAS and other storage appliances. By focusing on one or two key functions, storage appliances are more efficient.

Many high-end NAS devices have the ability to scale to very large sizes, into the multiterabyte range. This is more than a typical file server can often handle in a single file space. Recent NAS software has the ability to create a single file space across many NAS devices. This feature lets the system administrator connect multiple arrays and have them appear as one file space, expanding the file space by adding new arrays when needed.

For some time, the NAS market has been divided into three spaces: low end, middle tier, and high end. The low-end NAS market has targeted products to the small office–home office (SOHO) and as desktop backup devices. These are little more than a large hard drive with an Ethernet network connection and an embedded network operating system. They are small, simple to install, and easy to maintain but have practically no features suited for a large data center. The Achilles heel of products in this category is cost. Although total costs are lower, owing to quick and easy installation and negligible maintenance needs, the cost of acquisition has traditionally been higher than for a general file server with similar capabilities. This has made these products unattractive to small businesses.

Most NAS falls into the mid-tier category and is designed for web servers and departmental file servers. Network Appliance is a leader in this arena, along with storage giant EMC. Arrays in this space often have high availability features, a faster network connection (usually 10/100/1000 BaseT Ethernet), software protocol support for enterprise-level management, and high performance. The storage capacity of these arrays ranges from 250 gigabytes to roughly 1 terabyte.

The high end of the NAS market is defined mostly by capacity and management features. High-end NAS disk arrays can scale up to multiple terabytes and include features such as global file management and virtual volume capabilities.

The File Head

What turns a bunch of disks into a NAS array? It is the file head. Often called the NAS head, it is a specialized server that contains at a minimum a processor, memory, network connections, storage connections (usually SCSI or Fibre Channel), and a network operating system. From the network's perspective, the file head is a file server, communicating via one or more common or proprietary protocols.

The file head may be external to the disk array or embedded in it. In many cases, the file head is physically integrated into the NAS device. The software it supports may be nothing more than the TCP/IP stack, simple web-based management software, and a stripped-down network operating system. On the other hand, it may contain specialized volume management, advanced device management, support for NAS backup, clustering, and other high-end storage software. It all depends on what type of applications the NAS device is targeted to.

NFS and CIFS

In beginning, a lot of NAS manufacturers used their own protocols for communicating between a host and the NAS array. There were certain drawbacks to this, chief among them being locked into one vendor. It also required special drivers, which limited the number of supported platforms.

Soon, most vendors of NAS products began to use two popular protocols for file sharing: the Network File System (NFS) from Sun Microsystems and the Common Internet File System (CIFS). NFS provides for file access and integrity when accessing files across a network. It was created by Sun Microsystems in 1985 and since then has been widely deployed on UNIX and Linux systems. Client-side NFS drivers are available for a variety of platforms, including all major versions of Microsoft Windows.

CIFS is an updated version of the Server Message Block (SMB) protocol, which also dates back to 1985. Originally developed by IBM, it was adopted by IBM and Microsoft as LAN Manager, and forms the underpinnings of file and print services common to all Windows platforms. An open-source implementation of the client and server side of SMB/CIFS—called SAMBA—is available on Linux and is widely used to create Linux file servers for Windows environments.

Some manufacturers still ship products using their own protocols, often for specialized applications or to gain some performance advantage. Most, however, use NFS, CIFS, or both.

Storage Architectures Using NAS

NAS can be used anywhere that a file server would be deployed. It can be supported on the same network infrastructure as servers or other network devices.

The most common uses for NAS are in web server farms; as departmental file servers; and for storing large files, such as GIS data or engineering drawings, that are typically shared among many users. For these applications, the high performance, efficient design, and ease of use of NAS devices makes them cost effective. NAS disk arrays are often called *filers*. The term originated with Network Appliance but has become a generic term.

File Server Replacement

In environments where there are limited or no IT resources, the ease of use and simple maintenance required of NAS makes it a worthwhile investment. Very small organizations tend not to have file servers at all because of the complexity of the software and skills needed to maintain them. NAS is an excellent choice for these organizations.

For larger companies, the need to change or add new file servers on a regular basis makes NAS a viable option. The ease of installation means that NAS arrays can be deployed quickly without draining IT resources.

WEB SERVER FARMS   One of the most popular applications for NAS is web server farms. ISPs, commercial sites, and large company web sites usually deploy many web servers for performance and availability reasons. By spreading the load over many computers, these web server farms are capable of handling many users simultaneously without performance degradation due to processor loads. Web server farms usually have a very large number of files that must be shared among all the servers. Copying files to many individual arrays is both costly and time-consuming when changes are made. NAS centralizes the files into a single space.

Because NAS is file-based, it matches the structure of the main components of web sites: HTML files. HTML files can now be housed on only a small number of high-performance NAS arrays and remain accessible to all web servers. This is clearly more cost effective and easier to maintain than many individual arrays. Web servers provide a processor and memory; the NAS devices provide file services.

Hybrid NAS-SAN Devices

For a long time, NAS and SAN were independent, often hostile, technologies. Unfortunately, that's not what system architects and storage administrators wanted. The IT community understood one thing that vendors were slow to catch on to—it's just a bunch of disks. The network interfaces were no longer much of a concern, especially with iSCSI using an Ethernet network to create a SAN architecture. All that differentiated SAN and NAS disk arrays was the file head and other supporting software. A file head could be placed in front of a SAN to produce a NAS system and iSCSI used to get block I/O over Ethernet.

The data storage industry responded with a series of hybrid devices. First, SAN disk array manufacturers and resellers began to place a file head on the Fiber Channel SAN to produce NAS and SAN together. NAS vendors responded by allowing iSCSI commands to pass through the file head and perform block I/O. These hybrid systems are flexible and make the best use of expensive resources. Most IT managers will buy separate systems when they can, for the sake of efficiency. They deploy hybrid systems when cost control is more important.

Most hybrid arrays require that different volumes be used for the SAN and NAS portions of the disk space. It would not be very safe to allow changes to the data underlying the files without the knowledge of the file system. Reading blocks of data won't hurt anything, but writing could corrupt files and directories. Different protections can be set on volumes to accommodate this.

STORAGE AREA NETWORKS

Storage Area Networks is not a specific technology. It has become so closely associated with Fiber Channel that some people think they are the same, but they are not. A SAN is a storage system architecture, and Fibre Channel is one way of implementing it. There are other technologies that can be used to build a SAN. iSCSI is emerging as a way of creating a SAN without the expense and aggravation of dealing with Fibre Channel. It uses the more common Ethernet and IP infrastructure instead.

The SAN architecture replaces the I/O channel bus (Figure 2–6), common to technologies such as SCSI and ATA, with a network. Whereas NAS is file storage on a network, SANs are a network architecture for storage, capable of block I/O.

The storage bus architecture, developed for SCSI, suffers from a number of common restrictions. Distance, address space restrictions, number of supported devices, and a one-host/several device limitation make scalable, highly resilient storage systems difficult (and costly) to build and maintain. SANs, being network-based, overcome these limitations. Maximum distance is measured in many kilometers. Address space can be in the millions. The number of devices is usually limited only by the address space. SANs are many-to-many systems and can easily support multiple paths between devices. This makes SANs less susceptible to failures due to path failure.

A related benefit is better cable plant management. Because SANs use serial networking technology, the cables are thin and flexible. SAN cables can be dressed inside cabinets. They can be laid under floors and in ceilings, something that is very difficult with big, fat, rigid SCSI cables. This is a major concern in large installations.

DAS is difficult and expensive to scale. There is a one-to-one relationship between servers and storage. If more storage is needed, often, more servers need

Direct Attach Storage

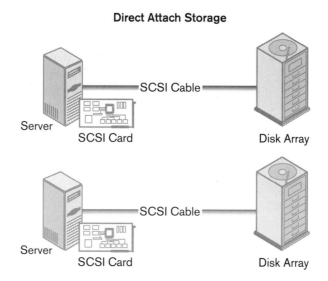

Storage Area Network

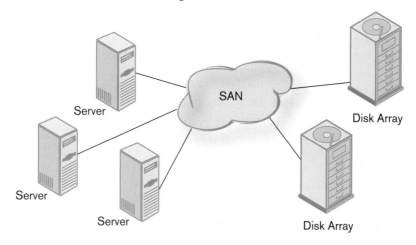

FIGURE 2-6 THE SAN ARCHITECTURE REPLACES THE DAS ARCHITECTURE

to be added as well. In a SAN, adding more storage does not mean more processors. Adding more servers does not mean adding more storage, either. The storage and server architectures can be *scaled independently.*

The implementation and topology of a SAN varies greatly by the technology used. An IP-based SAN will be designed differently from a Fibre Channel one. SANs may also use more than one type of technology, mixing Fibre Channel, iSCSI, and WAN or MAN elements, depending on system needs and cost constraints. Whatever is used to build the SAN the effect is the same. The servers and storage are decoupled and a multipoint network placed between them.

SAN COMPONENTS A SAN needs to have only three components: a host, a network, and storage. Hosts can be computers of any type but are usually servers. Storage can be of any type, such as disk arrays, tape libraries, or CD-ROM jukeboxes. Most often, a SAN is deployed when there is a need to share storage or hosts. If the goal is to consolidate a data center, for example, there is a need to share equipment. In this instance, a SAN may be justified. For a high availability infrastructure, the ability to perform failover to a similar device often makes SANs an important option.

That said, there are a lot of variables when it comes to SAN components. The applications involved drive the type of network needed, which in turn defines the components.

Is It Possible to Just Add More Storage?

It would seem that scaling a SAN should be a relatively easy thing. If something more is needed, simply add it. It's never that simple. To begin with, adding more of anything to a SAN means more network ports are consumed. That presents a problem when adding one more port means buying an entire switch at considerable cost. This is a problem typical of all networks.

The bigger issue is with *provisioning,* or allocating resources. Depending on the type of network, there may not be enough bandwidth available for the application in question. Allocation of the storage space itself is a problem. Just because the storage is available doesn't mean that a server can use it effectively. If the volume manager doesn't allow a system administrator to change the size of the volume to encompass the new disk space, it may have to be set up as a separate volume. That's often fine for files but not for a

(continues)

database, which may not be able to span volumes. In any event, the application is likely to have to be taken offline for the changes to be made. That is not an attractive option in a high availability environment.

Fibre Channel (FC)

The most common technology used to build SANs today is Fibre Channel (FC). Fibre Channel combines serial network and I/O channel technology to create a high-performance, low-latency interconnect. Although there are copper wire implementations of Fibre Channel, fiber optic support was included from the beginning, giving it excellent long distance capabilities (Table 2–4). Today, fiber optic cables are preferred for Fibre Channel networks.

Fibre Channel is very fast. Current implementations have signaling speeds of 1 or 2 Gigabits per second; speeds of 4 Gigabits per second are also available, with 8 and 10 Gigabit implementations in development. The majority of the installed base of Fiber Channel is 1 Gigabit, with 2 Gigabit likely to be implemented in new SANs; 4 Gigabit FC is deployed mostly for switch-to-switch links and inside very-high-performance arrays.

Links, whether optical or copper, are full duplex, with each port capable of transmitting and receiving at the same time. Data is packaged in frames, and frames from different channels are interleaved. Because of these characteristics, data from one channel does not have to wait for all the data on another channel tobe sent to perform its I/O. This is very important when writing to several disks or devices simultaneously. Unlike Parallel SCSI, there is no contention for a bus, though as in Ethernet, there can be network congestion issues.

FIBRE CHANNEL NETWORK STACK

Like most network technologies, Fibre Channel has a stack that defines the various layers of functionality. Each layer is defined by a set of standards and specifications that are maintained and expanded by the INCITS T11 committee (www.t11.org) in the same way that the T10 committee manages the standards for SCSI.

Each layer in the stack (Table 2–5) describes the behavior of Fibre Channel at a certain level, starting with the FC-0 level and progressing to FC-4.

TABLE 2–4 FIBRE CHANNEL CABLE DISTANCES

Cable Type	Maximum Effective Distance
Multimode fiber optic	500 meters
Single-mode fiber optic	2 kilometers
Copper	30 meters

TABLE 2-5 FIBRE CHANNEL STACK

Fibre Channel Layer	Description
FC-0	Physical
FC-1	Transmission
FC-2	Framing and signaling
FC-3	Common services
FC-4	Upper-level protocol mapping

FC-0 defines the physical layer including signaling, media, cable requirements, and receiver and transmitter specifications. FC-1 specifies the transmission encoding scheme. It uses 10 bits to encode 8 bits of data, the other two bits being used for error correction. This is why it is called 8b/10b encoding. The FC-1 layer also includes a set of specifications that define link layer behavior.

FC-2 specification defines the format of the FC frame, flow control, fabric login and logout, classes of service, and frame delivery characteristics. FC-3 provides specifications for common services, such as multicasting.

The top layer, FC-4, is most responsible for the success of Fibre Channel as a technology. FC-4 defines the mappings of common protocols to the FC infrastructure. From the beginning, FC was designed to allow all types of networking and application protocols to ride on top of the network infrastructure. The most common is the Fibre Channel implementation of SCSI (FCP), but many others are also available. Internet Protocol, or IP, is another common protocol readily available in an FC environment. IP is often used to carry management information in-band and has been used in the specialized applications in the same fashion as IP over Ethernet. Fibre Channel is capable of accommodating storage protocols over a network while maintaining a high-performance, low-latency environment

FIBRE CHANNEL TOPOLOGY: POINT-TO-POINT, FABRICS, AND LOOPS

Fibre Channel supports three topologies: switched fabric, point-to-point, and arbitrated loop. *Point-to-point* refers to connecting two devices without the benefit of a network. Although fairly uncommon, it is sometimes used when there is no need to share devices but distance or performance is a problem. It has become less common since the advent of SCSI Ultra3 and SCSI Ultra 360.

Switched fabric, usually referred to simply as *fabric,* uses a Fibre Channel switch to provide *full-bandwidth connections* between nodes in the network. Fabrics may consist of one or many switches, depending on scale, availability, and cost considerations. Fibre Channel fabrics also provide other network services. Switches implement naming, discovery, and time services as part of the fabric. This is different from many other network architectures. Unlike Ethernet or IP, these are *required* to be implemented in the switch. DNS for IP networks does not require that it be part of a switch or router and is often a separate device. In Fibre Channel fabrics, these services are integrated into the fabric.

The terms *fabric* and *switch* are often used interchangeably. They are not the same and should not be used as such. Fabric refers to the topology and services, but not a device. A switch is a network device that implements the fabric.

Switches and Directors

Another type of Fibre Channel switch is called a *director*. Directors are switches, just large ones. They are loaded with high-reliability features, but at a higher cost. Switches can be quite small, as small as 8 ports, although 16-port versions are more common. Directors tend to have 64 ports or more; the largest have hundreds of ports. All directors have high-end reliability features such as two or more power supplies, automatic failover of critical components, and the ability to perform firmware upgrades without powering down the unit.

The third Fibre Channel topology is called *Fibre Channel Arbitrated Loop*, or just *loop.* Arbitrated loops were conceived of as an inexpensive way to implement a SAN by eliminating the relatively expensive switch, along with its integrated services. In an Arbitrated Loop, all nodes are connected in a loop, with frames passing from one node to the next. All nodes on the loop share the available bandwidth, which inhibits the scalability of Arbitrated Loop. The more nodes that are transmitting on the network, the less bandwidth is available for any individual node. As fabric switches have become less costly, Arbitrated Loop has fallen from favor. It is used mostly inside storage devices such as arrays.

FIBRE CHANNEL ADDRESSING All Fibre Channel nodes carry an address called a *World Wide Name* (WWN). The WWN is a unique 64-bit identifier. Much like an Ethernet MAC address, part of the WWN is unique to manufacturer of the equipment, and the rest is usually a serialized number. However it is created, the WWN is unique and specific to a physical port.

Changing the World Wide Name

Although it would seem that the WWN is immutable, there are some instances in which it can be changed. WWNs are often placed in nonvolatile memory (NVRAM) and as such can be changed, given the right utility. A utility such as this would need to be available at boot time, before the port was fully initialized. In the early days of Fibre Channel, it was not uncommon to find host bus adapters with this capability.

Why would anyone want to do such a thing? Having the same WWN would have a similar effect to having the same MAC address in an Ethernet environment. At least one of the devices would not be able to log into the network, or devices would become confused as to the origin of a frame.

The reason this facility sometimes exists is that the NVRAM that holds the World Wide Name can become corrupted, making the port unusable. This used to happen with host bus adapters placed in poorly shielded computers. It is a dangerous utility to have around (as will be evident in Chapter 6: Storage System Security) and should be locked away, where no one can get at it.

Some devices do this on purpose. In certain multiport devices, some ports are kept offline in case a port fails. If one does, the spare port becomes active with the original port's WWN. This makes it look like the original port to the network. This method of failover has the advantage of not requiring hosts or applications to do anything. On the other hand, I/O is usually lost, and some applications may fail during the changeover.

A 64-bit address is very large. Needng to have a frame carry two of these—one for the source and one for the destination—makes routing packets between ports cumbersome. To combat this problem, Fibre Channel also uses an alternative addressing scheme within Fibre Channel switched fabrics. Each port is assigned a 24-bit port address within the fabric when the port logs in. There are two advantages to this. One, it is faster to route packets on a smaller address (and takes less processor time). Second, the addresses are dynamically assigned and managed by the fabric operating system. This also makes it easy and faster for the OS to deal with changes in the fabric.

FIBRE CHANNEL SAN COMPONENTS Like other network technology, Fibre Channel needs certain basic components to create the network infrastructure and connect to it. In addition, a Fibre Channel SAN needs to have storage; otherwise. it's not really a SAN.

There are basically three major components to a SAN. The first is the host bus adapter (HBA). Deriving its name from the SCSI HBA, the FC HBA allows host devices to connect to the Fibre Channel network. Almost all FC HBAs support fabric, point-to-point, and arbitrated loop topologies. The host connector depends on the type of computer that it is intended for, but most support the PCI bus. Newer HBAs support PCI-X, and a smaller number of older adapters have support for Sun Microsystems' S-bus technology.

The second piece of the Fibre Channel SAN is the network equipment. Because most FC networks are installed as fabrics, switches are needed. The type of switch will depend on the nature of the SAN applications. A small SAN will likely use one or more 16-port switches, whereas a large, high availability SAN is a good candidate for a director.

Finally, it would not be a SAN without storage, so Fibre Channel-enabled disk arrays, tape libraries, and other storage devices will be deployed in the network. There are other components that can be added, including device management software, storage resource management (SRM) software, gateways to other networks, and various appliances. However, with HBAs, a switch, and some storage, the basics of a SAN are in place.

ZONING   A concept important to Fibre Channel SANs is *zoning*. In a nutshell, zoning is a crude method of limiting access to SAN resources. It is specific to fabrics (it is a fabric service) and allows a set of nodes to see only other nodes in the same zone. Similar to LUN masking, zoning doesn't restrict frames from being sent from one node to another. Originally conceived of as a way of keeping operating systems from seeing and grabbing hold of resources that were already claimed by other hosts, zoning has become important as a tool for managing large SANs.

There are two types of zoning. The first is based on the World Wide Name of a Fibre Channel port. Called *soft zoning,* it has the advantage of flexibility. Zones do not need to change when you move a device to a different port. The disadvantage is that it is a less secure method of zoning. This is discussed in detail in Chapter 6, Storage System Security.

The second type of zoning is called *hard zoning.* Hard zoning creates zones based on the switch *port* address. In some ways, this is less amenable to changing environments, because the zone has to be changed when devices are moved from one port to another. There are some security benefits to hard zoning.

The default zone for new devices is no zone. *There is no default zone.* **It is considered good practice to zone all ports, even ones not in use.**

PORT BLOCKING   Fibre Channel switches do not have unlimited bandwidth. The amount of bandwidth available to service connections is a function of the amount of memory in the switch, the speed of the internal processors, and the design of the switch chips. It is hardly ever cost effective to provide enough bandwidth to handle full-bandwidth connections to all ports at the same time.

Instead, switches deploy a strategy of port blocking. When the devices on the Fibre Channel SAN are trying to transmit a quantity of data that exceeds what the switch is capable of handling, some ports will be temporarily blocked and applications forced to wait until system resources are available. This is not usually much of a problem. It is unlikely that all ports will want to receive and send at full bandwidth at the exact same time. Even when that does happen, which can occur in some very demanding environments, the amount of time that a port is blocked is small enough not to be noticed by an application.

TIP Some director-class switches claim to have all ports nonblocking. Read the fine print to see if this is really the case. It may be true for limited configurations but not for a full port count.

IP-Based SANs

For many years, the terms *SAN* and *Fibre Channel* were nearly synonymous. Although there were crude SCSI SANs using specialized and quirky devices, any real SAN was a Fibre Channel SAN. That has since changed. SANs using IP over Ethernet have proved to be a viable alternative for many applications.

Because Fibre Channel SANs already exist, it begs the question "Why bother?" FC SANs are proven technology, and IP networks are not nearly as deterministic and, hence, not as conducive to block I/O. Why introduce the SAN architecture into a new environment? The answer is cost and stability. Fibre Channel is still very expensive to implement. The components are specialized and very costly for many applications. It needs a specialized skill set within the IT department, as well as specialized management software that is largely not integrated with other networking suites.

An IP SAN, in comparison, leverages existing skills and knowledge in the IT department. It uses equipment common to other networking needs, including switches, NICs, test equipment, and software. Having one homogenous network architecture also reduces management costs by providing only a single problem set to deal with. For many IT professionals, maintaining an entire separate network just for storage is difficult to justify.

Many of the components are less costly, especially switches, on a per-port basis. Even where equipment is on par, from a cost perspective it is expected to drop faster, because Ethernet products sell in much higher volume than does Fibre Channel. Over time, the cost of an IP network should be less than that of a Fibre Channel one.

Fibre Channel has been plagued by incompatibility issues since its inception, and IT professionals are tired of having to deal with these problems. There is the perception that Ethernet and IP products are more stable. There is some truth to this. Ethernet and IP have been around much longer than Fibre Channel (by more than 20 years) and have very strong standards.

Simply put, Fibre Channel gives some people sticker shock, is overkill for many applications, and has a history of incompatibility problems. IP is a known problem set. Most IT departments understand IP and are comfortable with it.

IP SAN Performance: When Is It Good Enough?

The biggest drawback to implementing a SAN using IP networks is performance. Fibre Channel fabrics are *deterministic,* meaning that they can be relied on to deliver frames within a certain amount of time. Block I/O was originally built around a bus architecture that delivers all the data requested right away, as soon as the data transfer starts. Thus, block I/O depends on deterministic behavior to some degree. Fibre Channel can deliver that.

IP networks are by nature nondeterministic. Packets are delivered based on best effort. Congestion, loss of connection, and other disruptions in data delivery are common. This mode of operation can give high-performance storage applications fits, causing timeouts and other undesired behavior. It is fine for file I/O but can cause problems with block I/O.

That doesn't mean that IP networks are unusable for block I/O. Instead, there are limitations as to what can be reasonably expected in terms of performance. For many applications, it won't matter at all. Tape backup, for example, benefits from a SAN because of connectivity, not performance. Most backup is already done over IP networks, and the slow speed of most tape drives does not put demands on the network.

In situations where performance is not the chief concern, but cost and connectivity are, IP SANs are good enough.

iSCSI   Many protocols have been introduced for building SANs over IP networks. Most were brought out by now-defunct companies. The industry settled on iSCSI instead, and it has emerged as the standard for SANs on IP networks. iSCSI, as its name implies, is a form of the SCSI protocol that operates over an IP network instead of the Parallel SCSI physical layer. It has the same general architecture, with initiators sending commands from targets, which deliver data and responses.

Like Fibre Channel, iSCSI allows for many-to-many configurations, very long distances (though how long remains to be seen), and a much larger address space. iSCSI maps SCSI LUN addresses to IP addresses and port numbers, allowing for millions of potential addresses.

iSCSI uses IP as its transport, which means it can work on any physical network that supports IP (including Fibre Channel). Gigabit Ethernet will be needed to do almost anything useful. Storage applications are heavily affected by bandwidth and latency. The high speed of Gigabit Ethernet will be necessary for applications to perform effectively. New generations of NICs that place the TCP/IP stack on a chip will also help with high-performance applications.

> ### Storage NICs
>
> Some iSCSI interface cards use the term *storage NIC* instead of *host bus adapter*. This is, in part, a recognition that iSCSI runs over Ethernet and IP, where NIC is the term of choice. A storage NIC differs from a standard Ethernet NIC only in that the iSCSI protocol is onboard and not in the OS network stack. Even then, some manufacturers have chosen to call storage NICs host bus adapters.

EXTENDING SANs OVER MAN AND WAN

SANs based on Fibre Channel are isolated installations. Because Fibre Channel is a switched, not routable, protocol, it cannot be routed over a wide area network or metropolitan area network. There are many good reasons to want to connect SANs over a long distance, data protection being chief among them. Copying blocks of data in near real time over a distance is a key component of data protection. Fibre Channel can reach to 2 kilometers, which is enough to get across a campus or over a river. However, doing so requires the laying or leasing of a dedicated fiber optic cable. That can be extremely costly. The solution is to find ways to interact with public networks available from telecommunications providers. That provides a balance between cost and function.

There are several ways to extend a SAN beyond its own cable limits by using public networks. The most popular is to change the transport by using the IP network to carry an FC frame. A protocol called FC-IP was developed to do this. The FC frame, including its payload, is encapsulated in an IP packet. The frame can now be routed over a public network. At its destination, the FC frame is stripped out and placed once again onto the Fibre Channel network. There are several SAN appliances that perform this function, as well as blades that integrate into Fiber Channel switches. A similar protocol called FC-BB sends FC frames over SONET.

Another way to get FC packets over a WAN or MAN is to crack open the frame; pull out the data; and place it in another type of packet, such as iSCSI. Converting to and from another type of protocol can be processor intensive and can lead to interesting address-mapping issues, but several products do this.

Finally, raw bits can be sent over an optical network. Optical switches convert electrical signals to wavelengths of light and send them out over a fiber optic cable. Several optical switches have blades available that convert physical Fibre Channel signals to optical and then send them over optical fiber. Flow control and other network functions have to be handled by the Fibre Channel switch. The optical network basically acts as very long, fat, fast cable.

Extending IP SANS

The problems of routing FC frames do not exist for IP SANs. IP SANs use a routable transport protocol, and IP switches already have interfaces for WANs and MANs. What remains to be seen is whether applications can tolerate the latency inherent in a WAN or MAN.

KEY POINTS

- Direct Attach Storage was the original storage architecture. The term *DAS* came later. One of the first disk systems was called Direct Access Storage Devices, or DASD, and was popular in the IBM mainframe environment. The choices of storage architecture changed in the 1990s with the introduction of Network Attached Storage (NAS) and Storage Area Networks (SAN).

- Hard drives are the primary online storage media, with high speed and high capacity. Tape, CD-ROM/RW, DVD-ROM/RW, and magneto-optical systems are used mainly for backup and archive, as well as software distribution.

- Aggregation into large systems provides benefits in speed, logical capacity, and data protection. Removable media libraries and jukeboxes reduce the chance of error, increase availability, and allow multiple computers to access different media simultaneously.

- When data is accessed directly as blocks, it is called *block I/O*. If it is accessed through a file system, it is referred to as *file I/O*.

- RAID is a way of increasing performance and data protection by writing and reading data to multiple disks at the same time. Major RAID functions including *striping*, the writing of different data to many disks simultaneously, and *mirroring*, which is the writing of the same data to several disks.

- SCSI is a high-performance standard for transferring data to and from devices. It is used extensively for mass storage, and it encompasses both hardware specifications and a software protocol.

- ATA is the most popular storage technology today. It is used in most desktop and laptop computers. It is an in-the-box technology, almost never used to attach storage externally. There is a new serial implementation called SATA or Serial ATA.

- Network Attached Storage (NAS) devices are highly optimized file servers. They use standard protocols to communicate with a large number of clients. They provide high performance, can be quite scalable, and are easy to install and inexpensive to maintain. NAS uses a file head, sometimes called the NAS head, to provide a file system, management, and an interface to the network.

- A SAN is a storage architecture that performs block I/O over a network. SANs have advantages over DAS in terms of distance capabilities, address space, the ability to support many-to-many device configurations, better cable plan management, greater scalability, and higher availability.

- Fibre Channel (FC) is a high-speed, low-latency technology that marries networks with I/O channels. It is often used for SANs. Fibre Channel supports three topologies: fabric, arbitrated loop, and point-to-point. Fabric is the most common and allows for full-bandwidth connections between all nodes in the network. It also implements naming, discovery, and time protocols as part of the fabric.

3

BACKUP AND RESTORE

In This Chapter:

- The First Line of Defense
- Designing Storage Systems for Backup and Recovery
- Recovering from Disaster: Restoring Data
- Tape Backup
- Disk-to-Disk Backup
- Disk-to-Disk to Tape
- Backup and Restore Practices
- Application-Level Backup and Recovery
- Case Study: Bingham McCutchen
- Key Points

THE FIRST LINE OF DEFENSE

Backup and restore is the cornerstone of data protection. Because the earliest computer systems began to collect and manipulate data, having an extra copy of the data for later retrieval has been the most common method of protecting against data loss.

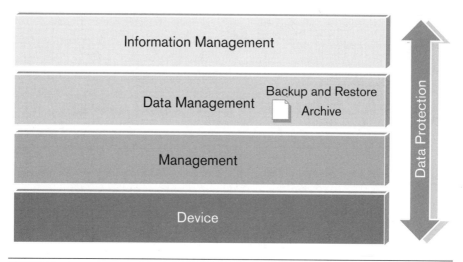

FIGURE 3–0

Backup simply means making copies of data to a different device from the original one, for purposes of restoring it later. The difference between backups and copies made for other purposes is the goal. Whereas other copies of data are made to transfer information or provide for failover, backup data is not meant to be immediately available. The data on the backup media cannot be used in place of the primary system while it is down. Instead, it must be restored to the original or a replacement system, using a process called *restore*. Backup is useless without restore, and restore can't happen without a good backup.

There are many ways to back up data. In some instances, making a copy on a floppy drive is sufficient. That works well for individuals but not for an enterprise of any size. The classic backup media is magnetic tape. Until recently, tape was almost synonymous with backup. All backup and recovery software was designed to work with tape. So prevalent is tape that newer disk-based systems often try to emulate tape backup for compatibility reasons.

For many years, backup and recovery were dull backwaters. Although backup represented a point of pain for IT departments, most of the energy of the data storage industry was focused on making tape systems work better. Tape drives have gotten faster, and media can hold more data than ever before. SAN architectures allow for faster backup of more computers. Very little that was fundamental to backup changed until the late 1990s. At that point, tape was no longer able to keep up with the demands of many businesses. Since then, new ways of supporting backup and recovery operations have been devised.

Now the system architect can choose among many different methodologies and technologies when designing a backup system. Although this makes for more efficient backup and recovery operations, it also complicates design and implementation. It is worth the effort, though. The demands that businesses place on the backup process are increasing and will continue to do so as corporate information becomes more and more valuable.

The Backup Window

Performing backups during heavy system usage times creates problems. Application data may be locked when the backup software needs to copy them. The backup software might do the same, causing applications to fail. Backups tend to create heavy system loads, which slow servers and cause network congestion. All of these cause adverse effects on the system response time and annoy end-users immensely.

For these reasons, backups are usually run when the system load is the lowest, to prevent slow system response times and application timeouts. Typically, this means that backup is done in the middle of the night. The interval when backups can be performed without affecting other systems is called the *backup window*.

DESIGNING STORAGE SYSTEMS FOR BACKUP AND RECOVERY

Storage systems must be designed with backup and recovery in mind. All too often, they are afterthoughts to primary storage systems. This has led to a number of problems, including:

Inadequate backup capacity for the amount of data stored. A constant problem is the need to match backup capacity with the amount of potential disk storage. Often, there is too much data for the available media storage capacity. This leads to failed backups or data being left unprotected.

Backups take too long. The classic point of pain for the IT department is the time it takes backups to complete. If backups take too long, the backups will exceed their backup window. Overlong backups affect systems running during the working day or keep systems from running at all.

Recovery takes too long. It is axiomatic that restore operations take much longer than backups. Unfortunately, restore is always something that you need to do as quickly as possible. If it takes hours or even days to restore data to a critical system, an organization will notice the negative effects. For some organizations, a slow restore of critical data can shut down the entire operation, perhaps for good.

Backup data is corrupted or damaged. As is the case with all complex procedures, things can go wrong. Somehow, the data on the backup media is damaged and unusable. This is often discovered when an attempt is made to recover from a data loss.

Bad data is saved; good data is not. Another common problem is backing data that is damaged. Something has caused the data to be corrupted on the primary storage system, which is then backed up. When the bad data is found, a restore of the data will be attempted. Because the backed-up data is only a copy of the corrupted data, restoring from the backup yields the bad data again.

Critical data is not saved; unimportant data is. To compensate for limited backup capacity, not all data is backed up. Perhaps only data on servers is copied. Maybe only data placed in certain directories or folders is saved. In any event, sooner or later a critical piece of data won't be in the right place and will not be backed up.

Backup data gets copied over by accident. It could be as simple as mislabeling media. Perhaps a system administrator doesn't have the right tape when performing backups and chooses to use another one. Some system administrators, when rotating media, accidentally use the wrong media or get one out of order. There are many ways that the current backup can get overwritten, taking away the insurance that backups are supposed to provide.

The cost of performing backups is skyrocketing. As the amount of data increases, the cost of performing backups is increasing as well. More media is constantly needed as more servers are deployed. Soon, the media begins to cost a considerable of money and takes a lot of time to manage.

Backup media is old and in poor condition. Because nothing is indestructible, all media wears out over time. This is a problem that archivists know well; they are accustomed to paper that dissolves, and to stone that chips and cracks. Electronic media is fragile, too. Over time, tapes stretch and can break. Hard drives can fail (which is one of the reasons we perform backups in the first place), and CD-RW dyes can fade. It is typical to discard a tape when it reaches a certain age, rather than risk breakage. Tape replacement doesn't always happen on time. If there *are* no tapes available, old ones might get used, even when they are past their useful lifetimes.

It is *hard* to recover just one piece of data. Backup software is very good at copying large amounts of data and then restoring it all at once. It is commonplace to back up an entire volume, hard drive, or disk array and then later restore it to the exact state it was in before. When only one file needs to be restored, it can be extremely difficult to find and recover that one file. Tapes do not allow for random access, and it is slow to find and recover a single piece of data.

Good system design can alleviate these problems. In the same way that products are designed for manufacture, storage and server systems must be designed for backup and restore from the start.

Doing the Math Behind Backup

Several factors affect the speed at which backup can occur: the speed of the interface to the backup unit, the access time of the drives being backed up, the speed of the computer's I/O bus, how much memory is available in the computer doing the backup, and the speed of the backup drives. The factors that have the most impact on backup speed are the I/O bus data transfer rate, the speed of the interface, and the access time of the backup drives. The access time of the hard drives rarely comes into play, because it is either very fast or aggregated within an interface that is at least as fast as the backup unit's interface.

As in most computer systems, total throughput is determined by the slowest component in the system: the bottleneck. Usually, that is the tape drive, which is the most common backup media. A very fast tape drive might operate between 35 megabytes per second and 30 megabytes per second uncompressed. Even when transferring compressed data, most tape drives top out at less than 75 megabytes per second. These transfer times are much less than the bandwidth of common storage network connections. Most networks can transfer data at 1 to 10 gigabits per second—roughly 100 to 1,000 megabytes per second.

Two sets of design principles can be derived from this. First, match the interface to the backup drive carefully. It is not worth spending money on a fast interface for a slow drive. Second, aggregation is very cost effective. When data can be streamed to multiple drives, the device's interface's bandwidth is better utilized and larger amounts of data can be backed up.

Recovery Time Objective and Recovery Point Objective

When designing backup systems, two important metrics must be considered. They are Recovery Time Objective (RTO) and Recovery Point Objective (RPO). *RTO* is the amount of time that a system must be up and running after a disaster. In enterprise data centers, the RTO is a matter of a few hours to mere minutes.

RPO is the point in time to which data must be restored. An RPO may require that data be restored up until one hour before the failure, for example. In other situations, it may be acceptable to restore data to the close of business the previous day.

Different systems and types of data often have a dissimilar RTO and RPO. The recovery metrics set for a departmental file server are often different from those set for an enterprisewide database.

Internal DAS Backup

The simplest backup method is to mount a drive internally within an individual server or other computer. A drive is embedded in the computer, and software writes a copy of the primary storage drive's data to the media on a regular basis. This drive can be almost any media, including tape, CD-ROM/RW, another hard drive, or a flash memory device. Tape is the usual media for a server, whereas desktop PCs often use other types of media, such as CD-RW.

The advantage of internal DAS backup is that it is easy to build, configure, and manage. Also, it doesn't create network congestion problems, because no data is being sent over the LAN. Internal backups are self contained and have less chance of being interrupted by forces outside the server.

On the other hand, internal DAS backup subjects a computer to a heavy strain on its memory, I/O bus, system bus, and CPU. It is not unusual for the load on the server to get so high that it can't function at all during the backup. Fine-tuning the backup software and setting a proper backup window are critical and worth the time.

Managing lots of separate media is also a chore and can lead to costly mistakes. It is an especially difficult task, especially when servers are spread out over some area. There is a tendency to leave media in the drives and just let the backup happen automatically. This causes each previous day's data to be overwritten. Not changing media ensures that data can be restored only from the most recent backup. If it takes several days to discover that a critical file was accidentally deleted or corrupted, there will no longer be a credible backup of the file. Unless there is another version on a different computer, the data is lost forever. This defeats the purpose of doing backups.

A similar problem arises when the amount of data to be backed up exceeds the capacity of a single target media. The backup will fail if there is no one around to change the media. It is important to have spare media available and equally important to have someone to load them into the drive. When it is impractical to run around and change media, look to network backups or DAS systems that can change media automatically.

Have the End-User Change the Media: A Really Bad Idea

When the computers in an enterprise are geographically dispersed, it is tempting to have the on-site people change the backup media, even if they are not skilled IT personnel. This is a *very bad* practice. To begin with, the people at some remote location are not trained in the arcane ways of back-ups. They are apt to make bad choices if something goes wrong. It is also likely that they will choose to do nothing at all, leading to backup failures or no backups. Process failures such as this tend to go undiagnosed for long periods of time.

Worse, end-users are more likely to make serious process mistakes. They might choose to leave the media in the drive, for example. They do this because they are too busy with tasks that are central to their jobs (changing media is not).

There are several choices for unattended backup, including external libraries, jukeboxes, and autoloaders, as well as network backup. A service provider might also be a good option to offload remote backup. These are better choices than relying on end-users to perform backups.

External DAS Backup

When the amount of data becomes large or the backup resource load becomes too disruptive, it is important to look to external DAS solutions. With this type of architecture, the backup unit is mounted in its own chassis, external to the computer being backed up, and attached by a cable. The internal DAS model is extended past the computer chassis and into a separate unit. The most common technology used for this is parallel SCSI. A SCSI Host Bus Adapter is mounted in the server and a cable attached. The far end of the cable is attached to the backup unit. The backup software sees the device as though it were mounted in the computer and works the same way as the internal DAS system (Figure 3–1).

There are several advantages to this type of architecture. To begin with, the backup unit has its own processor and memory. This immediately takes a portion of the load off the computer's resources, because some I/O is offloaded to the backup unit.

By having a larger chassis, external units can accommodate multiple sets of media. Media is loaded automatically by robotics or mechanical loading trays. This takes away the problem of having to change media or making mistakes while changing media. External backup devices also allow for multiple drives and SCSI connections to be used for backup, enhancing performance and availability. Media management software is often included with these units, which helps manage unattended backups. Features such as bar code readers keep track of which media belongs to which backup set, and sensors can tell when media is wearing out.

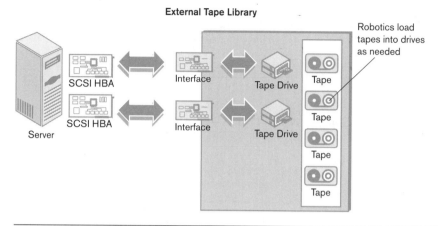

FIGURE 3–1 EXTERNAL DIRECT ATTACH STORAGE TAPE UNIT

TIP In general, storage systems that deploy external DAS primary storage, such as a disk array, call for external DAS systems. That way, capacity and performance can be more easily matched.

LAN-Based Backup

At some point, managing individual backup units for each server, whether internal or external, becomes difficult and costly. It becomes more effective to centralize backup in one or more large backup units that can be used for many servers. When bandwidth to the backup unit is not an issue, but management and cost are, LAN-based backup should be considered.

LAN-based backup uses a server with a backup unit attached to it, usually by some form of Parallel SCSI, to perform and manage backups. The backup server is in turn connected to the network via a standard Ethernet connection with TCP/IP support. This server, unlike an external DAS solution, is dedicated to backup and is used to back up the primary storage of other servers on the LAN (Figure 3–2).

A common variant of this model is to have a separate server control the backup process. The server to which the backup unit is attached only manages the I/O to the backup drives. This has the advantage of allowing one server to manage several backup units, centralizing management of the backup process.

The third variant uses a backup unit that is network enabled. Sometimes called NAS-enabled backup, it has an operating system and NIC embedded in it. The system administrator can then attach the backup unit directly to the network without the need for a server to host it. For small installations, this greatly simplifies installation and management, but at the expense of flexibility (Figure 3–2).

LAN-Based Backup

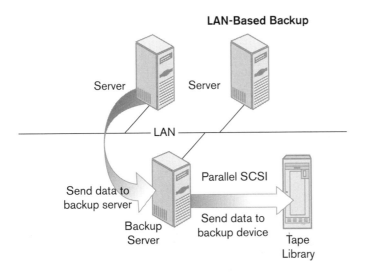

LAN-Based Backup Variants

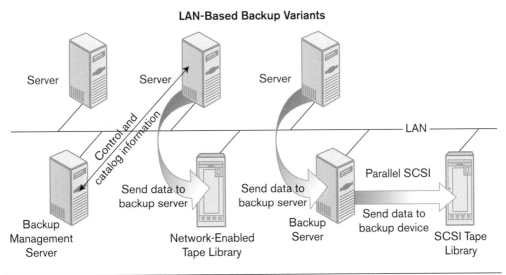

FIGURE 3–2 LAN-ENABLED BACKUP

NOTE NAS backup and NAS-enabled backup sound very similar. *NAS backup* is the practice of backing up NAS devices. *NAS-enabled backup* is LAN-enabled backup, which uses an embedded operating system to eliminate the server to which the backup unit normally would have been attached. It is analogous to NAS disk arrays for primary storage.

In all cases, the backup software on the server reads and writes the blocks of data from the primary storage and sends the data across the LAN to the backup server. The backup server in turn manages the I/O to the backup devices. Often, several backups can be run simultaneously.

The advantages of LAN-based backup are scalability and management. Rather than deal with many different backup drives in many hosts, backup is consolidated into a single unit capable of serving a collection of hosts. Adding a new server does not necessarily mean adding a new tape drive. Instead, excess capacity on existing units is utilized, saving money and time. Backup windows can also be scheduled centrally, with all the backups taken into account. Tape management is much easier when all the tapes are stored in a central location, rather then spread out over a building or data center. LAN-based backup also allows backup devices to be located in a different part of a building or data center from the servers they are backing up, providing flexibility in physical plant design.

The problem that most system administrators run into with LAN-based backup is the strain it places on network resources. Backups are bandwidth intensive and can quickly become a source of network congestion. This leaves the system administrator with the unattractive choice of either impacting overall network performance (and having angry end-users) or worrying that backups won't complete because of network-related problems. Worse, both can occur at the same time.

At some point, the only way to alleviate the network problems is to create a separate network and have a very low server-to-backup-unit ratio. Either method takes away much of the advantage of deploying the LAN-enabled backup solution. Separate networks mean many additional and redundant network components, reducing cost savings and increasing management resource needs. Having few servers backed up over the network reduces the scalability of the architecture until it eventually approaches that of the external DAS solution.

Some backup systems need to read and write data through the file system if they are to deliver it over the network. The backup server needs to mount the remote file system, open and read the files, and then write them as block data to tapes or other media. As is often the case with productivity applications, the files are small but numerous. Backing up a file server in this way means opening and closing many small files. This is very inefficient and slow. Software that can prevent this situation by placing agents on the servers may limit platform choices but allow the software to sidestep the file system.

Another important problem is the issue of the backup window. Unless the backup design calls for a separate network, there will be some impact on the network when backups are being performed. The backup window has to be strictly adhered to, or end-users will feel its effects, even those who do not use the system being backed up. With many companies operating around the clock, the backup window may be very small or nonexistent when network effects are taken into account.

Interrupted Backups: Slamming Your Fingers in the Backup Window

Few things cause IT personnel more pain then interrupted backups. All system administrators would like backups to operate in an unattended fashion without fail. This rarely happens consistently. Some common reasons that backups fail are system failure, network congestion (which causes timeouts), damaged media, backup time exceeding the backup window, excessive CRC check errors (for example, corrupted data), or a full tape or disk without a handy replacement.

When a backup cannot be completed, there are several paths one can take. The first option is to start over from the beginning. If the backup media is tape (which is likely), restarting in the middle of the backup is usually not an option. This is not too bad if the backup is ten minutes into a five-hour backup; it is generally not acceptable at hour three of that same operation. Restarting the backup process is likely to cause it to exceed the backup window, causing other problems.

Another option is to ignore the error and move on with the backup. In some cases, this is possible. If a single piece of data fails a CRC check, the software likely can continue, with only an error log entry being generated. Excessive CRC check failures are a cause for concern, because much of the data is now suspicious.

Sometimes it is impossible to move on, owing to some underlying problem that cannot be fixed immediately. If the backup is exceeding the available media's capacity, there's little that can be done until more of the media is available. If a bad drive controller is causing too many errors, the underlying cause may need to be repaired before backups can continue.

SAN Backup

The single most prevalent reason for the first deployments of Fibre Channel Storage Area Networks has been to alleviate the backup woes that large enterprises experience. By moving to a separate, high-capacity network, tailor-made to storage applications, many issues with backup windows, network congestion, and management can be addressed.

As is always the case, things have not worked out that way. There are many special challenges to performing backups across a Fibre Channel SAN, including the performance of systems on the SAN when backups are running. Still, the basic value proposition remains. FC SANs are an important step in having more reliable and less intrusive backups. With SAN Backup, the backup unit is connected via a Storage Area Network, usually Fibre Channel, to the servers and storage that will be backed up.

Much of the benefit derived from SAN backup comes from the fact that it is performed on a separate high-speed network, usually Fibre Channel. It is arguable that switching backup to a separate Ethernet network without changing anything else provides much the same advantage as a SAN. In many cases, that is true. The problems with network congestion are fixed, and there is enough bandwidth to back up more data.

SANs, however, have the advantage of being able to perform block I/O over a network. Unlike other network backup schemes, in SANs, blocks of data can be read from a disk and delivered directly to the backup unit, which writes the blocks as they are. There is no need for intermediate protocols or encapsulation of data. This makes even IP-based SANs, such as iSCSI, more efficient for backup. Fibre Channel SANs provide the additional benefit of having a very efficient network stack, which again boosts performance.

The SAN also provides connectivity with performance. Many storage devices can be backed up at the same time without impact on the primary LAN or servers. The high bandwidth of Fibre Channel and Gigabit Ethernet relative to tape drives, the most common backup media, allows data from several storage units to stream to multiple drives in the same library at the same time.

It is important to remember that all networks enable the distribution of functions from a single entity to several entities. LANs allow us to break processing and memory resources into many computers, some of which have special purposes. This way, expensive resources can be shared for cost-control purposes, scalability, and increased performance. SANs do the same by distributing storage resources. This is a big part of the attraction of SAN-based backups. By distributing the resources needed to back up data across a network, greater performance, scalability, and cost savings are realized over the long term.

There are two common architectures for a SAN-based backup system. The first, and most common, is *LAN-free backup;* the other is called *server-less backup* or *server-free backup.* Both have certain advantages and disadvantages, though they share the overall advantages of SAN backup.

LAN-FREE BACKUP   As the name suggests, LAN-free backup occurs off the LAN and on the SAN. The storage, servers, and backup units are connected to a network, across which block I/O can occur. This is a basic SAN backup system. All I/O goes across the storage network, and none travels through the LAN. Management and control information may still rely on the presence of a IP network, making LAN-free not completely free of the LAN (Figure 3–3).

Common Misconceptions about SAN Backup

Although SAN backup has some important advantages, the disadvantages are often overlooked. Two common misconceptions about SAN backup are that it has no network impact and that you can eliminate backup system components.

To begin with, the *N* in *SAN* stands for *network*. Performing backups still consumes bandwidth and creates congestion. With an IP SAN, the backup is perhaps more efficient, but dragging large amounts of data across the network will still have a negative effect on performance. Assuming that a separate network is used for the backup system, running several backups at the same time will eat up network capacity until backups fail.

With a Fibre Channel network, the bandwidth in the switch and between ports is still finite. If the SAN is used for more than just backup, which is almost always the case, performance to and from storage devices may be affected by backups. There will be changes in the performance of applications that perform heavy I/O, such as databases, during times when several backups are being performed. SANs do not eliminate the backup window.

Another common fantasy that system architects have is that SAN backup systems will somehow need fewer components and, hence, cost less than LAN-based backup systems. That's not necessarily the case. The storage devices are still needed, as are the backup server, HBAs, and switches. SANs do offer an opportunity to consolidate storage devices and servers, but new network components are also added. In backups as in life, there is no free lunch.

If the primary storage is also on the SAN, the backup server only interacts with servers to get system information. The backup server uses system information for purposes of maintaining catalogs and ensuring proper locks on objects. Actual data is copied by the backup server directly from the storage devices to the backup drives. *The data path does not go through the application server.* The immediate effect is to reduce the backup load on the application server. It no longer needs to read and write data during backups. This allows backups to be performed while the server continues to operate with reasonable efficiency.

LAN-free backup is a good method of relieving stress on servers and the primary LAN. As is the case with all I/O-intensive applications, performance of the SAN is impacted but does not affect the end-user much. LAN congestion and slow servers are more obvious to the end-user. They impact on their ability to get their daily tasks done. The server I/O can be slower than peak performance without the majority of end-users feeling inconvenienced. Let network response time become too slow, and the help desk will be flooded with angry calls. Customers will abandon the e-commerce application the company spent millions to build and roll out.

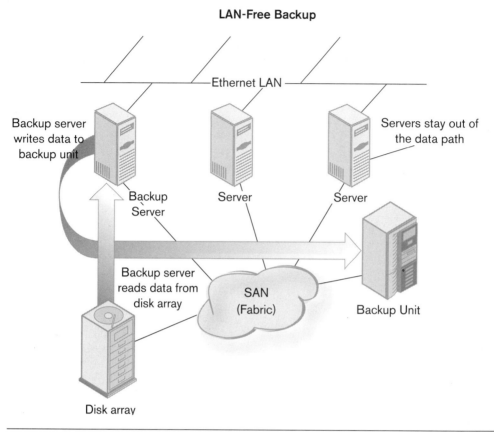

LAN-Free Backup

FIGURE 3–3 LAN-FREE BACKUP

LAN-free backup provides welcome relief to networks and servers overstressed at backup time.

There is another form of LAN-free backup, in which the backup software resides on the individual servers rather than on a dedicated backup server. This is easier to deploy and less expensive then a dedicated backup server. The downside is that the server is still in the data path; also, resources are still taxed during backups. It is also not a particularly scalable architecture. As the system grows, each server will need additional backup software, which will have to be managed separately. If the drag on servers during backups is not all that onerous, and there aren't enough servers to warrant consolidation of the backup function, the argument for performing backup across a SAN is weak.

SERVER-LESS BACKUP The ultimate backup architecture is the server-less backup. There is no server in the data path at all. The data is moved from the primary storage to backup by an appliance or through software embedded in one of storage devices. Software on a server tells the storage devices what to transfer to the backup unit, monitors the process, and tracks what was moved. Otherwise, it stays out of the way of the data. The data is moved from primary storage to the backup unit directly (Figure 3–4).

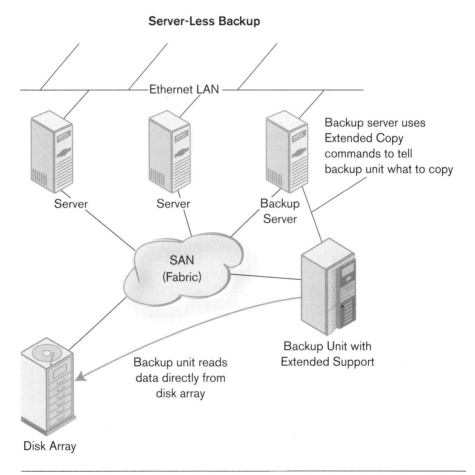

Server-Less Backup

Ethernet LAN

Server

Server

Backup Server

Backup server uses Extended Copy commands to tell backup unit what to copy

SAN (Fabric)

Backup Unit with Extended Support

Backup unit reads data directly from disk array

Disk Array

FIGURE 3–4 SERVER-LESS BACKUP

This is superior to the LAN-free backup because data moves only once and in one direction. Data does not have to be copied to a backup server before being written to the backup unit. An important performance bottleneck is eliminated, and more backup servers are not required to scale the system. Data travels through the SAN only once, reducing the amount of network bandwidth consumed.

From a system perspective, two things are needed for this design to work. First, there needs to be an appliance capable of handling the data transfer, called a *data mover*. The data mover has to be either embedded in one of the storage devices or in an appliance that sits in front of one of them.

There also needs to be a protocol that would tell the data mover which blocks of data to move from primary to backup storage while monitoring the results. This is provided by a set of extensions to the SCSI protocol called *Extended Copy*. By issuing commands to the data mover, the backup software causes the backup to commence and is able to monitor results without being involved in moving the data itself.

TERMINOLOGY ALERT   Never have so many names been given to a protocol. Extended Copy is also commonly known as Third Party Copy, X-Copy, and even E-Copy. Many vendors refer to this SCSI extension as Third Party Copy, because it enables a third party (the data mover) to perform the backup. Technically speaking, Third Party Copy should refer to the architecture and not the protocol.

Server-less backup has never been fully realized. Products claiming this capability have been finicky, exhibiting serious integration and compatibility issues. The performance gains did not outweigh costs for many IT managers. Network and server bottlenecks also turned out not to be as serious an issue as the throughput of the backup media. Disk-based backup is producing a greater impact on backup systems than server-less backup.

Backing Up NAS

There are three models for backing up NAS devices. The first mimics the DAS backup mechanisms of servers. A backup device is embedded within or attached to a NAS disk array system, which has specialized software to perform the backup. It provides a very fast and convenient method of backup and restore. The software can perform dedicated block I/O to the backup unit from the NAS disks. The software also already understands the NAS file system and does not need to use a network protocol to transfer the data on the disks. This is important, because many high-performance NAS arrays have file systems that are proprietary or that are optimized versions of common file systems such as NTFS. Backup software companies typically design custom versions of their software for these environments, or the NAS vendor will produce its own.

Although this is a solution optimized for performance, the backup unit embedded in or attached to the NAS array is dedicated to it. It cannot be shared, even if it is underutilized. Use of a shared backup unit for failover is not feasible. To have a robust system requires duplicate backup units, which are rarely fully utilized.

The second common architecture for NAS backup is via a LAN-enabled backup. As far as the LAN-enabled backup server is concerned, the NAS array is a file server or similar device using the CIFS or NFS protocol. The backup software queries the file system and reads each file to be copied. These files are then backed up through the backup server as usual. This approach has all the advantages and disadvantages of network backup. It is flexible, robust, and makes good use of resources. It is also slow if the NAS array has many small files, which is often the case. Opening and closing each file produces overhead that can bog down data transfer and negatively affect network and NAS system performance.

NAS arrays can also be backed up over a SAN. Most backup software vendors have SAN agents specific to common NAS. SAN backup of NAS devices eliminates the network overhead associated with copying files over a LAN. What detracts from this design is cost. A SAN needs to be in place or built. Additional agent licenses cost more money as more NAS devices are added to a system.

NAS and SANs in Backup Many NAS arrays use SANs for the back-end storage system. In most cases, this SAN is self-contained within the unit or rack in which the NAS system is mounted. There is a definite advantage in terms of scalability to this architecture. A backup system may be part of this back-end SAN. If this is the case, it is no different from a DAS backup unit contained within the NAS system. To the outside world, the backup devices are embedded. The advantage is that as the NAS device scales, there is opportunity for scaling the backup system as well.

NAS-SAN hybrid systems are another story. With access to the data on the disk at file *and* block level, different configurations are possible. A NAS device that can be attached to a SAN may utilize the resources of the SAN for backup. This marries the ease of use and file I/O performance of a NAS while offering excellent backup options.

NAS Backup Using NDMP To back up files, a tape backup program has to access the data on the NAS array. The open protocols available (such as NFS and CIFS) allow backup software to see only the files, not the underlying blocks. The backup then has to be performed using file I/O. Each file has to be opened, the contents read and streamed to a backup device over the network or via an internal SCSI bus, and then closed. This is not a big problem if you want to back up only very large files or a small number of files. If you want to back up *many small* files, files must be opened and closed constantly, and the overhead associated with that will make the system very slow.

The network model is often preferred for backing up NAS devices, yet going through the file system creates problems. Many NAS vendors have implemented their own protocols for streaming data to backup software. The downside of this approach is that the protocols are proprietary, requiring backup software vendors to support many different protocols.

In response, vendors involved in NAS backup developed a standard protocol to manage NAS backup while using standard backup software running on a network. Called the Network Data Management Protocol (NDMP), this protocol defines a bidirectional communication based on XDR (Extended Data Records) and a client-server architecture optimized for performing backup and restore. NDMP allows for a standard way of backing up NAS arrays over a network while removing much of the complexity.

NDMP requires that the backup software support the protocol and that the NAS array have an NDMP agent running on it. The agent is the server, and backup software is considered to be the host.

What's the Best Way to Perform Backup?

Because backup is the most common form of data protection, getting the design right is very important. It is impossible to say what the "best" design is, just as it's hard to say what the best song ever recorded is. It is relative to the system's desired level of protection, backup window, budget, and overall storage architecture. Backup architectures offer different advantages and disadvantages. These are described in Table 3–1.

TABLE 3–1 ADVANTAGES AND DISADVANTAGES OF BACKUP ARCHITECTURES

Architecture	Advantages	Disadvantages
DAS internal	High performance No LAN load	Lacks flexibility and scalability High server loads Can back up only small amounts of data
DAS external	High performance No LAN load Can back up large amounts of data	Lacks flexibility and scalability High server loads
LAN-based backup	Flexible Can back up large amounts of data	Low performance Substantial LAN load Lacks scalability High server loads

SAN backup (LAN-free, FC)	High performances Very flexible and scalable Can back up large amounts of data Low load on LAN	Moderate to high server loads High cost, especially if no SAN is already in place.
SAN backup (server-less)	High performances Very flexible and scalable Can back up large amounts of data No load on LAN Low server loads	High cost, especially if no SAN is already in place. Limited software and hardware support
SAN Backup (LAN-free, IP SAN)	Flexible and scalable Can back up large amounts of data Lower server loads Moderate cost No load on LAN	Moderate performance Lower cost than FC SAN backup
NAS (NDMP)	Moderate to high performance Flexible Can back up large amounts of data Low cost structure	Limited scalability Substantial load on LAN High server loads

The backup architecture has to fit the overall storage system. If it is a SAN being backed up, it is likely that a SAN backup architecture will fit best. The cost is incremental compared with the cost of the rest of the SAN. A SAN backup solution isn't a requirement—LAN-based backup can still be deployed, for example—but has advantages over other solutions.

Backup and Restore Software

Software is the primary ingredient in backup and restore systems. Almost any type of backup unit can be used successfully, but without backup software, it is as inert as a doorstop, except less useful.

All backup software must perform three important functions. First, it must copy the data to the backup media. Without the copy, there are no backups and no protection for the data. Second, it must *catalog* the data objects so that they can be found later. To restore data, the software has to find it and copy it back to the primary storage media. The catalog provides the mechanism for identifying what is on the backup media, what the characteristics of the original primary storage (including name, location, and assorted state conditions) were, and where on the backup media it is located. Catalogs provide the backup software the ability to restore data objects to the state they were in at backup time.

Finally, it must be able to restore data to the *exact* state it was in when it was backed up. That may mean that an entire disk is re-created on a new disk or a single file is restored to what it was last Tuesday.

Other common features that must exist in any enterprise backup and restore software are:

Include support for multiple backup devices. Different versions of the software may support different architectures or methods of backup, but the extended functionality should be a simple add-on or upgrade. Most backup software will work with tape and disk-based backup units. Some software offers options for CD-R/RW, DVD-R/RW, and magneto-optical drives.

Include support for multiple architectures. Most backup software supports SAN, DAS, and LAN-enabled backup models. The software should be able to access various types of disk drives, using either block or file I/O. Unfortunately, an upgrade to the "enterprise" version of the software (which costs much more) is often required to get multiple device or architecture support.

Have the ability to perform unattended backup. One clear difference between robust, enterprise-grade backup software and simple desktop software is how well they handle unattended backup. Desktop backup software usually relies on time-delay programs, such as Windows' Scheduled Tasks or the UNIX `cron` utility, to schedule a backup. Most don't gracefully recover from errors without human intervention. Enterprise-level backup software should be able to initiate and monitor backup, detect and recover from errors, and provide for remote administration. The key is to be able to recover from errors with specific objects, such as an incorrect CRC, without aborting the entire backup.

Have at least 2:1 compression. Considering the disparity between disk storage capacity and most backup media, compression is an important feature. When compression is used, more data is squeezed onto the backup media. It is slower but is often necessary. Most backup software also has provisions for hardware-assisted compression. The hardware assist may be on the backup unit's controller or through an external unit. Support for hardware-assisted compression is a must for enterprise-grade backup software.

Have the ability to back up open objects. It is important to be able to back up files and other objects that are in use, a feature often called *shadow copy*. Backups can often fail if the software lacks this capability. The software encounters an open object and either hangs or skips the object.

Be able to restore at different levels. One of the biggest problems with restore (besides the time it takes to do so) is the level of granularity of the recovery. The software should be able to restore individual files, directories, volumes, and entire disk images. The ability to do this effectively is hampered by what is reasonable for the media to do. The software, however, should support it.

Provide detailed error reporting. Backups are processes that the backup software automates. For proper management of backup, auditing, and error detection, detailed reports are necessary. Besides managing the catalog file, backup software maintains logs that detail (to various degrees) the success or failure of a backup or restores process. These logs are a valuable source of information when something has gone awry or for fine-tuning of the processes.

Include NDMP support. Clearly, if NAS is a major part of the environment, NDMP is a feature worth paying for. It will allow the backup system to adapt to a growing environment without having to rearchitect and rebuild it completely.

Old-Fashioned UNIX Scripts and Applications

Some system administrators swear by their tried-and-true collection of UNIX scripts and utilities. Typically, the `tar` utility is combined with `cron` to create a form of unattended backup. `tar` creates compressed or uncompressed archives, which can be created or copied to any mounted UNIX (or Linux) device, including tape drives. `cron` is used to schedule jobs in the background. By combining these two features of UNIX and Linux with other utilities, such as `grep` (to parse out errors) and the various scripting languages available, a rudimentary backup system can be assembled.

The major advantages of this type of system are that is costs nothing—except the programmer's time, of course—and is completely under the control of the creator. That's about all that is good about this approach. It might work well for a single UNIX system with an embedded tape drive but will do very poorly for any other form of backup.

There are severe limitations to this approach. For one, scripts break very easily. Error conditions that normally would be logged and dealt with by backup applications can cause a script to cease functioning. Error reporting itself is limited, and error handling in scripts can be difficult to implement in a robust fashion. Making changes to the backup procedure or devices is a programming job instead of a point-and-click operation.

For something as important as backup and restore, spending the money on professional software, constantly revised by an entire company, backed by technical support and field service, and with the support of all major backup device vendors, is worth it.

RECOVERING FROM DISASTER: RESTORING DATA

The reason for backing up data is to be able to restore it later. Restore differs from failover in that it is an offline process. With failover, a duplicate of the data and an approximation of the computing environment must be available all the time, in case of loss of the primary system. In the event of such a loss, the failover system uses the secondary resources—be they servers, network paths, or storage—instead of the primary ones, to ensure that the applications keep running. Failover can be very expensive, owing to the need to have sufficient duplicate resources that are seldom used available all the time.

The restore process uses copies of data to recover a system to the state it was originally. Data previously stored on backup media is transferred by the backup software to the repaired or new storage devices. These devices will then act as the primary storage system. In some cases, only specific objects are restored, such as files and directories. At other times, entire volumes and disk sets need to be recovered from backups. While data is being restored, applications that are dependent on the data cannot be used unless a failover data store is available.

The two most critical issues associated with restoring data are the speed of the restore and the validity of the restored data. Many factors are involved in how fast a restore operation can occur. One of the most important is the speed at which the data can be streamed from the backup media to the new disk drives. The speed of the interface is also critical to overall restore time. The time it takes to perform a restore over a 100-megabit-per-second network is vastly different from what can be accomplished over a 2-gigabit Fibre Channel SAN. How fast the backup server can facilitate the transfer of data (which itself is a function of the server resources) also figures in the speed with which data can be restored. The speed at which the disks can accept and write data is a minor factor in the performance of restore operations.

Architecting for restore is an exercise in finding and eliminating bottlenecks. Simply changing one component of the system may not achieve the performance goals for that system. Consider the case of a backup system that is based on a 100-megabit Ethernet network with a backup server using Windows 2003. Attached to the server, via an Ultra2 LVD SCSI host adapter, is a small autoloader deploying a Quantum DLT VS160 tape drive. (An *autoloader* is a tape backup device that has one tape drive but can load tapes automatically.)

The backup solution is designed to back up three servers, each roughly 100 gigabytes in size and each running a moderate-size database, with another 30 gigabytes taken up by system software. Given that the tapes hold 160 gigabytes of compressed data each, only one tape is used for each server. Because the tape drive can stream compressed data at about 16 megabytes per second under optimal conditions, the best case for restoring any one server is around 4.5 hours. In reality, it will take longer when network congestion and server resources are taken into account, perhaps much longer.

Several bottlenecks need to be addressed if the restore time is to be cut down. The Ultra2 LVD SCSI connection can be ignored, because it is capable of transferring data much more quickly than any of the other system components, at 40 megabytes per second. The tape drive and network interface are serious bottlenecks, however. Even under the best of circumstances, the 100-megabit Ethernet connection has a *wire speed* of 12.5 megabytes per second of throughput. Overhead from the Ethernet frames, collisions, and the TCP and IP protocols often takes this down further, to between 8 and 10 megabytes per second, if the servers and network have low loads. The tape drive operates at a maximum throughput of 16 megabytes per second for compressed data. The real throughput is probably a bit lower, because decompressing data often introduces some overhead into the system.

It would seem that the network is the major bottleneck. If the 100-megabits-per-second network connection is changed to Gigabit Ethernet, the bottleneck would shift to the tape drive. Even if the tape drive stayed the same, the theoretical restore time would be reduced to 2.25 hours, or about half of the current best time. Upgrading the tape drive to a SDLT 220, with a maximum throughput of 22 megabytes per second, would further drop the restore time to 1.6 hours. Clearly, changing the network interface has a major impact, and upgrading the tape drive has a lesser one.

THINGS THAT GO WRONG WITH RESTORE OPERATIONS

Many things can cause a restore operation to fail. Unfortunately, most of these are due to factors that occurred long before the restore was attempted. The best policy is to rotate media beforehand and to enable options to read back and verify data written to the media. Check error logs from backups as well, to see whether there were recoverable errors. Too many recoverable errors signal that something is wrong. An analysis needs to take place to identify the cause of the problem.

TIP Try to determine the cause of any error encountered during backup. It may look like backups are being performed correctly despite errors. Errors, especially read verification errors, mean that something is not right and may become an issue when you least want it: during restore. Recoverable errors are still errors and need to be explained and fixed.

Bad Media

Bad media is like bad tuna—something to be avoided at all cost. One reason that restore operations fail is damaged media. Improper storage and overuse of volatile materials like magnetic tapes can lead to situations in which backups are complete, yet restore is impossible.

It is assumed that if, during backup, the media is noticeably damaged or worn, it will not be used. The problems begin with borderline media, such as an old tape. It may complete a backup without error or with only small errors, but when it is time to perform a restore, it breaks or can no longer be read from reliably. All removable media, including floppy drives, CD-RW, and magnetic tapes, have these problems.

The best way to avoid this situation is to rotate the media on a regular basis, discarding media that has become too old. The data sheets of most media list an average lifespan or durability specification. This specification translates into the number of uses the media can reasonably withstand.

Bad drives can also lead to bad media. A tape head that needs cleaning may damage a tape, or a misaligned laser may ruin some data on a CD-RW. The backup may complete, but the data is damaged. To avoid this issue, clean and maintain all drives on a regular basis. Use of read verification options in the backup software will detect whether data has been written incorrectly. This alerts system administrators that there is a problem that needs to be addressed.

Poor media storage is another culprit. It is all too common for system administrators to leave tapes and CDs in hot cars, causing damage to the underlying plastic. Keeping anything magnetic near a magnetic or electrical field is another media-storage-related issue. One interesting mistake is keeping magnetic media on top of a computer. Computers, despite shielding, generate low-level electromagnetic fields that can erase portions of some media over a long period of time.

Data Corruption

Nothing is worse then a perfectly good backup that has perfectly bad data on it. Corrupt data can also lead to a bad restore operation that the backup software doesn't even detect. The restore worked perfectly—it was just bad data that was restored.

Some causes of data corruption are random errors, failing but not failed hardware, and data that was damaged to begin with. In some cases, only selected objects may be corrupt; sometimes, the entire backup set is.

Random errors do occur. No hardware is perfect, and the laws of physics apply. Everything from electromagnetic interference to stray neutrinos can change the data on the way to the media or after it's already there. Enabling read verification usually detects this and allows the backup software to rewrite the corrupt data.

Another cause of corruption is hardware that has become unstable but has not failed completely. Controllers that have damaged components may act erratically and write data erroneously to the media. This can occur in all types of media.

A laser or tape head that is damaged may also corrupt data. Having read verification enabled will detect errors caused by failing hardware. Rewriting data to the media provides a quick fix but not a permanent solution. Regular maintenance of system components will prevent some of these problems. A few read verification errors may be random; a larger number are media or hardware failure about to happen.

A source of near failures is the environment within which the hardware is kept. Hot system rooms will cause components to overheat, but not to the point of complete failure. Monitoring the environment in the data center can help eliminate data corruption caused by components operating outside their environmental specifications.

The most insidious data error occurs when the backed-up data is already corrupted. Technically speaking, the backup and restore worked perfectly. Unfortunately, bad data was backed up and cannot be relied upon. This occurs quite frequently. One reason to restore data is because the primary storage hardware failed. There are plenty of opportunities to ruin data before complete failure kicks in.

Network Congestion

Just as network congestion can cause backups to go wrong, it can cause restore operations to fail. Quite simply, if it takes too long for data to get between the backup device and host, the backup software will time out. It may even assume that the devices are no longer reachable and abandon the restore instead of retrying.

There are two good ways to avoid this. First, design the backup system so that it provides necessary bandwidth all the time. Many system architects have used Fibre Channel networks for this purpose. Even if Fibre Channel is not used, a dedicated network for backup would give the system a better chance of avoiding congestion during restore (and backup) operations. Simply having enough bandwidth to perform a restore should suffice, though there is clearly a cost involved with it.

Another way to ensure that a restore operation can complete without interruption is to cut off all other traffic on the system. Shutting down other high-volume systems or disconnecting end-users from the network while restore takes place will ensure that there is sufficient bandwidth to complete the operation. This is highly disruptive to operations. To shut down a large portion of a network to restore data should be a last resort. Shutting down noncritical systems while building the network with enough overhead to accommodate critical restore operations should suffice.

What If the Backup Is Bad?

Every system administrator's bad dream is trying to restore a system, only to find that the backup is corrupt or ruined. Applications can be restored from original disks, but the data is unrecoverable. For some organizations, the costs of restoring from paper records could destroy them.

There are some options, depending on how the backups were conducted. Using a rotating backup scheme, rather than reusing the same media every day, means that only data since the previous backup is lost. Ideally, that is only a day's worth of data. Recovering a single day's data from paper and other electronic media is a chore but not an organization-killer.

If the backup process simply reused the same media each day without provision for making a copy of that media, the problem is more acute. Some database data may be recoverable through transaction logs. Perhaps static content, such as web pages, is archived as well as backed up. If not, there are few options outside of hiring specialized companies to try to recover data from the damaged disks and backup media. They may be able to cobble the recovered data together into some semblance of the original data.

The best solution is to take preventive action and not reuse media each day. It takes a lot of media, but it's cheap insurance.

TAPE BACKUP

The most common backup and restore media is magnetic tape. Disk-based backup systems are quickly becoming an important tool in the system administrator's toolbox, but tape is still predominant.

Like the cassette tapes used for music, magnetic tape is a thin piece of plastic with magnetic media on its surface. Data is encoded on the tape by causing magnetic particles in the tape to align along the length of the tape. Analog and digital tapes differ in how they represent data on a tape, but both use magnetic particles embedded in a plastic binder as the method of storing information. When writing, the tape is moved past the tape head, and a magnetic field is applied that polarizes the magnetic particles. To read, tape is moved past the heads again, and the state of the magnetic field from the particles is detected. The read sensor in the head transforms the magnetic field into an electrical signal, which represents a bit of data.

Tape has several important features that make it desirable for backup. It is reliable; has high capacity; and is inexpensive, reusable, and removable. It has been around since before the dawn of the computer age and is a well-understood technology. Vendors know how to make *reliable* tapes, tape drives, and robotics. Failures, outside of those caused by overuse and poor handling, are small.

As discussed in Chapter 2, tape data storage capacities are high compared with those of other media, with the exception of hard disk drives. CD-ROM/RW,

DVD-ROM/RW, and other media are orders of magnitude smaller in capacity than common tape drives. The cost per megabyte for the media is also quite inexpensive. A 160-gigabyte (uncompressed) cartridge—a typical capacity for backup tape—can be found for less than $50. That's roughly $3.20 per gigabyte.

Tapes can be overwritten many more times than can other media, with the exception of hard disks. CD-R and DVD-R can be "rewritten," but that means that only the sections that are unused can be written to. Portions of the CD or DVD previously written to are no longer available for more data. After a short while, the CD or DVD capacity drops to zero, and it cannot be written to again. CD-RW and DVD-RW can be completely rewritten, but only a fixed number of times.

What makes tape technology so valuable to backup and restore is that it can be removed from the drive and placed in another location. This is a foundation component of a good backup strategy. The backup does little good if it is destroyed in the same accident that ruined the primary storage. Disks cannot be easily removed, and copying data to another location requires an off-site facility housing a backup unit.

Several types of tape technology are available. Tape systems sold today use digital tape. Several formats exist, with the most common being DLT, SuperDLT (SDLT), EXO, AIT, SuperAIT, and LTO. All come in models that can be mounted internally, externally, and in a network.

In large-scale enterprise systems, it is usual to find tape drives mounted in a library. *Tape libraries* are medium to large units (often as big as an industrial refrigerator) with several tape drives, a series of slots to hold tapes, and sophisticated robotics to move tapes in and out of the drives. High-end units have high-speed Ultra320 SCSI and Fibre Channel interfaces, along with embedded software that can perform automatic failover without losing I/Os already in progress. Libraries are a good option if you have a large amount of data or many nodes that need to be backed up. The robotics eliminate much of the drudgery associated with changing tapes while reducing errors caused by poor tape handling.

When media management is the issue, rather than capacity or performance, an autoloader is a good option. Autoloaders have only one drive but can hold many tapes. Tapes can then be grouped into backup sets and rotated. A typical autoloader has a carousel (similar to the old-fashioned slide projectors) that moves the tape into place and loads it into the drive.

Both libraries and autoloaders are tools to automate tape management. Libraries have the added advantage of being able to handle a large amount of data and many backup jobs. Autoloaders are much less expensive.

DISK-TO-DISK BACKUP

Although tape is inexpensive and reliable, it suffers from several deficiencies that have become less acceptable to IT management. Tapes wear out and can degrade much more quickly than other media. Tapes are relatively slow, causing problems with backup windows. Just-in-time or continuous backups are nearly impossible with tape.

These issues pale in comparison with the problem that tape presents for restore. When disaster does happen, and important data has been destroyed from primary storage, it is always desirable that the data be restored as quickly as possible. Tape systems are often too slow to accommodate required service levels. Take the case of a 1-terabyte array backed up to a SDLT 600 with 2:1 compression. Backing up that much data would take two full tapes, each holding 600 gigabytes of data. Further assume that these tapes are in a library with a fast interface and have hardware assist for the data decompression. This allows the full throughput of 72 megabytes per second, with only a minute or so to change tapes. At this rate, it will take nearly four hours to restore the array completely.

This is a highly optimistic analysis. It presumes using one of the fastest tape drives available, no loss of throughput due to decompressing the data (which is not realistic), and nothing going wrong. To restore a terabyte array in the real world is going to take much longer, perhaps twice that time.

Disk drives, on the other hand, have much faster throughput. A typical disk array is capable of keeping a 200-megabytes-per-second Fibre Channel connection completely full. Restoring a 1-terabyte array at that rate would take only 83 minutes. Even if this is an optimal calculation, it can still be assumed that restoring the array would happen in about 90 minutes—a huge difference when recovering critical data.

To address problems with restore, a new approach to backup and restore was devised, using disk arrays instead of tape libraries (Figure 3–5). Some vendors focused on entirely new ways of backing up data, but the data storage industry has settled on a method called *virtual tape.*

Virtual tape allows a disk array to emulate a tape system. It does not require rewriting the backup software, reconfiguring systems, or revising backup and restore procedures. From the point of view of the backup software, the disk array is a very fast tape drive. The controllers in the array translate commands intended for a tape drive into those used by the disk system. Nothing else in the system has to change except the backup unit itself, which is designed as a drop-in replacement for the tape drive.

Disk-based backup has several other benefits. It is much easier to find data on a disk drive than on a tape. On analog tape systems, finding data on the tape requires that the tape first be rewound to the beginning. It is then slowly searched until the data is found. This is not the case with modern digital tape, but the tape still has to move slowly (by disk standards) to get to the point where the requested data is. If the requested data is at the end of the tape, it might take a while to get to where it is. Not so with disk systems. Random data can be found quickly (the forte of disk systems), making selective recovery of data a more reasonable operation.

The speed difference is also an advantage for system administrators who need to shrink their backup windows. Because it is faster to write to disks than to tape,

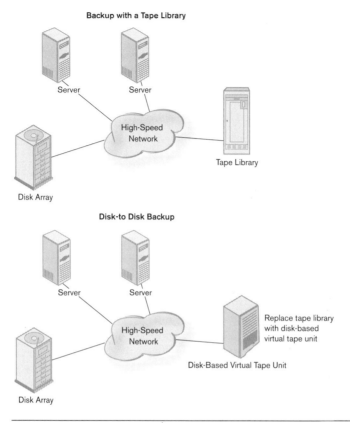

FIGURE 3–5 Converting to disk-based virtual tape

it is possible to back up information much more quickly. This allows the backup window to shrink to nearly zero, enabling near-continuous backup. *Point-in-time backup,* or making backups at different points throughout the day rather than once a day, makes more sense when the system can perform the backup in seconds or minutes.

Because of the large capacities of disk subsystems, many backups can be kept constantly available. It is feasible to perform a full backup each day, with incremental backups throughout the day—something that is very difficult to do with tape systems.

Is This the Death of Tape?

With all the obvious advantages of disk-to-disk backup, many analysts and vendors have predicted the demise of tape backup systems. Although no one

(continues)

can predict the future, it seems unlikely that tape will disappear any time soon.

Tape has one major advantage over disk-based systems: The media can be moved off-site. Getting the backup to a safe off-site location requires only shipping, driving, or walking it somewhere else. Doing the same for a disk system requires building a new facility off-site and setting up a wide-area network connection with enough bandwidth to do the backup. For many companies, that is more expensive than the convenience and faster restore speed are worth.

There are other factors. Tape is still inexpensive, well known, and reliable. At the end of the day, tape is good enough for most needs and will continue to be so for some time.

Disk-based systems suffer from the same network limitations that tape system do. On a slow network, the interface is the bottleneck, not the media. Performing network backup across a 100BaseT TCP/IP network will not keep a high-end tape streaming at full speed. Moving to disk-based backup will have no positive effect at all. Disk-to-disk backup systems tend to be deployed in Fibre Channel SANs, Ultra3 or better SCSI, and Gigabit Ethernet environments, which can take advantage of the speed of the disk systems.

Because there are many benefits to disk-to-disk backup for large installations, why has it taken so long for viable disk-based backup systems to become available? The short answer is cost. For disk backup to make sense, there can be only a small premium over tried-and-true tape systems. Fibre Channel and high-end SCSI drives are too expensive to build cost-effective backup systems. The performance and high reliability that FC and SCSI drives offer are more than backup applications need and cost more than they could bear.

Enter ATA and Serial ATA drives. Long thought to be too unreliable or slow for enterprise applications, these drives were found only on desktop machines. When they were placed inside high availability enclosures with high-speed RAID controllers fronting them, however, a balance among performance, reliability, and cost was achieved. This has allowed the technology to proliferate and become another tool for system administrators.

DISK-TO-DISK TO TAPE

As mentioned earlier in this chapter, disk-based systems have certain disadvantages compared with tape, especially a lack of mobility. Disk-based backup systems can suffer the same failures as primary disk systems. Without off-site backups, system administrators may find themselves with two inert storage systems instead of a viable backup. The rapid restore qualities of disk-to-disk systems, however, are a critical benefit of this technology. For some system administrators, the only way to bring backup windows within service levels is with disk-based backup. By combining disk and tape backup, they may achieve the best of both worlds.

One way of accomplishing this is to have the disk-to-disk backup system periodically dump the contents of the backup set to tape. This has the advantage of not affecting the primary backup's performance. The backup to disk might occur several times a day and serve as the primary restore point, while the tape backup might only occur occasionally and be designed to maintain an off-site capability. As long as the tape backup can be completed by the time the next disk-based backup is to occur, which may be several hours, there are no problems.

A variation on this design is to *stage* the backup to disk and then use tape for the actual backup. The disk system acts as a large *buffer* for the tape device. From the point of view of the system, it *is* a tape backup that can be completed in minutes instead of hours. The disk-based system can also act as a restore point (in essence, a very large cache) for the last backup performed. Previous backups would need to be loaded from tape.

Finally, the tape unit may be used for archive purposes only. Every so often, the contents of the disks are dumped to tapes, which are then carted off-site. This may happen only when data is to be removed from the system, but it still needs to be maintained.

Physically, there are many ways to design a disk-to-disk-to-tape system. The tape system may be fully integrated into the disk-based system and may not even be available directly to any other server or host. Software in the system will automatically handle the transfer of data to tape. This is a common design for smaller, self-contained units. The tape drives may be plugged into a common backplane with the disks or utilize a SCSI or SATA DAS connection.

It is also possible simply to place the disk-based system on the network that connects the backup units to the servers. Now the backup server can choose when and where to back up data to disk or tape. This loose integration has the advantage of flexibility. Some systems may still be backed up to tape, while more critical systems are backed up to disk-based systems. The disk-based backup system is then backed up to tape. If there is a tape library already available on the network, it would continue to be used rather than be replaced.

BACKUP AND RESTORE PRACTICES

Backup and restore cannot be implemented in a haphazard manner. A clear strategy needs to be designed before any hardware is purchased or software is installed. A system architect's or administrator's strategies will be driven by the needs of the organization. Most policies and procedures are unique to an organization and its goals. Certain practices are common to most backup operations, however.

Single-Tape Backup

An all-too-common and unfortunate practice for backup is to stick a tape into a drive and overwrite it each night. Smaller companies with limited resources often fall back on this method. The behavior is rationalized as the only thing they can do, given the resources available. They tell themselves that at least they're doing backups. This is a strategy (or nonstrategy) doomed to failure. Media will wear out quickly and fail. If a time does come when data needs to be restored, and there is a failure of the tape media, the data is lost.

The bad part of this practice is that if the tape is taken off-site, it can easily be lost or forgotten, making the next day's backup impossible. At that point, a good practice—off-site storage—has turned into a bad one, namely leaving data unprotected. Worse still, if the tape is simply left in the tape drive and a disaster hits, the backup will be destroyed along with the original data store. So although it may seem convenient to keep a tape in the tape drive of a server, it is a very dangerous practice.

Rotating Backups

The best way to manage backups is to rotate the backup media. With this practice, a backup is performed, and the media is removed from the backup unit. A new set of media is then used the next day, and so on. At the end of some period of time, the media can be reused.

This rotation can happen in any period, but the longer, the better. Having backups that go far back in time not only keeps wear and tear on the media down, but also makes it possible to recover objects that have been lost since the last backup. If, for example, the backups are rotated on a weekly basis, files deleted as long as a week ago can be retrieved. The deleted files may not have been noticed as missing until days had gone by, and the backups from the past few days would not have the files on them. The backup from a week ago will have the files, however, and the "lost" data can be recovered. Backup schedules that rotate tapes monthly provide the same protection going back an entire month.

Typically, a monthly rotation is established. A backup is done each day—often, an incremental backup—and a full backup is performed each week. These backup sets are moved off-site at the end of each day and week until a month's worth of backup sets is created. At the end of the month, a monthly full backup is performed and moved off-site, and the media from four weeks ago is reused.

This rotation schedule provides a great deal of protection. Objects deleted as long as a month ago can be retrieved. The chance that data will be corrupted on all the backups is quite slim unless the original was corrupted a very long time ago. Even then, the monthly backup from the previous month might still have a good version of the object, which can then be restored.

There is a downside, of course: the number of media to manage. Let's take the previous example of the 160-gigabyte disk being backed up each day to tape. Assuming that daily incremental backups take only one tape, and that weekly and monthly ones each require two, more than two dozen tapes are needed each month. Each week, four tapes are used for incremental backups, two more for the weekly, and two each month for the monthly. In a typical month, that is 26 tapes—(4 x 4) + (4 x 2) + (1 x 2) = 16 + 8 + 2 = 26—to manage.

In an enterprise with a large amount of data to back up, media management can become a real source of cost and error. With so many tapes to deal with, it is not unusual to have wrong tapes placed in tape drives, ruining entire weekly backup sets. Media can also get lost, losing entire weeks of backup protection. Certain backup units, such as tape libraries, mitigate the management problem by automating media management, but even this is not a complete solution, because problems can still occur when media is sent off-site.

Disk-to-disk backup systems can support a rotational backup schedule automatically. The backup unit has to provide enough disk space to accommodate the sheer amount of data that needs to be backed up—usually a week's worth of backups. Because of the speed of disk-based systems, schedules based on hours can be accommodated, assuming that sufficient disk space is available for the data. These systems also make doing full backups each day easier to perform.

A disk-to-disk to tape system has some advantages over tape or disk-only systems, depending on how it's implemented. If the disks are copied to tape each night, it is likely that the media management problem will persist. It could get even worse. *More* tapes are often used, because incremental backups are being performed throughout the day, and a daily full backup is performed each day. On the other hand, if only weekly and monthly full backups are copied to tape and sent off-site, the media management problem will be somewhat alleviated. The tradeoff is that any problems with the disk-based backup system mean that data will have to be restored from tapes that are a week old. The potential for lost data goes up considerably.

Full and Incremental Backups

A *full backup* is just what it sounds like: All selected objects are copied to the backup media. The advantage to a full backup is that you get a complete copy at a point in time. When it becomes necessary for a restore operation to be performed, the full backup set will have all the information necessary to restore the system completely. Full backups take a long time and require more backup storage space, whether it is tapes, disk space, or other media. Overall full backups make restore easier and backup more difficult.

An *incremental backup* copies only those objects that have changed or that are new since the last backup. Other objects are not copied to the backup media. Much less data is created or changed on any given day than is stored in the primary storage. Even though large amounts of data may be read during a period of time, much less is written.

The advantage of an incremental backup is that it takes much less time to perform. There is simply less data to back up. For the same reason, incremental backups require fewer media. When it is time to restore data, however, incremental backups take more time. The last good full backup has to be restored first; then *all* incremental backups from that point on have to be loaded. The full backup has the system state at that point in time, and the incremental backups have all the changes after that. If a hard drive crashes on Day Five of the backup cycle, the previous week's full backup will be restored first. The four incremental backups will also have to be loaded to bring the system to its original state. The additional time to restore data to its last good state can be considerable.

The use of full and incremental backups together over the course of a week provides a balance between the advantages and disadvantages of each type of backup. This is why it is rare to perform only a complete backup each month and incremental backups thereafter. The number of tapes and amount of time needed to restore a system to its proper state are unreasonable.

TIP   A group of backups, incremental and full, is called a *backup set*. One full, weekly backup plus the four incremental backups are a *weekly backup set*. With the monthly backup added, it's a *monthly backup set*. A complete cycle is often called a *complete backup set*.

Selective Backup and Restore

Most backup processes center on backing up entire volumes and disks. The events that most commonly drive backup procedures are hardware system failure (especially hard drive crashes), wholesale disasters that destroy data centers (such as earthquakes and floods), and corruption of a volume's header information resulting in an unrecoverable volume. The best remedy for these situations is a restore of the entire disk or volume from a full backup.

Backing up entire volumes and disks is usually wasteful. Operating systems and application software come on CD-ROMs or DVD-ROMs that are nearly indestructible, if kept in a safe place, and that can be replaced quickly if necessary. A great deal of media, be it tape, disk space, or CD-RWs, is wasted backing up software that is on another media already. It's the data that needs protection, not the purchased software.

It also creates the "needle in the haystack" problem. The chance that a disk will fail is lower than the chance that an important file will be deleted or damaged accidentally. The more data on the media, the more difficult it is to restore a single object. The backup software has to sift through all the data just to find a single object that needs replacing.

One option is to back up only select objects, especially those that are most subject to change. It makes sense to back up the database every day, but not the actual database software. Even configuration files and databases do not change very often. They can be archived instead of being backed up every night. Some items change so often that a backup is not worth it. System log files, for example, are important to detecting and diagnosing problems. They change constantly, and the data in them is rarely necessary to the operations of a server. Making copies of log files during the analysis of a problem makes sense; keeping them around on a monthly backup is wasting backup storage space. The same is true for virtual memory space.

For those system administrators who have very limited backup resources, selective backup is a time- and money-saving option. Very sophisticated systems, especially disk-to-disk backup systems with advanced backup software, reduce the advantages of selective backup.

Snapshots

Although often looked at as part of backup strategies, snapshots are not backups. They are point-in-time *virtual* copies of the file system. No data is copied to a backup media. Instead, the state of the file system at a particular point in time is recorded. Similar to transaction tables in a database, snapshots allow the file system to be rolled back to a known good state if something is changed in an undesirable manner. Although snapshots are a good tool for managing data, they do not take the place of a backup.

APPLICATION-LEVEL BACKUP AND RECOVERY

General backup software makes copies of data either by opening a file and copying the bytes out of it or by transferring raw blocks of data from a disk to a backup media. In either case, general backup is a binary copy. In the event of catastrophic failure of the object, such as corruption of the volume or a disk crash, the entire object can be recovered from the backup medium and the object restored to its state as of the last backup. This is called an *image copy*.

This creates problems for multielement, structured objects such as databases, e-mail systems, and similar applications. The elements inside structured objects are unknown to the general backup software. A database, for example, is copied to the backup media as a file or volume (depending on how it is implemented). It can be restored only as that type of object.

What if the event is not a catastrophic one? Perhaps a critical table was accidentally deleted, and the database is unusable. An important e-mail may have been deleted and needs to be recovered. It would be unacceptable to return an e-mail or database system to a day-old state, losing all changes that have occurred since then, just to retrieve a single element.

With image copies, the data is copied precisely, but there is no catalog of the elements within. Individual elements are inaccessible, because the software does not record what is in the structured objects. A Microsoft Exchange Server database can be copied to backup media as a whole volume or a file. General backup software does not know about the e-mails, attachments, contacts, and calendar items that are in the database and, hence, has no way to find them later. When it comes time to restore a single e-mail, the software has no way to reference it.

To alleviate this problem, many applications that use structured data stores have backup software that can catalog the elements within the structured objects. Oracle's Recovery Manager, also known as RMAN, is one such utility. Capable of backing up a database to various media, including disk, it allows for selective restores of database elements.

Most backup software vendors have application-specific versions of their software. They offer versions of their software that catalog internal elements of structured data objects. It is easy to find support for Oracle, Microsoft SQL Server, Microsoft Exchange Server, and IBM's Lotus Notes/Domino, either as a product or as an add-on to the primary backup software.

Structured Object Backup Constraints

Structured data objects have certain constraints that must be taken into account when backing them up. To begin with, many of these objects are outside the normal file system. The server processes that create and manage these objects use direct block I/O to access data on the disk. Subsequently, the normal discovery mechanisms that backup software uses cannot find application data. As far as the backup software is concerned, the data doesn't exist. Luckily, most backup software vendors and applications vendors have add-ons that allow for discovery of these objects. During installation of Microsoft Exchange Server, for example, a new version of the standard Windows backup software that is capable of seeing and backing up the Exchange database is loaded with it.

Most structured objects are difficult to back up when still in use. Many applications, especially database-oriented ones, require complete control over the underlying data store to ensure the integrity of the data. The database or application software has various controls built in to ensure that two processes do not try to change data at the same time. The software does this by placing locks on certain elements of the data. Other software is unaware of these controls, in much the same way that they are unaware of the internal structure. Backup software, by the very act of reading the data, can cause disruptions in the data. Many system administrators take database-oriented applications offline while backing them up. Because this practice makes the application or group of applications unavailable, it is not always desirable. Application-aware backup alleviates this constraint. By understanding the internal structure and locking mechanisms of the underlying databases, application-aware backup software can run backups without disrupting database operations and application availability.

Backup Software for Structured and Unstructured Objects

Backing up structured objects and backing up unstructured objects are dissimilar processes. Different software is required to perform backup and, more important, to restore lost data. This requires general backup software for normal file system objects and specialized versions for structured objects.

"Enterprise" backup software handles this process fairly well. This type of software generally has a server that sits on the network backup server and an agent that resides on the host managing a particular data store. Even more modest backup software may integrate general and application backup into one package.

Unfortunately, many system administrators are forced by budget concerns to use native application backup and a general package for the file system. This creates a process problem, as uncoordinated backup programs are running on different servers in the network. The use of a variety of software for backup creates management issues, especially when the hardware system is heterogeneous. Training, tweaking, and network behavior can all be dissimilar and unpredictable. It is always better, whenever possible, to purchase one product, with agents or plug-ins, for application servers and general file system backup.

Off-Site Backups

An interesting option for smaller organizations is to have a service provider perform backups to an off-site location. When the backup process is outsourced, most of the headaches are removed, and capital costs can be reduced to a more manageable monthly fee. This is a boon for capital-poor organizations or those that want to put their dollars into other projects.

A WAN link or virtual private network (VPN) over the Internet is established that connects the service provider's network to the customer's. The service provider runs backup servers on its side of the connection, which interacts with agents on the customer's servers or desktop computers. The service provider then takes responsibility for ensuring that backups are performed on a prearranged schedule and that the data is available for restore operations as needed. Pricing for this type of service is usually based on the amount of data backed up, though some service providers prefer to charge by the host.

For a small company with limited IT resources, using a service provider has benefits. Money is not tied up in capital equipment, and capital expenditures do not increase as the amount of data grows. Limited personnel are not stretched as backup needs grow, and the organization gains the extra protection of having off-site backups without the mishaps, hassles, and expense of having to move tapes.

What is given up is control. People outside the company are making decisions for the company. The service provider has to be trusted to provide for the security, safety, and availability of the data it holds. A reasonable amount of bandwidth on an Internet connection is also needed; for some companies, that can be expensive.

Backing up Home Systems

Most people do not have backup devices at home. Although some people in the computer industry and IT do, they are the minority. Home systems are often not included in backup strategies. Who cares, anyway? The organization will not suffer if a hard drive full of MP3 files is lost forever!

That's true, but along with those MP3s and the children's homework will also be work files. As more and more people bring work home or telecommute part time, a considerable amount of corporate data ends up on home PCs.

A strategy for backing up just the corporate data is necessary. In many cases, home workers are able to copy files to a corporate server, which is then backed up regularly. It might be over a VPN through the Internet, by dialing into the corporate network directly, or simply by carrying around a solid-state memory stick. This hardly ever works well. People forget to copy files to the server, and e-mail postboxes on home computers get ignored.

Instead, consider using a service provider that all workers can access through the Internet or backup software that can work across relatively slow links. Mobile workers and occasional laptop users can also be covered. As an incentive for users to participate, offer to back up other files of their own (with the exception of MP3s and graphic files, which may be illegal and are certainly huge).

It is bad policy to assume that home computers don't matter. Remember that the next time the CEO calls from home on Saturday and says, "I just lost an important file, and . . . ".

SAN Backup Deployment Steps

Relieving the stress of backup has been one of the most important justifications for installing a SAN. SANs remain an important tool in architecting efficient backup and restore systems. They provide fast I/O and allow for consolidation of backup resources. This in turn saves money, as fewer personnel are needed to run systems as they grow and storage resources have higher utilization rates. SAN-based backup is an important technique for improving performance and efficiency, as well as saving money through consolidation.

A SAN-based backup system deployment does not happen all at once. The amount of new equipment alone creates a lot of work for systems personnel and is usually done in stages. First, the basics of the SAN are put in place, including switches and host adapters. After the infrastructure is in place, it is time to build the rest of the system. The basic SAN should be fully tested and operational before any live storage systems are placed into the system. Otherwise, data corruption and downtime may occur, crippling the applications that depend on these data stores.

Next, the backup drives are consolidated into one larger unit. This means replacing individual tape drives with a library. It is also an opportunity to build in a disk-to-disk virtual tape system. All backup jobs are now pointed at the consolidated backup storage.

Even with storage consolidation, there is still redundancy in the operations, because there are still several uncoordinated backup jobs running. Software designed for a single machine may run well in a SAN environment, but it is inefficient. Backup software designed for a SAN, on the other hand, has a more distributed architecture that better mirrors the design of the SAN itself. Software that utilizes a dedicated backup server and agents running on different computers is installed once the backup system is up and running on the SAN.

Last, in the interests of even more efficiency, a data mover may be brought in to perform server-less backup. It should always be deployed last, after everything else in the system is running well.

A SAN is great technology for backup. A staged deployment helps bring components online gradually, allowing for less disruption of operations.

Archive Is Different from Backup

Archive and backup seem to be very similar on the surface. In both cases, data is copied from a primary to a secondary media. The goals, however, are very different. The purpose of backup is to store copies of data so that it can be available in case of disaster, allowing a recovery operation to take place. The primary data is left in place.

Archive assumes that it is no longer necessary to have the data online. Much of the purpose of archiving is to make room for new data. Whereas backed-up data is expected to be restored in a short amount of time, archive

(continues)

is considered to be much less accessible. When data has to be brought back from archival stores, there is not supposed to be a rush. Archive is also selective, copying only data that is specifically slated for removal and not entire volumes.

For these reasons, archive systems can be much slower than backup systems, both for read and write. On the other hand, they need to be able to last a long time in less-than-hospitable environments. Though tape is still the dominant archive format, CD-ROMs and DVD-ROMs make excellent archive media. They are tough and long-lasting (some predictions of CD longevity are in the hundreds of years) but have a small capacity and are slow relative to disk and tape.

CASE STUDY: BINGHAM MCCUTCHEN

As is the case with all large law firms, information is the lifeblood of Bingham McCutchen, LLP. With more than 850 attorneys and 12 offices throughout the United States, Europe, and Japan, Bingham McCutchen has data spread out over 200 servers that need to be backed up each night. The firm currently backs up over 12 terabytes of critical data each day.

Each night, full backups were performed for each server's data store. Because each server had its own tape drive, between 50 and 60 backups had to be performed at one location alone. All tapes were then taken off-site. A weekly and monthly full backup were also performed and sent off-site. The monthly backups were left off-site permanently. This procedure was performed in each of Bingham McCucthen's offices each night. At headquarters, backups consumed more than 66 tapes every night, week, and month.

The success of the firm had created backup process and media management headaches with accompanying costs. It was also recognized that e-mail had become a vital part of the firm's ability to provide service to clients. Restoring the Microsoft Exchange databases quickly in the event of failure was critical to business operations. The firm had always bought new tape drive technology when it bought new servers. This created a secondary issue of dealing with a large number of different *types* of tape drives and media.

Realizing that change was necessary, the IT department of the firm began the process of re-architecting its backup solutions. Led by Michael Carey, a senior security and network engineer, the department took a new approach to backup and restore. The project had two major objectives. First, IT needed to enable the backup system to restore a 100-gigabyte Exchange database in one hour, instead of the nearly one day that it had taken in the past. The second objective was to reduce the number and type of tape drives and media, simplifying nightly backups in the process.

To accomplish these goals, Bingham McCutchen brought in a series of Quantum DX30 disk-based backup systems for the large offices. The DX30 is a virtual tape system that minimized the software changes necessary to make the system compatible with the firm's existing backup software. A SAN was installed that allowed backup to be consolidated. The smaller offices replaced the multitude of tape drives with dual-drive robotic libraries. The result was better media management and fewer tapes overall. This made sense, because the amount of data was much smaller.

Primary backup is now done each day to the DX30, with the backup images cloned to tape. The tapes in turn are removed to an off-site facility as they always have been, and the normal backup schedule is maintained as usual. A week's worth of backups is kept on the disk systems to allow for rapid restore of critical systems.

The result is that Bingham McCutchen now requires only 7 to 9 tapes at its biggest office instead of 66, and restores can happen much faster. A single file restore, which used to take system administrators as much as four hours to perform, now takes *six seconds*. The system is faster, more scalable, and less costly to manage.

KEY POINTS

- Backup and restore are the cornerstones of data protection. They are the methods most used to protect critical data. The purpose of backing up data is to be able to recover it later.

- Backup consists of copying data to another place for safekeeping. Restore is the operation in which data is copied back to primary storage after data is lost or damaged. The most popular is magnetic tape, with disk-based backup becoming more common.

- Backup architectures include internal and external DAS systems, network-based or LAN-based backup, NAS backup with or without NDMP, and SAN backup. These architectures represent different levels of cost and performance. Backup software is also a critical component of backup systems. Depending on the architecture of the system, backup software may be a single program and process or a highly distributed server-based software system.

- Tape has the benefit of being well understood, reliable, high capacity, inexpensive, reusable, and removable. The disadvantages are that tapes break and are slow relative to disk systems. Disk-based systems are fast but more expensive. Disk-to-disk-to-tape backups extend the disk-based backup model to include the cloning of the backup image to a set of tapes. This provides for a removable backup set that can be taken off-site.

- Though archive also entails copying data to media, it is fundamentally different from backup. Archival data is not expected to be restored in a timely fashion and instead is expected to be stored away for long periods of time. Archive systems tend to be slower but have greater media longevity than backup systems.

4

REMOTE COPY AND REPLICATION: MOVING DATA TO A SAFE LOCATION

In This Chapter:

- How Remote Copy and Replication Are Different from Backup
- Remote Copy
- Design Considerations for Remote Copy
- Replication
- Case Study: PdMain
- Key Points

HOW REMOTE COPY AND REPLICATION ARE DIFFERENT FROM BACKUP

On the surface, remote copy, replication, and backup seem to be the same things. In all three cases, data is copied from a primary storage device, such as a disk array, to a secondary one. They all sit in the same layer of the information model (Figure 4–0). The goals are the same, too: to safeguard data by making a copy of it.

There would also appear to be similarities between remote copy, replication, and RAID. RAID copies data to multiple disks so that a hot copy is available at all times. This protects against total system failure due to a disk failure. It also provides protection in the form of a second copy in case the drive failure renders the original data unrecoverable. Remote copy does compare closely with RAID, but on a grander scale.

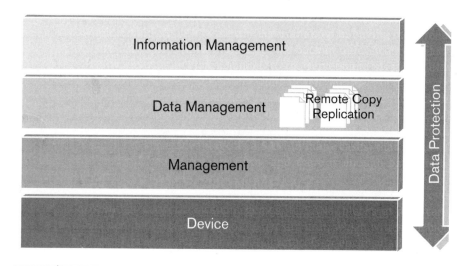

FIGURE 4-0 REMOTE COPY AND REPLICATION RESIDE IN THE DATA MANAGEMENT LAYER

Backup protects data by moving it to another location. RAID protects data by continuously copying an entire disk's worth of data so that every change is recorded. Remote copy and replication do both. With remote copy and replication, data is copied to a safe location continuously or nearly so. This ensures that complete, up-to-the-minute copies of data are safe and immediately available for failover in the event of disaster.

What is distinct about remote copy and replication is the scope. Backups and RAID are designed to guard against local failures and disasters—the loss of a disk or array. Remote copy and replication guard against wholesale, regional destruction, including natural disasters and terrorist attacks. It allows data to be tucked away in a safe place, awaiting widespread disruptions in telecommunications, electricity, buildings, and other essential infrastructure.

Another important aspect of remote copy and replication that differs from backup is its quick recovery time. With backups, a new storage device may need to be purchased or installed and then the backup data placed on it. Even for the fastest backup systems, this can be a time-consuming operation. With remote copy or replication, an exact duplicate already exists on another storage device that can be accessed immediately. Even complete failure of a system may not be noticed by end-users if the system fails over to the secondary array immediately.

How Far Is Far Enough?

A key question when considering remote data copy techniques is how far away the data should be placed from the main facility. It depends on the threat against which you want to guard. There are numerous local threats that affect only a single building or two, such as fire, water-main breaks, and local electrical failure. To have a second copy of the data in a bunkerlike disaster facility on the other side of town is enough.

Natural disasters are different. Earthquakes, hurricanes, and tornadoes can destroy buildings in a wide area and disrupt communications and electricity in entire regions. Safeguarding against data loss from natural disasters means placing the secondary data in a different region, perhaps hundreds of miles away.

Some horrible disasters cannot be dealt with effectively. Nuclear war, for example, would bring destruction over such a wide area that it is nearly impossible to guard against data loss fully and be operational in anything approaching a normal fashion. Only governments should worry about this. Corporate enterprises should focus on those things that they can deal with—regional and local disaster. Analyze the threat to the data, and determine distance from that.

REMOTE COPY

Remote copy is the duplication of I/O from one set of disks to another similar set on a block level. All data written to the disks, including changes, will be reflected in the second set. This yields an exact duplicate of the first disks.

Although similar to RAID 1 (as well as RAID 10 and RAID 0+1), remote copy differs in three important ways.

First, it duplicates an entire set of disks, even those organized into a RAID group already. In a way, remote copy can be used as RAID of RAID.

The second difference is that data is copied to a set of external disks. RAID duplicates data on the same bus in the same enclosure; remote copy duplicates data over a network to a remote location. That location may be right next to the primary array, in the next building, or hundreds of miles away. Data is protected not only through duplication, but also by distance.

Finally, remote copy is a network application. It relies on network connections to transport data over a distance. This does not mean that the storage system must be a Storage Area Network (SAN), although this is quite common. It does mean that some network with sufficient bandwidth needs to be available to the remote copy agent.

The goal of remote copy is to produce a set of disks that can replace the primary set immediately. Servers that use the disks can begin using the secondary set as soon as failure occurs.

TERMINOLOGY ALERT   Another term for remote copy is *remote mirroring*. Some vendors and analysts like to use the term remote copy to encompass the entire spectrum of data movement to remote disks. Others prefer to treat it as a product name, dissuading others from using it as a general term. For these reasons, the term remote mirroring is often used instead.

The problem with the term remote *mirroring* is that it can be confused with the mirroring in RAID. They are different enough that the names should not be so similar. Remote copy, on the other hand, does not share that problem.

Failover

Failover simply means that a new resource is always available if the primary one fails. Failover techniques are used to maintain network paths when cables break, to continue to provide power when a power supply fails, to allow a server to take over from a crashed one, and to allow access to data when an array goes down.

There are a number of ways that failover can occur. It may be an automatic function in which consumers of a resource are immediately directed to the secondary set of resources. In other cases, a manual process has to occur to redirect consumers to the new resource. Components, such as power supplies, fail over immediately; others, such as hard drives, may not, depending on the design of the unit. Server system software determines the way that failover occurs when a set of drives fails. Most operating systems will immediately switch over to the backup drives in a RAID set. There are different ways that this occurs when networked storage fails.

There is disruptive failover, and there is nondisruptive (also called *stateful*) failover. *Nondisruptive failover* maintains I/Os in progress and completes all transactions as though the failure had not occurred. Many IP routers and switches are capable of nondisruptive failover during path failure. This is not always the case for Fibre Channel switches. Very high-end FC directors provide for nondisruptive failover to a new path, whereas smaller switches and even some directors do not.

Load Balancing

A popular technique is to use load balancing as a way of providing for failover while increasing performance. A duplicate resource, such as a network path or cooling fan, is used throughout normal operations. This increases the capacity for that type of resource when things are normal. In the event of the failure of one of the resources, the others take on a greater load. This can continue until the load is too great for any one resource or all resources are expended.

There is one instance in which load balancing is used in remote copy. Because the bandwidth requirements can be very high, redundant network connections, or *trunking,* may be used when performing remote copy. I/Os are sent over multiple network connections to the remote array and the aggregate bandwidth used. If any one connection fails, I/Os will be spread out over the remaining active connections. This keeps the remote copy application from failing and gives it the bandwidth it needs.

Remote Copy Topologies

To perform remote copy, a system needs to have the primary disks, the disks to be copied to, a network connection between them, and a processor with software at each end to move the data and manage the process. Given these simple requirements, there are several ways that remote copy can be implemented.

The two most common topologies for remote copy are host based and storage system based. A new model is emerging in which remote copy occurs within the storage network switch. Although unproven at this point, it promises to be an exciting new design option for those building remote copy systems.

HOST-BASED   The basic idea of remote copy is to duplicate the I/O between a host and a networked storage unit. The first way to accomplish this is called *host-based* remote copy (Figure 4–1). Software running on the host system sends two duplicate sets of I/O to two different storage devices. All I/O sent to the first disk array is then sent to the second array.

The remote copy software intercepts all I/O going to the primary disk array and sends exact copies of the I/O to the remote array. It then waits for acknowledgment of both I/Os.

The advantages of this arrangement are that it is less expensive than other forms of remote copy and easy to implement. One need only load and configure the software on the host server and ensure functioning network paths, and the system is ready for operation.

Performance, on the other hand, is usually worse than in other remote copy designs. The load on the server can be very heavy, because the host is responsible for sending two sets of I/Os and must wait for two sets of acknowledgments before it can process another one. Server performance is also diminished, owing to the amount of resources used by the remote copy software.

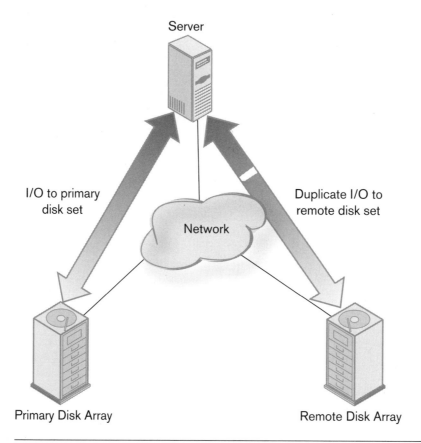

FIGURE 4–1 HOST-BASED REMOTE COPY

Host-based remote copy also is not scalable. Software has to be loaded on every computer whose data is to be duplicated, even if they sit on the same network or SAN. Adding servers to this protection scheme means loading and configuring new software for each new server. Because this is a low-level system function, for some operating systems, installation also requires that the system kernel be rebuilt. That particular task can be slow and may lead to system problems.

This form of remote copy is best used in situations where few hosts need to participate in remote copy and the amount of I/O is moderate. When the system scales above a few hosts, performance is inadequate, or a large number of hosts need to access a smaller number of disk arrays, host-based copy will not suffice.

DISK SYSTEM Another common topology for remote copy has the I/O copy performed by the disk system. A host sends a single I/O to a single disk array. Using software embedded in the array, the I/O is duplicated to a remote set of disks over a network connection (Figure 4–2). The disk system then handles all errors and acknowledgments from the remote array. If data needs to be resent, the disk system handles that. The host does not need to become involved in the transactions. It knows about the local array but not the remote one.

Whereas host-based remote copy is implemented as software on the host server, disk system remote copy is built into the disk array itself, usually by embedding a server in it. Some examples are EMC's Symmetrix Remote Data Facility (SRDF), Peer to Peer Remote Copy (PPRC) from IBM, and Hitachi Data Systems' TrueCopy.

Performing remote copy in the disk system instead of the host allows for greater scalability, better overall system performance, and less disruption of the servers. Because the far endpoint of the connection—the disk system, in this case —does the actual copying of data, servers can be added without altering the remote copy facility. There is no impact on server resources, because they do not

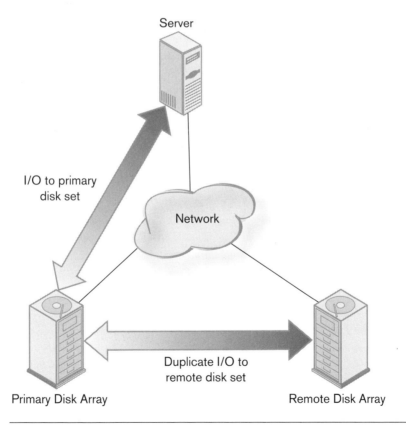

FIGURE 4–2 STORAGE SYSTEM REMOTE COPY

have to do the work of remote copy and are not waiting for acknowledgments. The impact on the disk array's performance is usually small, because the embedded server handles most of the heavy lifting. Only when there are a lot of errors or there is insufficient bandwidth to the remote device does performance degrade noticeably.

The tradeoff for performance is cost. Remote copy embedded in a storage system is very expensive, from hundreds of thousands up to nearly a million dollars. Embedded remote copy systems are complex and difficult to install, manage, and maintain. For large installations with many servers, large amounts of storage and data, and high availability and data protection needs, the cost is usually worth it.

NETWORK-BASED COPY   Until recently, the endpoints of a storage system have been the only devices with intelligence enough to perform remote copy functions. Storage switches were fairly dumb, with no extra processing power for hosted applications. Even the most advanced switch was concerned primarily with moving frames around the network as quickly and efficiently as possible. Features common on other types of network switches, such as traffic shaping and security, were nonexistent.

Starting in 2002, Cisco Systems and Brocade Communications introduced a different concept for Fibre Channel storage switches. They created intelligent *storage* switches with high-end management, traffic management, and other common network features. In addition to these features, the switches had the ability to host other hardware or software, giving them the ability to perform even more intelligent functions.

With the ability to add functionality to the network, companies that make remote copy products have been porting their products to these new switch platforms. This presents a whole new way of doing remote copy, turning it into a network service available to all nodes in the storage network. With remote copy software sitting on the switch, any I/O could be intercepted and copied to remote disk array, yet be completely transparent to the hosts and the primary disk array (Figure 4–3). Through traffic shaping and caching techniques, performance could be maintained at a high level.

Switches have the advantage of being able to manage traffic. With remote copy embedded in a switch, it has the opportunity to provide Quality of Service (QoS) to fit the remote copy application. The other remote copy topologies do not give the switch clues as to what the traffic is and require manual traffic shaping and QoS.

There is a downside to moving copy functions to the storage switch. Too much activity outside of core switching will degrade performance in the switch, dragging down all nodes. Instead of affecting the performance of a host or disk array, the excess activity could make the whole network slow if there is a lot of duplicate I/O, especially if there are many transmission errors to contend with.

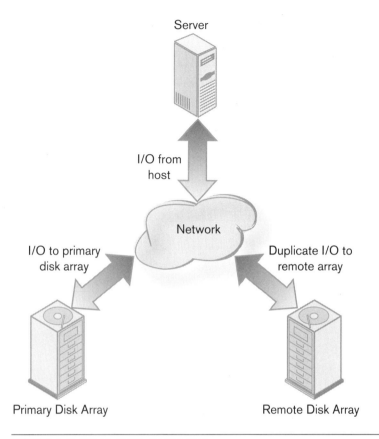

Server

I/O from
host

Network

I/O to primary
disk array

Duplicate I/O to
remote array

Primary Disk Array

Remote Disk Array

FIGURE 4–3 SWITCH-BASED REMOTE COPY

Another form of network-based remote copy uses a storage appliance to perform the remote copy. A specialized storage network device or server copies the I/O to a remote disk array by intercepting traffic to the primary one. The device uses the network in the same way as the host and disk system remote copy topologies (Figure 4–4).

The appliance topology has certain advantages over the switch topology. The most important one is that it does not affect switch performance. A dumb switch can also be used, because the intelligence is in the appliance. Not having to use an intelligent switch helps keep costs lower, because those features are paid for on every port, not just the ones that remote copy uses. A network appliance used for remote copy may also house other types of network services. Combining these storage network services allows for the creation of large managed pools of storage with a high level of data protection.

Like all network devices, the remote copy appliance suffers from reliance on a device external to the central switch. It is limited in how it can take advantage of

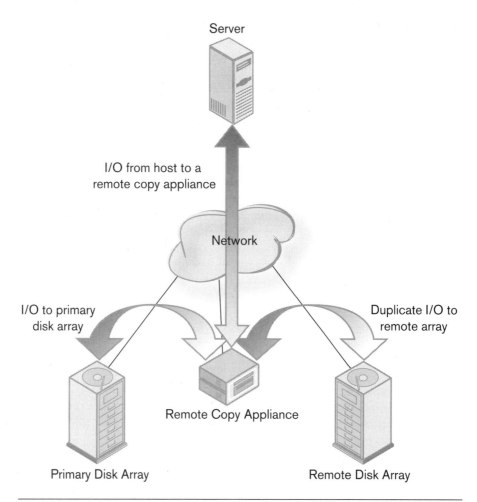

FIGURE 4–4 Remote copy using a storage network appliance

other network resources housed within the switch platform. QoS and traffic shaping do not happen in conjunction with the remote copy service. Redundant appliances are also necessary to guard against the appliance itself becoming a single point of failure. Because most appliances have a limited number of ports, redundant units are necessary to guard against simple link failure.

Design Considerations for Remote Copy

All kinds of networks can support remote copy, including Fibre Channel, Gigabit Ethernet, and a variety of wide-area networks. The choice of network depends on the topology, the distance that needs to be covered, the amount of data to be moved, and the amount of money that can be spent on the system.

Block-level storage applications are especially sensitive to latency and throughput. Distance drives network latency, and the amount of data to be moved defines the throughput requirement. Remote copy can easily fail if the round-trip delay is too great or if there is not enough bandwidth to move all the data. It is safe to say that more bandwidth and lower network latency are always better.

TIP   Network latency and storage latency are similar. In both cases, *latency* refers to the time it takes to send and receive data. What is different is the cause of the latency. For storage devices, the root cause of latency is the mechanical properties of the device and media. For networks, latency is a function of the electrical and software properties of the network connection. Both must be taken into account when designing remote copy systems.

Remote Copy and SANs

Remote copy is an application born for SANs. It is a network application that deals with block-level data, just like SANs do. Fibre Channel in particular provides high-bandwidth connections that can extend over 10-kilometer distances.

IP SANs can also be used for remote copy. There are questions as to whether the performance of these SANs is sufficient for remote copy applications. IP SANs based on Gigabit Ethernet and using dedicated storage switches may be capable of performing remote copy. With the advent of long-distance Gigabit Ethernet with distances up to 40 kilometers, IP SANs become an interesting option for moderate throughput remote copy.

SANs and remote copy are often deployed by the same types of organizations. Companies with large amounts of storage usually have a high need for data protection and have SANs in place. SANs become the natural network environment in which to locate remote copy services.

Bandwidth

Bandwidth needs are dependent on the remote copy application, which is different for each vendor. A good rule of thumb is to look at the underlying storage architecture and see what its bandwidth requirements are. If the storage infrastructure consists of 2-gigabit Fibre Channel, and the data transfer is operating at full rate, remote copy may need 2 gigabits of bandwidth.

The cost of network connections increases as more bandwidth is needed and distances increase. It costs much less for a 1-gigabit connection within a local-area network with Fibre Channel or Gigabit Ethernet than for a 1-gigabit connection from a long-distance carrier.

In practice, most storage applications do not run at full bandwidth. Most individual data transfers are less than the maximum bandwidth. Because more bandwidth costs more money, it is important to measure the actual bandwidth the application is using before buying expensive network services or components. Matching storage bandwidth needs with network connections is a key part of remote copy design. Table 4–1 gives a list of some storage connections and corresponding network connections.

The connection matching assumes that the applications using the storage need the full bandwidth of the connection. This would be the case in a SAN architecture or with an external disk array requiring high bandwidth. In most instances, full-speed network connections will not be necessary, because the applications using the storage will not use all the available link speed.

There are two methods of getting the bandwidth needed from a network connection. The simplest method is to obtain a high-enough bandwidth connection to handle the application's throughput. This can be costly, and in many areas, high bandwidth connections are not available.

TABLE 4–1 STORAGE BANDWIDTH MATCHED WITH NETWORK BANDWIDTH

Link Speed	Storage Connection Bandwidth (Gigabits Per Second)	Network Connection	Network Connection Bandwidth (Gigabits Per Second)
Ultra3 SCSI	1.6 GBPS	Fibre Channel	2 GBPS
		OC-36	1.866 GBPS
Ultra320 SCSI	3.2 GBPS	OC-96	4.676 GBPS
Fibre Channel (1 gigabit)	1.0 GBPS	Fibre Channel	1 or 2 GBPS
		Gigabit Ethernet	1 GBPS
		OC-24	1.244 GBPS
Fibre Channel (2 gigabit)	2.0 GBPS	Fibre Channel	2 GBPS
		OC-48	2.488 GBPS
SAS	3.0 GBPS	OC-96	4.676 GBPS
iSCSI (Gigabit Ethernet)	1.0 GBPS	Fibre Channel	1 or 2 GBPS
		Gigabit Ethernet	1 GBPS
		OC-24	1.244 GBPS

Another method is to aggregate several connections at the switch level to provide the required bandwidth. DWDM optical switching products do this well, combining several high-speed network connections into one fiber optic link. This method can also be used with long-distance WAN connections such as T-1/E-1 and T-3/E-3 leased lines. Though bandwidth is small by storage standards (1.54 megabits per second and 44.76 megabits per second, respectively), combining several connections can provide sufficient bandwidth for many remote copy applications.

The Causes of Network Latency

Network latency—the time it takes for a packet or frame to get from the source to the destination—depends on many factors. These include

- The type of medium through which data is being transmitted
- Delays in intervening network components such as routers and switches
- The distance being traversed

It is important to take these factors into account. Keep in mind the following:

- Fiber optic cables are not susceptible to radio and electronic inference, which slows signals. They produce less network latency.
- Optical switching is much faster than electronic switching. This reduces the network latency caused by switching packets.
- Shorter distances mean that packets don't need to travel as far.

What Causes Delays

There are three types of delays that affect network latency in a network connection.

Propagation delay is the delay caused by raw distance. The fastest that a packet can travel is the speed of light. The greater the distance, the longer the propagation delay.

Transmission delay is the delay introduced by the media and intervening network components. No signal can travel down a wire or fiber optic cable without resistance of some type. Small delays can be caused by radio or electrical interference in a wire or from the light pulses bouncing around in the fiber optic cable.

> The time it takes for routers and switches to process a packet and send it on to the next hop also increases the *overall delay*. The more times a packet has to pass through piece of networking equipment, the more network latency will be introduced. This includes the switching equipment of telco carriers as well as internal networks. These delays are cumulative. The more switches that the packet passes through, the longer the distance the packet travels, and delays caused by running through copper cables all combine to produce the latency of the network connection.

Because all storage was originally local, it works under the assumption that a long delay equals unavailable resources. This is in sharp contrast to network applications, which assume that network latency will happen and are willing to wait longer periods of time.

With remote copy, the problems occur when the application must wait for acknowledgment of a frame. To move on to the next I/O, the application needs to know that the last one was successful. When the application has to wait a long time for the last I/O to respond, it will assume that the storage is no longer available and will fail in some fashion. Long delays caused by the network latency will result in slow acknowledgment of the whole transaction and possible failure of the application.

Vendors of remote copy applications employ a variety of tricks to overcome network latency problems. All these techniques are designed to make it appear that the I/O was completed. Storage applications have also adapted to environments in which network latency is more of a problem, such as SANs. By queuing I/Os, retrying before abandoning, and through caching, applications have become more tolerant of delays in completing storage transactions.

DISTANCES   Distances for remote copy are thought of in the traditional networking manner. Network connections come in local, metropolitan, and wide area or long distance. Local remote copy is performed in the confines of the LAN or SAN within the same building or campus. It can assume very fast connections, usually Fibre Channel and Gigabit Ethernet, and few switches and routers to pass through.

The options are greater for metropolitan areas. The MAN distance is defined as being within the local area of a city or region, usually less than 100 kilometers. Intercity connections that are close together are also considered to be metropolitan. Direct fiber optic links can be leased or built. These can then be used directly by Fibre Channel and Gigabit Ethernet. Native Fibre Channel can be used when the distance is less than 10 kilometers and Gigabit Ethernet when the distance is less than 40 kilometers. High-capacity fiber optic connections such as SONET, OC-48, and OC-96 are also available within large metropolitan areas.

Long-distance remote copy can use any of the data communications connections available for long-haul transmissions, including T-1/E-1, T-3/E-3 circuits, and leased fiber optic lines (dark fiber). Remote copy at these distances, however, poses some difficulties for the system architect. The network latency caused by distance alone is significant and can create problems for remote copy applications. Another difficulty is the type of available network connections. The distances are too long for direct Gigabit Ethernet, Fibre Channel, and SONET protocols. A single fiber optic link is usually not available, so the packets have to be routed through the networks of a telecommunications carrier, adding more delay. To operate over long distance, a remote copy application needs to be fine-tuned very carefully.

Synchronous and Asynchronous Remote Copy

Problems with timely acknowledgment of remote copy I/O have led to two different ways of implementing remote copy. They are *synchronous remote* copy and *asynchronous remote* copy.

The synchronous form of remote copy has the host wait for acknowledgment of both the primary disk array and remote array. This is the more secure method of remote copy. The application is assured that all I/Os have been completed on both arrays and that an exact copy of the data and logs exists. If the I/O to the primary array fails, the remote can be rolled back to the same state as the primary and an error produced for the application. If the remote copy fails, the remote copy software can resend the I/O while the application waits for a response. If the response does not come in a reasonable amount of time, the I/O can be rolled back on the primary and an error code created.

Synchronous remote copy assumes that sufficient bandwidth exists on the network link to the remote array to perform I/Os normally. When the primary data path is using 1 gigabit per second of bandwidth, and the remote array is serviced by an OC-24 network link, there will be sufficient bandwidth for synchronous remote copy. In the case in which that link is shared by several applications, there may be times when the I/Os to the remote array cannot be completed in the allotted time, and the connection times out. Depending on the applications, the host may be able to wait for the packet to be resent, or an error may be generated.

With asynchronous remote copy, the remote copy software—whether it is housed in an appliance or within a storage device, or is host-based—acknowledges the I/O as soon as the primary storage completes it. The I/O is then sent to the remote array and is managed independently of the primary I/O. The host does not have to wait for acknowledgment from the remote array to continue (Figure 4–5).

Even when the I/O to the remote array does not fail, waiting for the acknowledgment can drag down the host's performance. Network latency, retries, and other delays can cause the host to spend time waiting instead of processing data.

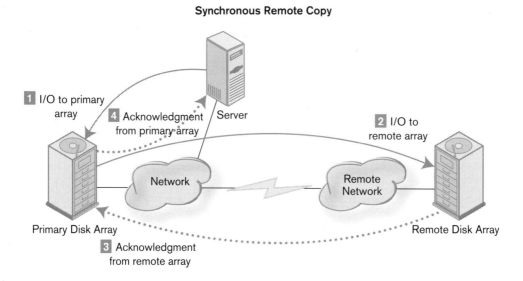

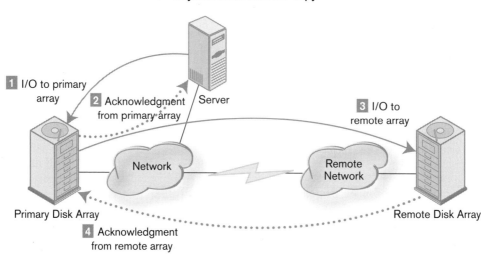

FIGURE 4–5 SYNCHRONOUS AND ASYNCHRONOUS REMOTE COPY

With asynchronous remote copy, there is no waiting. This is a vitally important characteristic when the network link to the remote array is slow or very long distance.

Asynchronous remote copy has allowed for less costly implementations. Slower connections mean more network latency and retries. With asynchronous remote copy, these have less effect on the overall performance of the host. Lower-bandwidth connections can be used, which cost much less on a recurring basis.

There is a downside to this approach. The host has no way of knowing whether the remote copy actually occurred correctly or at all. In the event of problems on the remote network link, the remote array could become out of sync with the primary array. To mitigate this occurrence, remote copy applications often have a facility for resyncing the data. That is a time-consuming process that has to happen offline, causing downtime in the overall system. With this form of remote copy, the state of the remote array cannot be verified at all times by the host.

It should be noted that the steps involved in remote copy are not always sequential. Some implementations of remote copy will write the I/O to the primary and remote array at the same time. What is important to note is that the host has to wait for both acknowledgments before continuing with the next I/O, whichever arrives first. With asynchronous remote copy, only the acknowledgment from the primary disk array is necessary before the next I/O can begin.

Bunkering

For some organizations, asynchronous remote copy does not afford the level of protection that is needed for critical applications. This is true in the financial-services industry, for example. Synchronous remote copy is used over a short distance, allowing for the use of a high-bandwidth connection such as direct Fibre Channel or Gigabit Ethernet. Metropolitan Area Network connections such as SONET are also used to get high bandwidth over short distances.

When the need exists for long-distance but high-performance remote copy, different architectures are needed. Otherwise, costs will be high and system performance less than what is desired. One such architecture is called *bunkering.*

With bunkering, a hardened facility (the bunker) is available at a short distance, housing only storage and networking equipment. A separate facility that contains not only storage but also application servers is kept at a far distance. Data is copied, using synchronous remote copy, to the arrays in the bunker, where it is available for use over a high-bandwidth local or MAN connection. The bunker storage acts as a staging ground for asynchronous remote copy over a longer distance but a slower link. From here, data is copied over long distance, using standard data communications links (Figure 4–6). Copies of the data are kept on the primary array, bunkered array, and remote array.

Bunkering solves several problems with long-haul remote copy: cost, performance, and link failure. Because the primary storage has already copied its I/O over to the bunker storage, the application is not affected by the slower, less costly connection. If the long-distance connection should fail, there is still the copy of the data in the bunker protecting the data. When the connection is

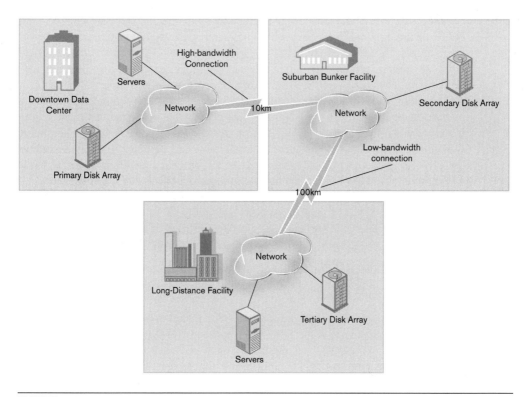

FIGURE 4–6 BUNKERING

brought back online, the bunker storage and long-distance storage can synchronize without disturbing the primary storage.

Bunkering provides other advantages over direct remote copy. By making three copies of the data instead of only two, the data is safer. In the event of a regional disaster that destroys both the primary data center and the second one, the third version of the data is far enough away to remain unharmed. It can also be an operating data center where employees travel to, allowing the company to return to normal operations sooner.

By staging the data, it is also possible to run backups at one or more of the remote facilities. Backups can be performed at almost any time without disrupting applications. Also, because bunkering requires three facilities, a network connection could be established between the primary and long-distance facilities, allowing remote copy to continue in the event of a major disruption at the bunker. With traditional remote copy, disruption in the network link or remote facility leaves no options for continuing remote copy. Bunkering provides an alternative for businesses that have very high availability and data protection requirements.

Optical Networking

One of the more popular ways of implementing remote copy is through optical networking. Optical networks use light instead of electricity to transmit information. Bits are sent down a fiber optic cable by a light-emitting diode (LED) or laser that pulses on and off. Optical networks have the advantage of high bandwidth and no interference from electromagnetic sources. Whereas a copper wire is subjected to electromagnetic interference (EMI) and radio frequency interference (RFI) from all the electrical and radio sources around it, optical networks are not. This yields a better signal over a longer distance than copper wire.

Fibre Channel and Gigabit Ethernet use optics only for transmitting the signal through a fiber optic cable. They are otherwise completely electrical. An optical network is completely based on light. Dense Wave Division Multiplexing (DWDM) is an optical networking technology used extensively in remote copy applications. It is can be used with leased fiber optic line or with public optical networks such as SONET. It provides 32 to 64 data channels at 2.5 gigabits per second of bandwidth each on each fiber optic strand.

Storage systems connect with optical networking products either through a blade in the storage switch that allows for outbound optical connections, by a converter box that takes in Fibre Channel or Gigabit Ethernet and interfaces it to the optical network, or through a Fibre Channel or Gigabit Ethernet blade in the DWDM switch.

Because DWDM is so costly, it usually cannot be justified for remote copy alone. With up to 64 channels available on one fiber optic cable, other voice and data traffic can be accommodated easily.

Cost Considerations

Remote copy can be a very expensive method of data protection, especially for long distances. When designing remote copy systems, it is important to keep these cost factors in mind:

- **Host software.** Often, the least expensive way to implement remote copy functions is with host-based software. Like all software products, host-based remote copy software becomes more expensive as more hosts are added and more licenses purchased.

- **Remote copy hardware.** Depending on the scale of the solution, disk array systems that perform remote copy can cost in the hundreds of thousands of dollars. Although that sounds like a lot of money, the cost per megabyte of data protected decreases as more storage and hosts are added. Aside from that, these solutions are used because they meet the needs of certain types of organizations better than less expensive ones do.

- **Local network connections.** All remote copy requires network connections, preferably high-speed ones. Gigabit Ethernet and Fibre Channel are the most common types of local network connection deployed for local remote copy. The cost of these types of network connections is dropping quickly, and many are already in use for SANs and server connections.

- **Remote network connections.** Unlike other storage applications, the recurring cost of the long-distance network connection for remote copy often far exceeds the cost of the components of the system. This is true even over the course of a single year. Even with the current glut of fiber optic lines, high-bandwidth, long-distance network connections are very expensive.

Belt and Suspenders: RAID, Backup, and Remote Copy

It is rare to see remote copy used alone. Instead, it is part of a comprehensive data protection plan. Primary data storage is almost always disk based, and the other techniques available for protecting disk storage are combined with remote copy to create widespread protection.

Because they all operate at a block level, remote copy is complementary to RAID and backup. RAID 1, mirroring, copies blocks of data destined for one set of disks to a second set; data is protected against local disk failure. Backups then make offline copies of the RAID volumes, which protect against local equipment failure. Remote copy further copies the data over a distance to protect against a disaster's affecting the entire data center. Used together, RAID, backup, and remote copy protect data against an ever-increasing set of threats.

REPLICATION

On the surface, replication would appear to be the same as remote copy. The primary goal is certainly the same: to make a copy of the data at a remote location. Replication, however, does it in a different way. Instead of duplicating every I/O produced by a host at a block level, replication works at the file or application level. It produces copies of the *elements* of structured or unstructured *objects* at a predetermined time interval. The disk image may not be exactly the same as it is with remote copy, but the important data will be duplicated

Replication is usually host based. There are replication servers and appliances, but these depend on either host-based agents or the ability to mount a file system, volume, or database remotely. This is not surprising, because replication requires that the software have intimate knowledge of the structures within the application or file system objects whose elements are being copied. Software companies produce third-party replication software, but it is often a feature or add-on to database and e-mail applications.

Although replication is used for data protection, it is also a management tool used to duplicate key information to a variety of data stores. If a company has two call centers using the same Customer Relationship Management (CRM) software, for example, performance is better when each site operates from a local copy of the underlying database. Caller information generated at one center would need to be duplicated to the other center in case a call is routed to it (Figure 4–7). Database replication would be used to ensure that the call records from each center are duplicated in the other center.

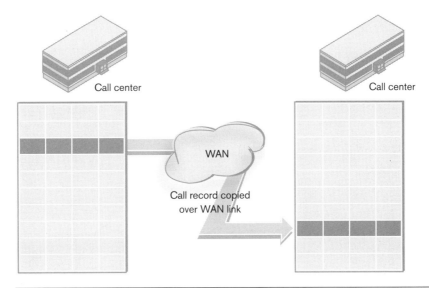

FIGURE 4–7 REPLICATION

The advantages of replication over remote copy are cost and the amount of bandwidth required. The cost of the software or add-on is usually much lower than for a remote copy system. Specialized hardware is rarely needed for replication, further reducing the initial costs. The overall cost of replication is also lower, because much less expensive telecommunications links can be used. T-1/E-1 WAN links (with a maximum of 1.55 megabits per second) can be used effectively for replication but rarely for remote copy.

Replication has its limitations from a data protection point of view. It duplicates information only for a specific file system or application to a *similar* file system or application. Data is copied, but the positions of elements, supporting metadata, and system files are not duplicated. When database rows are copied, for example, the row may be in a different place in the database from the original. The "remote" database may also have rows in it that are not replicated to the first one. Replication is less complete than remote copy, and failover is less automatic.

Replication does not guarantee timeliness. Whereas remote copy copies data to two places simultaneously, replication waits until the initial transaction occurs and then copies the data to the remote object. For some amount of time, the two objects will be different and the data not the same. There is the potential for data to be unprotected for a period, because the objects are not fully synchronized. A failure during replication may mean that the two data stores are out of sync. Although most replication software allows for a complete resynchronization of the replicated system, it is time-consuming and often requires the systems to be offline.

> **Event-Driven Versus Timed Replication**
>
> Replication usually occurs in one of two ways: event-driven or timed. *Event-driven replication* happens when a specific action occurs that triggers the replication of data. Each time a new customer row is created in a database, for example, that row is copied to the remote database.
>
> *Timed replication* happens at intervals specified by the system administrator. Data may be replicated once a day or every few minutes. It can be configured to happen during off-peak periods of network usage. This saves the costs of having to lease additional long-distance network links. It affords less protection, though. If new data in the primary object is destroyed during the period between updates, it is gone forever.

Database and E-Mail Replication

Databases and e-mail systems are two common applications that use replication. Because most e-mail systems are backed by some type of database, the mechanisms are the same. Application objects such as rows, columns, tables, and sometimes code elements such as stored procedures are copied to another database.

All major Relational Database Management Systems (RDBMs)—including Oracle, SQL Server, and DB2—support replication as a feature of the database server. Open-source databases, such as PostgreSQL and MySQL, have similar replication capabilities.

Most databases support several types of replication. One-way replication, sometime called *snapshot replication,* is when database objects are duplicated in the remote database only. This is fine for data protection. If the goals of the replication strategy also include sharing data among facilities, one-way replication is limited. One-way replication is less bandwidth intensive and takes much less time to perform. Two-way replication will synchronize objects between two databases. When the replication is complete, the two databases will have the same objects. Although it is a more complete form of replication, it takes more bandwidth and additional time to perform.

Databases support replication through special SQL commands, such as Oracle's `Create Snapshot`, external processes, or both. This makes native replication a nonportable process that is done differently from database to database. It also means that replicating from one vendor's database to another is impossible using the native tools.

Luckily, some third-party replication tools can copy data between disparate databases. These software products use a database's Application Programming Interface (API) to interact with the elements of different types of databases. This allows them to perform replication between different database systems.

File Replication

File replication copies files from one file system volume or directory to another. This is a popular method of protecting data as well as distributing files among servers. A software add-on product monitors changes in the file system and copies changed or new files to the remote file system. Although some replication software uses proprietary protocols, most use CIFS or NFS as the data transport protocol.

File replication tools need to understand the underlying file system and are OS specific. There are a variety of ways that the software can be designed, but all need some type of host-based agent to monitor the file system. Host-based agents either use low-level system calls or are built into the operating system kernel.

NAS systems often have replication features built into them. Many server operating systems also have some form of rudimentary replication as well, often as part of clustering software features. File replication is most popular with file-oriented systems such as file servers and web server farms.

CASE STUDY: PDMAIN

What do you do when there is no acceptable amount of downtime? That is a problem that PdMain, Inc., of Burlington, Ontario, Canada, has struggled with. PdMain provides integrated systems that are used to manage manufacturing companies as stand-alone systems or hosted systems. They also provide hot-site capabilities for those customers that prefer to host their own applications. To provide these services, PdMain maintains its own data center near Toronto.

Customers rely on the PdMain systems and data centers for the most basic operations, including running the factory floor and dealing with the challenges of just-in-time inventory. Typical allowable downtime for PdMain customers is less than *five minutes a year,* and recovery from failure must happen in *less than two minutes*. Traditional backups, no matter how fast, cannot meet this requirement.

The ramifications of system failure in this environment are simple—entire factories will shut down. Worse, the factories of the vendors feeding the factory will also shut down, because they will not know what parts need to be shipped where. The financial impact of a system failure such as this is enormous, with multiple sites and thousands of workers idled.

PdMain used all the traditional means for ensuring availability in systems. It deployed redundant, high-availability servers. Multiple telecommunications lines have been implemented, using two different carriers that use completely separate infrastructure. PdMain even maintains generators at the data center with fuel on hand for two days of operation. Unfortunately, this was not good enough. Even if the customer could cut over to a new set of servers and storage immediately, the data was old. This led to lost data and poor referential integrity. Simply put, the systems would not run without current data.

The solution was to provide continuous replication to a server at a hot site. Partnering with XOSoft, Inc., a maker of data replication software products, PdMain is able to replicate, in real time, all the databases that are the underpinnings of the application. All the data in the duplicate system is exactly as it is in the main system. The actual replication happens in milliseconds. In some cases, PdMain customers will bunker data, keeping a duplicate of the data on storage within their data centers and replicating it further to the PdMain data center. In this way, they protect themselves against local system failure and data center disasters. The use of asynchronous replication allows PdMain and its customers to use less expensive telecommunications, as low as a T1 or a DSL line, while maintaining high service levels.

By replicating data, PdMain customers are capable of continuous operation in the face of a variety of disasters. Replication is a necessary part of their business operations and the key to avoiding crippling data loss.

KEY POINTS

- Remote copy and replication protect data by making duplicate copies in a different array or location.

- Remote copy makes mirror copy of the data at a block level. Replication duplicates data at a file or element level.

- Remote copy can be implemented at a host level or storage system level. New forms of remote copy will allow duplication to occur at the network level.

- The most difficult part of remote copy design is balancing bandwidth, network latency, and cost requirements. Bunkering and asynchronous remote copy are two ways of achieving this balance.

- Replication is application or file specific. There is no guarantee that all data will be duplicated exactly. Instead, important data is duplicated in a usable form.

5

BASIC SECURITY CONCEPTS

In This Chapter:

- Least Privilege
- Defense in Depth
- Diversity of Defense
- Encryption
- Typical Attacks
- Key Points

There are thousands of books on computer security. They range from broad overviews written for IT managers to how-to books for system administrators to academic tomes about encryption. What they have in common is a language and set of concepts about security. It is important to understand this language as it applies to data protection. Protecting systems from intruders reduces the chance that data will be destroyed or stolen. System security must be part of the data protection strategy.

This chapter is designed to explain quickly some of this language and the key concepts. As one would expect, it does so from a data protection and storage point of view. The principles are, however, universal.

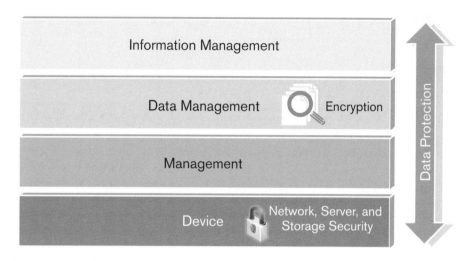

FIGURE 5–0

LEAST PRIVILEGE

Least privilege refers to the amount of access any user, host, or processor should have to system resources. It is always best to give just the least amount of access possible to accomplish the required tasks. If a server needs to see data on only one disk in a large array, it should be restricted to read access of that one disk. Because most end-users need to access the Internet only during working hours—say, between 7 a.m. and 7 p.m.—Internet access should be limited to that period. Other end-users may have different needs, and their access would differ accordingly.

The downside of least privilege is that it can place inconvenient restrictions on people. In the example of Internet access, what happens if a person has to work a different shift and now needs access between 7 p.m. and 3 a.m.? Temporary changes themselves can lead to security problems if the temporary changes are not revoked in a timely manner.

Least privilege is always preferred but not always practical. Compromises are inevitably made, but least privilege should be maintained as a policy.

SECURITY POSTURE

All security plans have a posture or philosophy about security. The posture determines the approach to security throughout the organization. The two most common postures are referred to as Default DENY and Default ALLOW.

In *Default DENY,* if something is not explicitly allowed, it is immediately denied. The default action for all security operations is to disallow access to a resource. Least privilege encompasses Default DENY. This is a more secure posture.

Default ALLOW is the opposite; it assumes that all things are allowed unless specifically denied. Systems are completely open except for specific instances where a resource is limited or closed off. End-users find Default ALLOW more convenient.

Some plans mix the two postures. A posture of Default DENY may be assumed for inbound network operations and Default ALLOW for outbound ones. File servers may be subject to Default ALLOW, whereas database servers are subject to Default DENY. In practice, this is what usually happens. A balance is then achieved between the ability for end-users to get to resources they need versus keeping hackers out.

Default DENY is still the better practice despite the limitations it places on end-users.

DEFENSE IN DEPTH

It is typical when discussing network security to talk about defense in depth. This concept comes from military science. It refers to the many layers of defenses that an attacker must penetrate to gain an objective. In computer system security, defense in depth refers to the layers of security and detection systems that inhibit a hacker from gaining access to corporate systems and data.

In a well-designed system, intruders first need to penetrate network perimeter defense to gain access to the interior network. Then they must gain access to hosts on the network. Finally, they have to penetrate the storage subsystem defenses to gain access to or damage data.

Perimeter Defense

Perimeter defenses are designed to inhibit attacks from outside the network, primarily from the Internet. The goal is to keep an attacker from gaining access to the interior corporate network. Besides protecting the network from intruders, perimeter defense includes the ability to detect attacks, whether they are successful or not. This gives system security personnel the ability to track the attacker and protect interior systems from future harm.

FIREWALLS The primary method of protecting the corporate or home network from intruders is the firewall. Firewalls are designed to examine traffic as it comes in and deny entry to those who do not have access rights to the system.

There are different types of firewall designs. Most combine several methodologies to protect the inner network from harm. The most common functions of firewalls are proxy services, packet filtering, and network address translation (NAT).

Packet filtering admits or denies traffic attempting to access the network based on predefined rules. A common version of packet filtering is *port blocking,* in which all traffic to a particular TCP/IP port is blocked to all external connections. Host-based firewalls, common in home and small-business situations, use this method to protect individual desktop computers.

Proxies place a device or server between all incoming and outgoing traffic. Rather than simply route traffic to and from the outside world, the proxy server appears to be the source or destination of the traffic itself. It is often used as a method of controlling user access to the Internet as well.

Network address translation services translate internal addresses into a range of external addresses. This allows the internal addressing scheme to be obscured to the outside world. It also makes it difficult for outside traffic to connect directly to an internal machine.

Firewalls can operate at the TCP or the application protocol level. Simple firewalls usually examine TCP headers only when making decisions about the traffic. Others might look at HTTP conversations to see whether the connections should be made. Some firewalls also incorporate antivirus and antispam filtering.

All firewalls provide a choke point through which an intruder must pass. Any or all traffic can then be examined, changed, or blocked depending on security policy.

INTRUSION DETECTION SYSTEMS AND INTRUSION RESPONSE SYSTEMS Another form of perimeter defense is *Intrusion Detection Systems* (IDS). An IDS does not regulate access to the network. Instead, it examines violations of security policy to determine whether an attack is in progress or has occurred. It then reports on the alleged attack. Some security software even claim to be *Intrusion Response Systems* (IRS). Intrusion Response Systems are devices or software that are capable of actively responding to a breach in security. They not only detect an intrusion but also act on it in a predetermined manner.

How Effective Is an IDS or IRS?

IDS and IRS are important and sophisticated technologies. The efficacy of these systems is still being debated, given their current state of development.

Problems with effectiveness exist because they generate too many false positive events. A *false positive event* is a detected event that is not truly an attack but only appears to be. These events needlessly alarm IT professionals, causing them to shut down systems and restrict access unnecessarily. Afterward, false positives initiate costly reviews and audits.

If an organization experiences enough of these events, the tendency is to ignore IDS alarms or set thresholds low. This opens the organization to undetected attacks that may persist over time—just the situation that the IDS is supposed to deal with. Attaining the right balance between protection and false positives is tricky and requires experience.

Host and Application Defense

Host security is usually accomplished by ensuring that a person or process that requests resources has rights to those resources. Verifying the identity of a host, group, person, or process to some degree of confidence is called *authentication*. Authentication allows for *access control* to be implemented to a particular level. Access control then limits access to resources according to rights granted by the system administrator, application, or policy.

The way access control is managed and which resources can be controlled depends on the operating system, file system, or application. One common problem with access control is that different mechanisms are used by applications, file systems, and the operating system. This makes system administration difficult and error prone.

Software exists to help manage access policies on a variety of operating systems and with a large number of applications, but none is all-inclusive. System administrators usually find themselves writing scripts to grant access control to various systems. This is especially true in smaller organizations, which cannot afford to purchase system management software.

Authentication and Access Control

Authentication is the ability to verify identity with some degree of confidence. It is based on something you are, have, or know. The reason that an airline passenger needs to present photo identification at the airport is to ensure that he is actually the person who has the reservation. This is not foolproof, of course. The ID may be forged. Even if it is not, it only identifies a person as being that person. It cannot determine whether that person means to do harm.

Computer authentication provides a method of ensuring that the person requesting access to a resource is entitled to it within some degree of confidence. Depending on the security needs of an organization, authentication may take many forms. Some of these are

- Username and password
- Smart cards and dongles
- Biometrics

The most common is the use of a username-and-password combination. It is easy to manage and understand. Although it is better then nothing, it is only as secure as the password. Passwords can be found out (often through user careless-ness), guessed, or discovered through the use of programs containing dictionaries of common passwords. Most security professionals suggest that passwords be changed on a regular basis to reduce the risk that an attacker will guess or purloin the password. Unfortunately, this burdens users. Users can become clever about working around password rotation schemes, defeating the purpose of them.

Smart cards, dongles, and similar devices require that a physical entity be present to access a computer and attached resources. Although fairly strong, smart cards can be lost or stolen. In this case, resources are temporarily unavail-able to the user. They also do not work for "users" that are really processes run-ning on a server.

Biometrics is the use of biological markers to determine identity. It is very strong security because it is difficult (though not impossible) to fake biology. A range of technologies have been used over the years, depending on the type of access required. Biometrics has been deployed extensively in ensuring physical security, especially handprint readers and retina scanners. For individual comput-ers, thumbprint readers have been popular. There are also several systems that rely on psychological traits, such as typing or handwriting patterns.

Two-Factor and Multifactor Authentication Use of any authen-tication system enhances security of computer systems. Still, there are numerous ways to defeat any one of them. A password may be captured by an attacker or a smart card stolen and used. There are even ways to defeat certain biometric systems. Relying on any one method may not be secure enough for many organizations.

Two-factor or multifactor authentication combines more than one form of authentication to create a more secure environment. A password by itself may not be secure, but combined with a smart card, it is much more so.

It is always best to combine different types of authentication methods. In the example of the password and smart card, it combines something the user has (the card) with something she knows (the password). Of course, if the user tapes the password to the bottom of the smart card or card reader, the system is useless.

User versus Host Authentication There are many levels at which authentication can occur. There are two types of authentication commonly used: user level and host level. *User-level* authentication verifies the identity of a person or process. *Host-level* authentication verifies a particular host computer.

They key issue with host authentication is that it forces access control to be implemented at a very high level. If an attacker is able to gain any level of access to a host, he is likely to be able to access all available resources. User authen-tication is stronger and allows access to be confined to individual people and processes.

DIVERSITY OF DEFENSE

In biology, there is a concept called biodiversity. *Biodiversity* is the number of different types of organisms living within a particular environment. It is believed that greater biodiversity leads to healthier ecosystem. Diversity ensures that a failure in one species does not destroy the entire environment. The same can be said of the workplace, where diversity of culture, opinion, and backgrounds leads to a more robust organization capable of adapting to changes in the marketplace.

The computer security concept of diversity of defense is similar. By deploying many different methods of defense in layers, a better defense is created. If an attack is successful against one type of defense, there are other forms of defense that continue to block the attacker's progress. The attacker has to change strategies constantly to penetrate farther into the system.

One example is the use of different types of firewalls. If a series of packet-filtering firewalls is being deployed to provide defense in depth, different types of filtering on each of the firewalls will provide better protection than all the same type. A firewall that is checking for HTTP attacks, such as malformed URLs, may be used for the first firewall. This would be followed by one that blocks access to certain ports. Further protection may be provided through the use of network address translation, which hides internal addresses from the outside world. An antivirus system can also be hosted on a firewall that scans high-level traffic for known virus signatures.

To succeed in an attack, an intruder would need to use different strategies to overcome each firewall, making the attack difficult to carry out. Deterring attacks and making intrusion as difficult and detectable as possible are what system security is all about.

ENCRYPTION

One of the most common methods for ensuring that data is not viewed by prying eyes and has no value to thieves is encryption.

Encryption is the encoding of data so that the plain text is transformed into something unintelligible, called *cipher text*. Because cipher text is unintelligible, the data is rendered useless to an intruder. This transformation comes about by combining the data with a key that is known only to the sending and receiving parties. The key acts as a code book that, along with the original data, is input into a series of algorithms that produces the cipher text. When the data is received by an authorized party, it is decoded into its original and more useful form through a reverse of the original process.

Two principal methods of encryption are used today. The first is *private key encryption,* also called *symmetrical* encryption. With this method, both parties have the same key and use it to encode and decode data. The advantage of this method is speed, but there are challenges in ensuring that the keys are distributed safely.

The second method is often called *asymmetrical* encryption. This method uses a publicly known key. The receiver then decodes the cipher text, using a key that is known only to the receiver but that matches the public key. In this way, anyone can send encoded text to the receiver, but only the receiver can decrypt it. Although often slower than private-key encryption, this method solves the problem of key distribution. No one can decode the text except the intended receiver.

Encryption is used to protect data on hard drives, as well as on tapes, and is the basis for most secure data and voice communications. In practice, asymmetrical-key encryption is used for quick transfers of information, especially the exchange of private keys, and to encode e-mails. Private-key encryption is used for secure communications channels.

TYPICAL ATTACKS

Some would say that there is no such thing as a "typical" attack and that each is unique. On some level, that is true, but certain types of attack are more common. The common denominator of all attacks is that they exploit defects in design, configuration, or implementation of systems. Before there can be an attack, there needs to be a vulnerability.

Denial of Service

The denial of service (DoS) attack is one of the most common launched across the Internet. DoS attacks are not meant to damage systems or steal data. Instead, they seek to deny the use of the system. Some common methods of performing DoS attacks are to overload a host or network interface, to cause a system or application to crash, or to fill up memory.

In many cases, recovery from a DoS attack requires little more than temporarily shutting down access to a computer or network port. Others are more persistent.

Exploiting Programmer Errors

Two words sum up why so many vulnerabilities exist in computer systems: bad programming. There are a lot of programming errors that create security holes, but the two most frequent are buffer overruns and poor exception handling.

Buffer overruns happen when a programmer has neglected to place boundary checks around an input buffer. The attacker then sends input to the program that exceeds the size of the allocated memory for the buffer. The extra data is actually executable code that is then placed on the system stack and run. What happens after that is up to the warped imagination and skill of the attacker. It might simply crash the application or OS. Worse things can happen, though, and often do. In many cases, the rogue program stays in memory and continues to execute until the system is shut down.

Another common and related problem is poor exception handling. One common attack against UNIX and Linux computers exploits poor exception handling in a piece of network code and crashes it. Now, on the surface, this seems more like a DoS attack. Unfortunately, many UNIX and Linux daemons and applications are run from high-level or even root level shells. If these programs crash, they will transfer control to a root-level shell. When that happens, commands sent along with the ones that crashed the application will run as root, giving them carte blanche to do tremendous damage.

Man-in-the-Middle Attacks

Man-in-the-middle attacks occur when a hacker has hijacked your connection. Using a computer that mimics both ends of a network connection, the attacker makes each end appear to be talking to the other when, in fact, both ends are talking to the hacker's computer. This allows the attacker to snoop on the data moving between the two computers.

With information gleaned from the man-in-the-middle attack, the hacker can launch a replay attack. Assuming the identity of one of the endpoints of the conversation, the hacker computer sends its own data and messages to the other end (Figure 5–1). An intruder might now request data from the remote computer or even damage it.

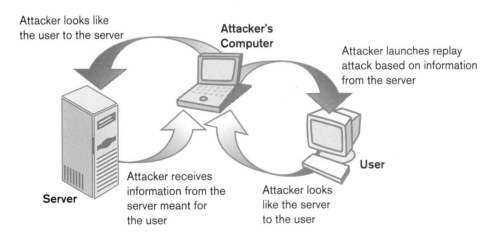

FIGURE 5-1 MAN-IN-THE-MIDDLE WITH REPLAY ATTACK

Viruses and Trojan Horses

A few years ago, network-based DoS attacks were in the news. Now all the press is about viruses and Trojan horses. Although downloaded files still represent a vector for these types of attacks, e-mail, web pages, and instant messaging have become major conduits for delivering these maladjusted programs.

Viruses consist of computer code, usually very compact, that is carried to a computer from a downloaded file, message, or e-mail. Viruses attempt to hide themselves and can often attach themselves to other programs. When run, they remain resident in memory and are reloaded when another infected program runs. Some viruses automatically duplicate themselves by sending an e-mail containing the virus to everyone in a user's address book. Others leave behind a small program that opens a network connection. This allows an attacker to get access to the infected host over the Internet.

Trojan horses are programs that seem innocuous but are really malicious code. Like the Trojan horse from the Greek epic poem *The Iliad,* they look harmless or even beneficial but are not what they seem. When activated, many act in a way similar to viruses. The most obnoxious thing about Trojan horses is that they rely on the assistance of the users themselves. This makes them malicious *and* rude.

Whether a virus or Trojan horse, these are programs that, when run, can do almost anything. This includes wiping out a hard drive and filling up memory so that the computer grinds to a halt. Viruses represent one of the greatest threats to data today.

KEY POINTS

- The concept of least privilege advocates that the most restricted amount of access to resources is the best. The best security posture, then, is Default DENY.

- Security should be deployed in layers to thwart attackers. This is known as defense in depth.

- Different techniques should be used together to cause attackers to change strategies constantly. This is known as diversity of defense.

- Encryption, or the act of encoding information to make it impossible to read, is one of the most common methods of protecting data.

- Typical types of attack modes are man-in-the-middle (with or without replay), denial of service, and the exploitation of programming errors.

- Probably the most common form of security breach is the virus or Trojan horse. These are malicious programs that hide from the user and damage or steal data.

6

STORAGE SYSTEM SECURITY

In This Chapter:

- The Role of Storage Security in Enterprise Data Protection
- DAS Security
- SAN Security
- Internal and External Vectors
- Risk
- Security Practices for Storage
- Secure Fibre Channel Protocols: FC-SP and FCAP
- Case Study: Transend Services
- Key Points

Storage security is an area that is often ignored in data protection plans. That's unfortunate, because protecting data from harm means making sure that nothing can happen to it. It's not enough to be able to restore damaged or destroyed data after the fact; it has to be protected from damage in the first place.

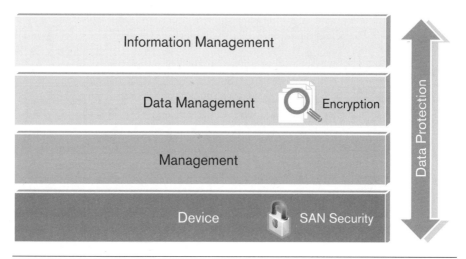

FIGURE 6-0

THE ROLE OF STORAGE SECURITY IN ENTERPRISE DATA PROTECTION

The goal of all security is to protect important assets. Whether it's putting jewels in a safe at home, posting a guard at the front gate to a plant, or setting up elaborate intrusion detection systems on your network, all security is about safeguarding something of value. Storage security shares that goal. Its chief objective is the protection of data from harm by intruders, malcontents, and the incompetent.

Backup and remote copy ensure that data is protected by having duplicates in safe locations and on different media. The purpose of these methods is to be able to restore data after it has been damaged. Storage security ensures that data is protected from harm in the first place. The best data protection plan falls short if an intruder destroys or alters the data before it can be replicated to a more physically secure site.

Storage security focuses on making the storage system environment safe. For DAS devices, solid server and application security are enough to secure the storage as well. Storage security becomes much more difficult when networked storage is involved. SAN and NAS systems allow hosts to have direct access to shared storage. Although these systems provide many advantages, they are more difficult to secure. This is especially true of SAN systems, which, in terms of security, are quite immature and lack basic features such as access control.

Moat, Bailey, and Keep

In medieval times, the security of a castle was based on a three-tier design. Called a moat-and-bailey design, it integrated three different obstacles that an attacker had to overcome to overpower the castle inhabitants. A moat was a big, deep ditch that surrounded as much of the castle as possible. The bailey wall was a high wall with a steep face that was originally made of earth. Finally, in the center of the castle complex was the keep. The keep was a high tower, usually made of stone, that provided the last refuge to the defenders. Defenders could hold out for very long periods of time in the keep.

System security utilizes a similar three-tier design. Network perimeter security, like the medieval moat, keeps the majority of external attackers at bay. Server and application security, the bailey wall of system security, provides yet another obstacle to people intent on damaging a corporation's data. The keep is storage security. It is the last line of defense from external threats and provides security from those already inside the corporate network.

DAS SECURITY

Direct access storage is so tightly coupled with the host computer that there is little one can do to add security to the storage. The level of trust between a DAS device and its host is, by design, very high, and almost any additional security would inhibit their ability to operate together. The best security for data on a DAS device is good application and server security. Security applications such as anti-virus software will protect data as well as applications and the operating system itself. Setting access controls properly, usually by denying users access to anything but their own data, is a good way to protect data at a file system level.

It Hurts When You Get Hit with Your Own Hammer

One common security problem with DAS systems centers on utilities. System administrators have many utilities that allow them to configure, manage, and change disk and file system attributes. Some come with the operating system or are purchased from an ISV; others are supplied by the storage vendor.

With the convenience of these tools comes an access path for the intruder. If these tools are themselves in an insecure location, it is easy enough for an intruder to use them to do great damage to the data on disks. Access to these

(continues)

tools can be controlled by limiting access to the directories that they are kept in. If an attacker can overcome the access controls on the operating system, however, this will not provide any protection. Instead, remove them from a host. Keeping tools on a CD-ROM that can be physically secured in a locked cabinet will make it less likely that they will be turned on the system administrator.

SAN SECURITY

It is easy to think of SANs, especially Fibre Channel SANs, as naturally secure. FC systems are, after all, closed systems. Storage arrays and tape libraries are not directly accessible from desktop machines or the network. They must be accessed from a Fibre Channel host bus adapter that is installed in a trusted server.

The safety of the SAN is, therefore, in the hands of the server. SAN devices have a *totally trusting* relationship with the servers that access them. The problems start when an intruder gains access to the server. When the intruder has access to the server, he gains an open path to the storage.

It is trust and openness that have made Fibre Channel SANs vulnerable. There is little or no protocol-level security built into Fibre Channel itself. Fibre Channel devices have always operated under the assumption that they are attached to a trusted server in much the same way that Parallel SCSI is. Devices require little or no real authentication for the same reason. When Fibre Channel host bus adapters (HBA) log into a fabric, they are not challenged.

Instead of providing a last stand against an attacker, Fibre Channel SAN architectures introduce new vulnerabilities that can be exploited by malicious hackers and may represent an unacceptable risk to IT infrastructures. IP SANs improve on Fibre Channel in terms of security but do not plug all the holes. Luckily, IP security is highly developed and, with IPSec, inherent in the protocols.

Fibre Channel Vulnerabilities

Some of the vulnerabilities that exist within Fibre Channel SANs are derived from a lack of security features common to other networks and servers. For example, Fibre Channel lacks common access controls and even simple challenge-response protocols that are used to provide authentication. All but the newest Fibre Channel switches secure the management port with only one known login and password. At the root of most of the security problems with SAN is the level of trust that servers have with the Fibre Channel network. All devices are completely trusted and have complete access to the storage devices available on the network. Some of these shortcomings are being addressed by the Fibre Channel standards bodies, others by storage system vendors. Fibre Channel security is getting better but is starting from such an abysmally low level that it will be a while before it is even adequate.

Lack of User Account Authentication

Fibre Channel networks have no native authentication mechanisms. Practically any device can log into the network without challenge. Zoning inhibits only what a host can access, not whether it is allowed into the network at all. Once on the network, host processes have access to the storage devices at a level below the file system and its access controls.

The login process of a Fibre Channel fabric does not support any type of *user-level* or *account-level* authentication. It uses only the World Wide Name and port address in the HBA. Users and accounts sit above the HBA in the OS layer and are divorced from the login process. When the HBA logs into the fabric, it is not challenged as to the authenticity of its identity beyond the WWN and port address. The application or file system interacts with the storage devices without challenge as well. If the Fibre Channel and SCSI addresses are as expected, the host can have whatever privileges have been associated with whose addresses.

In all fairness, this is not very different from Ethernet. If you have a valid MAC address, you are allowed onto the network. This is true even if MAC address filtering is being used, because the address is an expected one. What is different is what happens in the upper-layer protocols.

Most applications that are run on Ethernet networks use TCP/IP, IPX/SPX, or NetBIOS as transport protocols. These use higher-level, application-level protocols to communicate between processes and applications. These in turn provide the network services necessary for applications to access resources. Almost all of them require some form of challenge-based authentication, such as a valid username and password or a set of encrypted keys. Even primitive TCP/IP protocols such as Telnet or FTP require at least a simple username and password.

SAN applications behave differently. They access resources directly, using SCSI. SCSI has no native authentication, and its Fibre Channel implementation continues that tradition. Whereas the application-level protocols found on most networks have an intermediary application whose protocols require authentication, Fibre Channel SANs give direct access to resources without any authentication.

This security hole can be used by a malicious insider to run a program on a compromised server that accesses the SCSI driver directly. Using techniques such as WWN spoofing, hackers can also assume the identity of a valid HBA and access the fabric without challenge as though they were that HBA. Any device that has a path to a SCSI device and LUN (Logical Unit Number) can access the blocks on that LUN, whether it should or not. The attacker can then send bad information to the storage devices, produce commands that destroy data, or read the data.

Because there is a lack of user-level authentication, an attacker does not need root or system administrator access to interact with the storage devices on the SAN. She needs only to have enough privilege to be able to issue SCSI commands or use utilities that issue SCSI commands to storage devices. Many user accounts have these privileges so that they can legitimately access data on a disk.

TIP Hosts attached to a SAN should not allow any user account except root or the system administrator to add programs. This will help keep intruders from downloading utilities that send SCSI commands directly to storage devices.

The only real defense against attacks using SCSI utilities is to secure the server and its applications. When an intruder has control or access to a server on the SAN, he can bypass the file system and attack SAN devices directly.

It should be noted that the industry has developed a Fibre Channel protocol that addresses issues of authentication, called FC-SP. The goal of the protocol is to provide a secure connection between Fibre Channel devices. It includes the use of common authentication schemes to identify who has access to particular storage resources or services.

SOFT ZONING AND WORLD WIDE NAME (WWN) SPOOFING Fibre Channel fabrics use a technique called *zoning* to restrict hosts from accessing certain devices on the network. Zoning is a relatively weak form of security, and one form of it, *soft zoning,* is especially poor as a security mechanism.

Soft zoning restricts access to devices on the Fibre Channel network according to their WWN. This is convenient for system administrators who need to make changes to the Fibre Channel SAN on a regular basis. Because an HBA in the server has a WWN, the identifier for it travels with it if it is moved. If the port to which the server is connected changes, its access privileges remain the same.

This convenience comes at a price. Place the same HBA in a different host, and the zoning stays the same. The access rights to resources on the SAN are those of the original host, because they are tied to the HBA, not the host itself. If an administrator forgets to change the zoning, the new host will access the SAN as though it's the original one.

It is also possible to change the WWN on many HBAs. Changing it to another HBA's valid WWN is known as *WWN spoofing.* The computer that is spoofing the legitimate WWN will appear to be the same host, but on a different port. With soft zoning, this host will now have the same access as the original. As far as the Fibre Channel switch is concerned, the device has simply moved. All that an attacker needs is a WWN that is properly zoned, and access is assured.

Why Would Anyone Allow WWN Spoofing?

There are legitimate reasons for WWN spoofing. Some controllers and servers use spoofed World Wide Names so that they are able to assume the identity of a failed device. Using this method, a controller will present to applications the same WWN as the failed device and allow I/O to continue without first failing and restarting. Similarly, an HBA in a clustered server may spoof a WWN to appear to the SAN to be a failed host so that it does not have to request that data be resent from a storage device.

Despite these reasonable uses for WWN spoofing, it is a dangerous feature to have enabled on an HBA or a device controller, because it allows an attacker to hijack the identity of a legitimate server.

The best way to avoid successful WWN spoofing attacks is to not use soft zoning. Instead, use hard zoning, which uses the port name and WWN together. It is less convenient but more secure.

NO PROTOCOL-LEVEL ENCRYPTION SCSI never anticipated the need for sending data over anything but a closed, dedicated connection. With a closed system, there was no good reason to encrypt data as it moved over the wire. Data may be encrypted on the medium, but it was not worth spending the CPU cycles on encrypting normal I/O. This legacy carried over to the Fibre Channel implementation of SCSI. No protocol support exists for encrypting data in transit in an FC network. Unlike IP networks, which can rely on SSL or IPSec, connection-level protocols do not encrypt data in transit in a Fibre Channel network.

It is possible for a host application to encrypt data before sending it out over the network, even without protocol support. In practice, however, this is rarely done. It places a heavy burden on the application programmer and host CPU. It also requires that the device at the other end of the connection be able to decrypt the data before writing it.

INADEQUATE ISOLATION Zoning is a reasonable method of hiding resources from hosts that shouldn't see them. As a security mechanism, it is not particularly robust. Even *hard* or *port* zoning can be defeated by plugging an invalid host into a valid port in the zone. Without account-level authorization, only a port ID, port address, or WWN stand between the system and harm. All of these identifiers can be obtained with the right software and spoofed.

Within a standard Fibre Channel switch, zoning does nothing to isolate services such as the simple name server or the zoning service itself. Any malicious code, or even poorly designed code, that causes a disruption in these services disrupts the entire fabric. Zones do not isolate fabric services from failures that could bring down the switch or the entire fabric. This provides an opportunity for a denial of service attack.

There is some good news, though. Many of the latest generation of intelligent Fibre Channel switches provide for virtual fabrics that create better isolation of internal services. Although some errant or malicious code may be able to crash a particular virtual fabric, it is less likely to affect other virtual fabrics or the entire fabric. These are important features to consider when purchasing Fibre Channel switches.

FIBRE CHANNEL ARBITRATED LOOP AND LIPS In the early days of SANs, Fibre Channel Arbitrated Loop (FC-AL) was developed as a less expensive way to implement a SAN. The components were less expensive in large part because they lacked any intelligence and were only minimally managed. This was in contrast to switched fabric implementations that required many more software services and cost much more as a result.

Two services that FC-AL does not provide are a login service and a naming service. The result is that when any device enters an FC-AL SAN, the entire loop is reinitialized. A command called a Loop Initialization Primitive (LIP) begins the process of loop reconfiguration. This is why the process itself is often referred to as LIP, even though that is only the name of the command.

The problem with loop initialization is that it can cause disruptions in the I/O that is currently in progress. The loop effectively halts while the reinitialization sequence proceeds. A node that enters and leaves the loop repeatedly, or that issues excessive LIPs, can cause an arbitrated loop to basically shut down while it tries to figure out how to reconfigure it. One of the most common causes of this type of behavior is a hub port that goes on- and offline several times in a row.

This behavior represents a security threat. A hub or device port can be made to go in and out of bypass mode effectively, taking the node in and out of the arbitrated loop quickly. One method of doing this would be to gain access to the management interface of a hub or other FC-AL device via an IP network and use it to turn ports on and off. An intruder could exploit this behavior, causing disruptions within the entire FC-AL portion of the SAN or storage device.

Most storage system architects no longer build FC-AL SANs. The stability problems far outweigh the cost savings. One area where FC-AL is still prevalent is in the internal architecture of storage arrays, both tape and disk. There may be vulnerabilities inherent in the use of FC-AL in the internal architecture of arrays. If an intruder has gained access to the array's management interface, she is capable of creating a denial of service attack that would be hard to distinguish from other loop problems. Using managed hubs and securing the management port of FC-AL devices is the best method for halting these type of problems.

FIBRE CHANNEL OVER IP: EFFECTS OF GATEWAY DEVICES Although still a relatively new part of the SAN architecture, the need to support data protection applications, such as remote copy, is continuing to drive investment in what is commonly referred to as SAN extension.

As described in Chapter 2, there typically are two ways to connect SANs over long distances: directly, using a long fiber optic cable, or using existing WAN and MAN capabilities available from most data communications providers. Using the

WAN/MAN infrastructure requires the use of special devices or switch blades that provide the interface to the data communications infrastructure. These must also implement one of the common long-distance Fibre Channel protocols. The most commonly used protocols are FCIP (Fiber Channel over IP) and iFCP (Internet Fibre Channel Protocol).

There are no special security concerns associated with the direct Fibre Channel connection method. Unless someone can physically tap the fiber optic cable, it is a closed transmission and difficult to tamper with. There are, however, several security issues with moving Fibre Channel frames over WAN and MAN connections.

To begin with, they are susceptible to many of the same attacks that IP connections have. Leased lines and similar private data communications are more secure, because traffic doesn't move across a public network, such as the Internet, and is inaccessible to the outside world. That said, security can be breached when the same network infrastructure is used for storage and the Internet. In this case, portions of the storage infrastructure are now exposed to typical intrusion and denial of service (DoS) attacks.

Most exposed is the IP gateway device, which naturally has to be connected in some fashion to the LAN or WAN infrastructure. Many IP SAN gateways are designed to connect Fibre Channel to interior IP networks. These networks are vulnerable themselves and provide an attacker a direct channel to storage that didn't exist before. Most IP gateways do not provide firewall capabilities and must be married with a firewall product even for internal connections.

Because FCIP encapsulates Fibre Channel in IP packets, it would be very difficult to read or change the data in a way that would not cause the data to be corrupted. Probably the worst that can happen is that the data stream becomes so corrupted that the transactions fail, causing a DoS situation. The ability to launch an attack on a SAN extension gateway device would seem to be very difficult but not impossible, given the right set of circumstances.

MANAGEMENT INTERFACES: IP AND VENDOR API The Achilles heel of many Fibre Channel storage networking system components has been the management interface. Rarely afforded the level of security that the rest of the network has, the management interface often has only a single login and password, which then yields complete access to the device. Most do not use authorization schemes, encryption, or other standard security measures that one would expect from a server or network device.

System administrators can access many FC SAN devices from insecure web browsers or simply telnet in to them. This represents an excellent vector for an intrusion. Most IT professionals place management ports on separate networks, completely isolated from the main user network. Those that do not isolate the management port place their systems and companies at great risk. A management port should never be accessible through the main LAN and, especially, over a WAN.

Because they use embedded servers, management interfaces also suffer from similar vulnerabilities as most servers. Typically, intruders have used buffer overruns and poor exception handling to place arbitrary code on an operating system's program execution stack. This, of course, allows the attacker to run rogue programs at will. Although this is much harder in embedded systems, owing to the specialty of the embedded software, it has happened to networking equipment in the past. Many storage devices are based on commercial operating systems rather than proprietary ones. The knowledge to write dangerous programs for these software platforms is readily available and often exploited. This is yet another reason why management interfaces need to be physically isolated from other portions of the network.

BYPASSING THE FILE SYSTEM   SCSI is by far the most widely deployed storage protocol in FC SANs. The key advantage to SCSI over Fibre Channel is that the applications written for Direct Attach Storage do not have to change dramatically. For more information about SCSI over Fibre Channel, consult Chapter 2, "An Overview of Storage Technology."

When host security is compromised, an attacker has not only access to the file system to create mischief, but also the host SCSI commands. It is possible to run a program on a host that directly issues all kinds of SCSI commands to devices on the SAN. Because there is no SCSI packet filter on the network ensuring that these are legitimate packets, it is conceivable that a host that has been breached by an intruder can be used to do considerable damage to devices on the storage network.

There are a number of attacks an intruder can execute using SCSI commands. An intruder may choose to use SCSI commands for a DoS attack, for example. One way of doing this is to use something known as *FC Ping*. The legitimate function of FC Ping is to discover whether a device on a network is still operational, which is similar to the IP version. It is not, however, based on the same IP primitive command as IP Ping, the ICMP Echo command.

There is a variety of implementations of FC Ping. One freely available version, called *fc ping*, uses the SCSI Inquiry command to detect responses from devices on a SAN. This software and its source code are freely available on the Internet. It would not be difficult for an intruder to modify the source code to send SCSI Inquiry commands repeatedly to a device on the SAN.

This would be one way of launching a DoS attack against a SAN, similar to the Ping of Death. If it is sent to enough devices at the same time, other problems would occur in the FC SAN, including traffic bottlenecks and device timeouts. Situations such as this have occurred by accident due to badly behaving HBA driver code. A determined attacker could do much worse.

Having access to other SCSI commands means that data blocks could be changed or manipulated without the host file system or database being any wiser. With access to SCSI Media Control commands, an attacker could even manipulate or damage backups.

The good news is that other types of SCSI-based attacks would be very difficult because of the way FC HBAs are constructed. Most FC HBAs put both the Fibre Channel command processing and the SCSI command processing in silicon on board. Without altering the HBA microcode, it is very difficult to launch an attack based on SCSI commands.

USING FIBRE CHANNEL ANALYZERS One possible way to do extreme damage to an FC network is through use of a Fibre Channel analyzer or test instrument. These are invaluable tools to engineers and system administrators trying to debug problems in Fibre Channel equipment. In the hands of a knowledgeable malcontent, they can be used to siphon off information and to disrupt an FC network. The analyzer taps into the network but is usually invisible to the network. Better analyzers can decode FC commands and SCSI commands in a human-readable form and inject FC commands into the network.

This is a very difficult way to attack a SAN. To begin with, FC analyzers are hard to use and need considerable training and practice. Second, they are expensive enough as to be rare in most organizations. If one were to go missing for a while to be used as a tap, it would most certainly be noticed. Finally, the people who are trained in the use of an FC analyzer tend be highly paid and well-treated members of an engineering or IT organization. They have less incentive to do damage to the SANs they design and manage.

The real threat with a Fibre Channel analyzer is that it will be stolen by someone inside the organization. These analyzers are quite expensive, usually costing tens of thousands of dollars, and only as big as a laptop. They are valuable and easy to steal, making FC analyzers prime candidates for theft. FC analyzers need to be kept under lock and key, and subject to signout procedures.

IN A NUTSHELL: ALL ARE TRUSTED Fibre Channel is a network designed like a closed environment. Security was a major concern at the beginning of the technology's development. The same was true for other types of networks, which had back doors and security holes long before the Internet exposed them. Even now, there are many preventable security problems with networks at all levels.

One can sum up one of the key deficiencies of Fibre Channel from a security perspective by saying that all devices are considered trusted. Like PCs, which were treated as an extension of the mainframe environment, and the Internet, which was treated as an extension of the network environment, SANs were designed to extend the Direct Attach Storage (DAS) model. In the DAS model, all devices are trusted, there being a one-to-one relationship between the storage device and the host. In this type of relationship, there is no need to *not* trust the host or the device.

The Fibre Channel SAN concept opened up the DAS model and provided much greater connectivity and access. Unfortunately, it maintained the DAS trust model. Zoning, virtual fabrics, and LUN masking and locking are attempts to limit access between devices for the purpose of management, not security. If access has been granted to a WWN or port, it is assumed that the host attached to it is trustworthy. This is simply not always the case.

IP-Based SAN Vulnerabilities

As SANs based on the IP networking protocols—iSCSI SANs, for example—become more popular, a new set of security concerns is introduced into the storage arena. IP SANs have the benefit of mature IP security features, yet many storage security holes remain.

Some argue, however, that IP SANs may even be less secure then FC SANs. That argument is usually based on the fact that an external attacker can directly access IP storage devices without first having to go through a server or other host, and the devices are accessible from anywhere on an IP network. At least one layer of security has been removed, the skills needed to launch an IP-based attack are more common, and there are more avenues of approach for an attacker to use.

IP SAN devices may also be susceptible to a long-distance threat. For most FC SAN attacks to be successful, the attack has to come from inside the network. A person in the IT organization is the most likely attacker, which limits the pool of people capable of attacking the SAN. IP SANs are on the IP network and can expose storage devices to external intruders. An attacker capable of breaching the network defenses can now attack storage and servers separately, using different modes of attack. This greatly complicates system security by adding a new dimension to the overall security picture.

IP SANs do have a certain advantage from a security perspective. There are secure protocols, both open and proprietary, for IP networks. This is not the case for FC networks, especially those that use FC SCSI. IP networks can use various methods of securing data in transmission, including IPSec and SSL. In addition, IP networks have well-understood, field-tested, and commonly deployed authentication methods, including CHAPS and Kerobos. FC networks are still waiting for these.

AUTHENTICATION IN ISCSI   iSCSI, being IP based, allows for authentication of hosts. This is superior to Fibre Channel, which is only beginning to deploy authentication protocols. Unfortunately, the iSCSI authentication is host based, not user based. This presents a problem if a host is compromised. It is usually easier for intruders to break into a user or guest account that has very limited access to resources. In the case of iSCSI, this type of account is usable for launching an attack. This is another reason that a firewall must be between the iSCSI target devices and the hosts that access them, and that the firewall must be able to filter on users.

SCSI ATTACKS FROM UNKNOWN OR SPOOFED HOSTS One key advantage that FC has is that an attacker almost always needs to access the SAN from an internal and (ideally) trusted host. This creates a significant barrier to intrusion. For an attacker to access a Fibre Channel storage device, he would first have to penetrate the perimeter defenses (firewalls, secure routers, Intrusion Detection Systems, and so on) and then breach host security and perhaps even application security.

With iSCSI, one layer of protection—host security—has been bypassed. SCSI commands—iSCSI, in this case—can be sent directly from some point on the LAN, the WAN, or even the Internet to the storage devices. This has several effects. Unlike Fibre Channel, iSCSI devices on the IP SAN are now subject to *malformed SCSI commands,* similar to malformed URL attacks. The effect of this is unknown, but it may expose iSCSI devices to buffer overflow and exception handling problems that are more common among Internet-accessible devices.

Another possible effect is that correct iSCSI commands may be sent to a storage device that are designed to do damage. Assuming that the attacker can spoof a valid host (which is not hard to do), she will be able to retrieve, alter, or delete blocks of data from a remote computer.

DoS ATTACKS Any IP device is vulnerable to IP-related DoS attacks. This is true for IP SAN devices. iSCSI devices are also vulnerable to an attack similar to the fc ping attack. It is possible to send repeated SCSI Inquiry commands to a device, overwhelming it as it tries to respond. This type of attack can now be carried out without use of a compromised host simply with a breached network perimeter. The normal Ping of Death attack can also be used against an IP SAN device. Other, similar IP DoS attacks can be launched against iSCSI devices.

IP SANs are susceptible to another form of DoS attack, one not aimed at the iSCSI devices but at the infrastructure supporting them. Because iSCSI is built on Internet technology, attacks that can disrupt portions of that infrastructure may affect the ability to access iSCSI SANs.

Although these attacks are not likely to destroy data, they disrupt the ability to use the data. Continued loss of availability can have an effect on a business that is as profound as data loss.

Naming and Discovery Services

A particularly vulnerable portion of the IP SAN is the naming and discovery infrastructure used by iSCSI. iSCSI uses a URI type address to name resources. This has the advantage of allowing changes to the IP addresses of devices on the network without having to reconfigure all the hosts. Under-

(continues)

neath these names are still IP addresses. If the hosts are using standard network work directory technology like DNS, LDAP, or SLP to provide for discovery and translate iSCSI names into IP addresses, the IP SAN can be brought down by attacks on these network services, many of which are well documented and common.

This differs from Fibre Channel, in which the directory services are provided by the Simple Name Server (SNS) built into the Fibre Channel switches themselves. This network service is accessible only from nodes connected directly to the fabric. Access to SNS happens at such a low level that it would be incredibly difficult to attack it even from a compromised host. There is no FC naming and directory that can be accessed from outside the SAN to cause a DoS attack.

FIREWALLS DO NOT SPEAK ISCSI   A major security concern in IP SANs is that most firewalls are not designed to crack open an iSCSI packet. Different types of firewalls can examine incoming IP traffic and reject packets based on a variety of criteria and at different network layers. Some are able to filter packets at layers 3 through 7 and can even decode malicious HTTP traffic. iSCSI commands are new to firewalls, and none currently looks at that type of payload.

Some firewalls may simply reject incoming iSCSI commands, depending on how permissive the security is. This could cause problems for system architects who envision accessing IP over long-distance connections.

It is also likely that iSCSI traffic would be deployed over a secure VPN connection, which most firewalls will not be able to interpret because the payload is encrypted. It is unknown whether the VPN server's security filters will be able to understand external iSCSI commands and see them as malicious. This may cause undesirable iSCSI commands to pass through a secure connection right to a device. With a VPN, only the connection is secure, not necessarily the host at either end of the connection.

It is important to remember that iSCSI primarily targets small and midsize businesses. These businesses rarely have the most sophisticated network defense devices and often rely on integrated security appliances. If these devices do not know how to identify malicious use of iSCSI commands, use of iSCSI will create potentially dangerous system vulnerabilities. iSCSI is also being promoted as a less expensive way to perform replication and remote copy functions, which are important to disaster avoidance and business continuance. Security appliances set at very restrictive levels that do not understand iSCSI will make these architectures difficult to deploy, and setting them to more permissive levels will expose the SAN to hackers.

Detecting Intruders

Storage systems represent a special difficulty for security administrators. Most tools used to monitor illegal activity do not understand SCSI, Fibre Channel, or other storage protocols. There are many ways to tunnel storage protocols in standard TCP/IP and have it look like normal traffic.

Even if more sophisticated tools do not help much, simple techniques do. Log files on hosts and SAN devices will show some unusual activity and should be checked periodically. Changes in the behavior of the system may also indicate the presence of an attacker.

Unfortunately, the best way of knowing that an intruder has penetrated the security of a SAN system is by the effects. When data blocks begin to change unexpectedly, it may mean that an attack is in progress.

MULTIPLE TCP/IP CONNECTIONS When an application creates multiple IP connection to better use available bandwidth, the application data that is carried in the IP packets is spread out among many separate connections. This makes it very difficult for Intrusion Detection Systems (IDS) and firewalls to detect potentially damaging information sent to a device.

This is currently a problem with many packet filtering technologies today, because the firewall has no way of knowing that part of the payload is in a different data stream. Potentially harmful information can be sent to a device without security systems detecting it. Only when the application reassembles the information will the effect be noticed. The onus is on the application to detect harmful data. Because of this, many firewalls will not allow multiple data streams to travel between remote and local hosts and devices.

iSCSI uses multiple TCP connections to make better use of bandwidth in a network connection. Even if the firewall or IDS is capable of cracking and examining iSCSI packets, it may not allow multiple IP streams as part of the same session. If multiple connections are allowed, the security measures may not be able to detect harmful data contained in those connections, and iSCSI devices will have to be able to guard against attacks contained in iSCSI packets.

SOFTWARE AND CONFIGURATION HOLES EXPLOITABLE BY EXTERNAL HACKERS iSCSI devices are, by nature, TCP/IP devices. This makes them vulnerable to all the attacks that currently affect network devices. The use of commercial or open-source TCP/IP stacks means that methods of attacking these devices are well known. Fibre Channel benefits by security through obscurity, meaning that the skills and tools needed to attack it are not readily available.

IP SANs have no such advantage. In fact, the network interface may be the real target of a DoS or other type of attack. The attacker may not even know that the iSCSI device is primarily a storage device when launching an attack. The results will still be the same—a down or damaged storage device.

Another potential vulnerability is the management interface. If management information is run across the same network as the actual data—if both interfaces are connected to the same network—there is a chance that SNMP information will announce to an attacker that a storage device is available and what its key features are. An attacker can glean important information about devices from management data being broadcast across the network.

SAN Appliances

It is becoming more common to have special-purpose devices, or *appliances*, present in SAN architectures. They are commonly used to provide specific services for the storage network. Some examples of these servers are virtualization, backup, remote copy, clustered file services, and management appliances. Some vendors have created large storage servers, which integrate a large number of these features into one device.

Although these devices have an attractive Total Cost of Ownership (TCO) profile and allow functionality to be added incrementally to a SAN, they are basically servers and are vulnerable to many of the same problems as other servers. Often, they are based on a commercial or open-source operating system such as Microsoft Windows or Linux. Vulnerabilities in these operating systems are transferred to these appliances. If the appliance is accessible to a network of any sort, it may be vulnerable to attacks common to the underlying OS.

Attack Vectors Common to All SCSI Storage Devices

Any storage device that uses a form of SCSI has certain vulnerabilities. As previously discussed, SCSI was designed for a closed and, hence, trusted environment. SCSI devices traditionally have been held behind and subordinate to a server and inaccessible on their own. Storage networking changed this, opening storage devices directly to rogue hosts and Internet hackers.

INLINE MANAGEMENT THROUGH SCSI COMMANDS: SCSI ENCLOSURE SERVICES   There exists a set of SCSI command extensions called SCSI Enclosure Services (SES). SES was conceived of as a way for complex DAS systems to communicate information about the operating conditions of the device back to a host. This in turn allowed the host to alter some of the environmental and operational variables. Because the SCSI connection was always present, sometimes the only connection between the host and device, this was convenient. Typically, the host accesses the enclosure as a LUN on the target SCSI address.

There are several implications to having this type of command set at the disposal of an intruder. First and foremost, intruders need information about their intended targets, and SES provides information that would be hard to get otherwise. If the attacker has the ability to access the storage array from an IP network node or the Internet, he may obtain information that would otherwise be available only to someone who was standing in physical proximity to the devices or who had compromised a secondary network reserved for management. Even if an attacker cannot get to the management interface because it has been properly secured and resides on a separate network, it is possible for her to gain management information by using SCSI commands on a compromised host. SES creates a back channel for hackers to get at management features.

Gleaning information about devices is dangerous enough, but SES also provides the ability to change some of the operational parameters of a storage device. This allows management software to manipulate various elements within the storage device, including interfaces and fans. With access to these commands, an intruder can do quite a bit of damage.

LUN MASKING AND LOCKING UNCOVERED Storage system administrators rely on a feature called LUN masking to help secure storage resources. With LUN masking, devices will not respond to the SCSI Inquiry/Report LUN command unless it comes from an initiator that has permission to receive device information. This tricks the host into thinking that there are no devices available on that LUN. This approach works when certain LUNs must be hidden from certain hosts.

LUN masking is a weak form of protection against attack, because it does not make the LUN truly unavailable; the LUN only *appears* to be unavailable. Hosts can still send SCSI commands to a masked LUN, and devices will respond to it. There are diagnostic programs that attempt to send SCSI commands to all LUNs at a SCSI address incrementally to see whether any respond, in a manner similar to a TCP port scanner.

An attack on masked LUNs would try to send commands to a LUN and see whether it responds with anything, including an error code. Then it would write erroneous (probably random) information to the device. That could easily damage real information on the device. LUN masking offers no real protection against data loss.

Some storage array manufacturers have instituted a stronger version of LUN masking called *LUN locking*. With LUN locking, LUNs will not respond in any fashion to any command that does not come from a known initiator with proper permissions. This is clearly a more effective method of securing devices from attack. Even then, this provides no safety if the attack comes from a spoofed or compromised host that has permission to access certain LUNs. Without account-level, two-level authentication, it is still possible to get past LUN locking.

CONTROLLERS SUSCEPTIBLE TO SERVER TYPE PROGRAMMING ERRORS Controllers are used to provide a central access point for individual storage devices, such as the disks in a disk array. Many have higher-level features, including RAID, path failover, device failover, virtualization, and management. Although much of the functionality of a typical controller is in hardware, more advanced functions (management, failover, and virtualization) are provided by software and as such are vulnerable to the same type of security holes as are servers. Buffer overruns, off-the-shelf or open-source TCP/IP stacks, and poor exception handling are primary areas at which a hacker may launch an attack.

Patch management of controllers is as important as with server operating systems.

NAS Security

NAS devices are comprised of three main parts: the disk subsystem, RAID controller, and NAS or file head. The most vulnerable part is the NAS head. Often based on Linux, Microsoft Windows, or a proprietary NOS, the NAS head is still a server and susceptible to many of the same security afflictions that other file servers have, including vulnerabilities in the TCP/IP stack and file system. The good news is that NAS devices typically have had all other functions not vital to serving up files stripped away. This provides a hacker less opportunity to exploit other types of common vulnerabilities even when based on a commercial or open-source OS.

NAS devices, like all file servers, are also open to attacks via the protocols they use. Because all NAS devices use CIFS, NFS, or both, they are also susceptible to attacks aimed at those protocols.

CIFS and NFS Security

There are several security issues with CIFS and NFS. NFS, for example, uses *host-based* authentication instead of *user-level* authentication. User-level authentication is necessary to access the host, but when authorized, the user will have access to all exported mounts available from that server.

On the other hand, many implementations of CIFS allow user-level control over access but still show all available shares, including ones that the user can't access. This gives an attacker invaluable information about the resources available on a network.

The conventional security system vendors are now taking NFS and CIFS security seriously. Application firewall and IDS products are now available that can look at CIFS and NFS packets and scan for attacks. Software has also been introduced that integrates antivirus software into the NAS filer so that viruses and Trojan horses are removed as they are stored, not when a host accesses them.

Securing Files Through Access Control and Encryption

There are many ways to secure a file system. The two most important ones are *access control* and *encryption*. The former, access control, determines permissions for each user and process, thereby controlling access to system resources, including file system objects. Access control, in turn, relies on authentication to determine whether the person requesting access to resources is really who she claims to be.

TIP One of the most common methods of access control is by using an *access control list* (ACL). An ACL can cause performance problems though. It can take a lot of time to search an ACL to find what permissions a system object has. The most frequently used systems often have very long lists. Sifting through these lists can significantly reduce performance.

Access Control Posture

Access control is part of all file systems, to some extent. What is important to the system administrator is the default posture of the access control system. Many systems are quite permissive, allowing access to all resources unless otherwise stated. It is important to assume a Default DENY posture and set access to be as restrictive as possible within the file system.

Access controls make it difficult for unauthorized users to get at file system objects. Encryption assumes that an attacker can find a way to access an object. Instead, it makes the object useless to attackers, deterring them from trying in the first place. If the attacker tries anyway and is successful at cracking through the access control and other security measures, the data will not be of use to him.

Encryption is simply the encoding of data so that it is unreadable and unusable. Until it is decrypted, or decoded, encrypted data appears to be a jumble of incomprehensible characters. The method by which data is encoded is outside the scope of this book, but many books on security provide good descriptions of the algorithms used.

When to Encrypt: Data at Rest, Data in Motion

A typical problem for system administrators is when to encrypt data. Data can be encrypted while being transmitted over a network *(data in motion)* or after it has reached its destination *(data at rest)*.

(continues)

Encrypting data in motion defeats attempts to capture data while it is in transit between two nodes. This is what secure network protocols such as SSL and IPSec do, and it is the backbone of VPN services. If an intruder is able to tap into the data stream, the data will be indecipherable and of no value to the attacker.

Data at rest is often encrypted to secure data on storage devices. Encrypting data at rest is used more often for removable media, making it pointless to steal. With networked storage systems, critical data is also encrypted while at rest to safeguard information from those who might have access to the network.

It is important to encrypt sensitive data in motion and at rest. Both methods deter attackers from bothering with the data by making it unusable to them.

MANUAL ENCRYPTION There are two ways to encrypt and decrypt data: at a file system level and at a block level. The first is a manual process, and the second uses inline devices and software to automate encryption and decryptions.

With manual encryption, file data is run through a program that encodes the data and saves it to the same file or a new file. This type of program is available as commercial, open-source, and free software. Typically, the program asks for a key, which is a code word or phrase supplied by the user. The file to be encrypted and key are run through one or more algorithms that transform the characters in the file into different characters. PGP (Pretty Good Privacy) is an example of a program of this type.

To decrypt, the file and the key are once again supplied to the program. The data is run through the same algorithms in reverse to produce the original data.

Manual encryption products are a great way of securing small amounts of data. Many commercial programs will allow a user to set up a secure portion of her hard drive and to encrypt and decrypt data automatically. The downside to this process is that the user has to remember the key phrase. Key phrases suffer from the same problems as passwords. Users either forget them and cannot access their data, or they write them down—or worse yet, record them in an unencrypted file on their hard drive. When the key is accessible, electronically or physically, the purpose of encryption is defeated, and the data is no longer secure and protected.

TIP Don't lose your keys. Losing encryption keys is like losing the key to your house or car. The data is locked up, and there is no good way to get at it. Keys must be secured against theft and loss. Copies of keys should be kept in secure devices or locations.

AUTOMATED ENCRYPTION Encryption can be automated in several ways. In some cases, encryption is built into software used to write and read data. A prime example of this is backup software. As described in Chapter 3, most backup software vendors have encryption available, either as a feature or as an add-on product. When data is encrypted automatically, it becomes less of a target to an attacker, who can't use it.

Another method of automatically encrypting data is through use of a hardware device, either as an appliance or embedded in a storage device. These devices tend to be much faster than software devices. Another advantage over software encryption is that the devices exist outside the host and are not compromised if a host is. It takes additional attacks to get at the encryption device itself. Finally, one device can act to encrypt data for many hosts, centralizing key management and other security functions. Many encryption devices are also including authentication functions, as well as adding a layer of security to the storage system.

The downside of automated encryption is that a large amount of data is now accessible only if the software or hardware device is also available. Device or host failure can render data inaccessible.

INTERNAL AND EXTERNAL VECTORS

In biology, a vector is the way that a disease agent accesses a host. Sneezing is a vector, as are the surfaces in a bathroom. The vector for the Black Death in the Middle Ages was fleas carried by rats, and mosquitoes are a vector for yellow fever.

The same is true of computer attacks. Several vectors can be employed to attack systems. Storage systems have some vectors in common with other parts of a computer infrastructure and a few unique ones as well.

Generally speaking, attacks come from either an inside source or an outside one. In a recent study by the Computer Security Institute and the Federal Bureau of Investigation, internal attacks against systems were listed as the second most common type of attacks reported.[1] Because these attacks tend to be underreported or categorized as something other than computer intrusion, it is safe to say that internal threats are very dangerous and prevalent. Attacks against storage systems are more likely to be from internal vectors, owing to the difficulty of getting to the storage infrastructure from the outside. Many layers of network, host, and application security have to be breached before a typical SAN can be attacked. Fibre Channel networks in particular require an external source to have high degrees of access and uncommon skills to mount an effective attack.

---

1. 2003 CSI/FBI Computer Crime and Security Survey.

Besides the ability to mount attacks, insiders have the capability to do much more damage. They have superior *knowledge of and access to* sensitive information, such as passwords. Insiders can also cover their tracks better because they are knowledgeable of a company's security policies, practices, and capabilities.

That is not to say that external hackers aren't capable of attacking a storage network. iSCSI, being Internet based, is especially vulnerable to attack. The complete lack of authentication in a Fibre Channel network ensures that if a host is breached, the storage devices are wide open to attack. It is only a general lack of knowledge of FC SANs that keeps storage system hacking from becoming a more widespread problem.

Security Through Obscurity

Some systems are more secure because they are not well known. This is known as *security through obscurity*. The skills necessary to deploy and manage a SAN, especially a Fibre Channel one, are not at all common. SANs are still something of a specialty, and this has acted to protect SAN systems despite gaping holes in security.

This type of protection never lasts. As technology becomes more commonplace, so do the skills to attack it. With the advent of IP SANs and Fibre Channel SANs targeted to the small- and medium-size business market, IT professionals can no longer rely on SAN security by virtue of a lack of knowledge.

To attack a system from the outside, the attacker first needs to penetrate the perimeter network defenses. The intruder then needs to gain access to a host with sufficient privileges to access the applications and tools used to manage and access the storage system. There are several methods for doing this, including making use of a flaw in a running system process or application.

Despite the difficulty of all this, it is possible to launch an attack from outside a storage network. It is also conceivable that an actual attack will emanate from a different computer on the network that is acting as a relay. This is old hat for many hackers.

Unintentional Security Breaches

Another type of threat that is often overlooked is unintentional attacks. These are almost always insider mistakes. Perhaps a Fibre Channel switch is not zoned properly, and a new host is allowed to format a disk containing data from a different host or application. Maybe an iSCSI disk array is placed on the network without a firewall, and curious people snoop around, causing corruption of the data.

Well-meaning but poorly trained IT professionals are often a major reason why systems are damaged by insiders. Someone who thinks he can configure a Fibre Channel switch but doesn't really understand the management interface can cause as much damage as, or even more damage than, the most malicious attacker. Security systems are like locks on doors—they keep honest people honest.

RISK

It isn't worth talking about security if there is no risk. Risk is a measure of the negative economic results associated with vulnerability and threat. Without a negative outcome, risk does not exist. Practically any vulnerability can be used to do damage, of course, so risk goes hand in hand with vulnerability.

Risk is also a function of threat. Even if vulnerabilities exist, there must be someone willing to exploit them. In some cases, vulnerability exists, yet no one has the skills to carry out an attack based on it. This means that there is theoretical but not practical risk.

This is important when making security decisions. Security is much like insurance. The cost and likelihood of the negative outcome must be weighed against the cost of security.

Outcomes of Storage Security Breaches

Assuming that an intruder can breach a storage system's security, several outcomes can be predicted. Ultimately, an intruder has a goal in mind when choosing to launch a security attack. Knowing ahead of time what those goals are allows IT professionals to anticipate the attack and prevent it.

The first thing that an attacker may do is nothing. Many breaches of system security are carried out by self-styled "hackers" who do what they do for bragging rights or to feel smart and important. These types of attackers are likely to look around yet leave things alone.

The next possible outcome is that an intruder will simply look around for interesting things he can use or steal. For some intruders, it will be information they are personally interested in; others are looking for information that has clear market value, such as defense information, product plans, and credit card numbers.

TIP Encryption thwarts attackers. Few so-called hackers have the wherewithal or equipment to decrypt strongly encrypted data. If they can get this data and there is nothing for them to see, they will move on to greener pastures eventually. They may also spend a lot of time looking for unencrypted data. This gives the security response team time to analyze the attack, stop it, and safeguard against future attacks.

A third outcome is that data is made unavailable for some time, with the purpose of hurting the organization that the intruder is launching the attack against. Denial of service (DoS) attacks are often in this category. They may take down a company's web site for a time or remove a database from service. Sometimes, DoS attacks are precursors to other attacks, sort of a softening-up process.

Finally, the most malicious intruders will attempt to destroy or alter data. They attempt to disrupt an organization's operations by denying it key information. Even subtle changes in data can have far-ranging effects on an organization.

TIP Solid access control and authentication are the key to preventing these types of attacks. Commonly part of host security, they also must be instituted on management interfaces and storage devices where possible.

Connectivity as a Risk Multiplier

When the Internet was young, risks associated with it were relatively low. At the time, there were a limited number of computers (in the beginning, only four mainframes) tied together over dial-up lines that communicated most of their information via UUCP. It was easy to secure only four machines and a handful of modems. Access to the network was very limited, and the number of assets involved was low.

As the Internet grew, both in size and complexity, security problems became more prevalent, and the risk involved in using the network became higher. There were more devices of different types with many more access points. Attackers had access to thousands and then millions of computers, not just four.

Networking storage has had a similar effect on storage security risks. Even if the likelihood of a successful attack against a SAN is small, if a malicious attacker does get through defenses, she now has a greater number of devices to wreak havoc on at her disposal.

Because risk is based on outcome, a successful intrusion into a SAN could be much more devastating than an intrusion into an equal number of DAS devices. With a SAN, if one server is compromised, the attacker potentially has access to many storage devices. Even if there were no special risks associated with SANs, the *risk multiplier of a SAN* still needs to be a factor in security planning.

Vendor Lock-In

As Fibre Channel SANs evolved, it was clear that the incompatibility issues would persist for some time. Some argued that this was done intentionally by vendors who wanted to gain an advantage in the marketplace. Others would point to the loose standards that are indigenous to the data storage industry. Yet others claimed that it was a matter of evolution, and that all technology often starts in a proprietary form and eventually become more standardized.

Whether the reason is loose standards, competitive practices, or normal technology progression, it still stands that much of the Fibre Channel products that are available to IT professionals do not work properly in a multivendor environment. This has led to a rise in single-vendor solutions. A primary storage equipment provider builds entire solutions, either as standard configurations or a custom installation, for a customer using components that have previously been tested by the vendor and certified as interoperable. This has become one of the most popular ways to purchase SAN equipment. It has taken from the system architect the burden of making disparate components work together in a unified architecture.

The *monoculture* inherent in single-vendor solutions means that all devices may be susceptible to a *single set of flaws* in the devices that make up the solution. An error in a controller's microcode or web interface that generates a security risk will be amplified by the ubiquity of that code in a single-vendor solution. Diversity in infrastructure is important to mitigate risk within an environment. This becomes more worrisome as vendor consolidation creates less choice of vendors.

If the vendor of choice is unable to produce security features in a timely manner, vulnerabilities will exist in a vast majority of the systems within the storage infrastructure. Single-vendor solutions contain a risk multiplier owing to the ubiquity of the same type of device and the increased reliance on a limited set of underlying platforms.

Software Monoculture

Many storage system vendors rely on a similar set of manufacturers to supply major components such as RAID controllers and NAS heads. Many storage networking devices use the same operating systems from Microsoft and Wind River (maker of VxWorks embedded software), as well as Linux. The management interfaces also tend to use commercial TCP/IP stacks from a limited number of software vendors. Security flaws in these components and software may affect many different vendors' devices. It is important to know what software vendors are using when performing security audits of storage systems.

SECURITY PRACTICES FOR STORAGE

There are many hurdles for the system architect who is trying to craft a secure storage system. Foremost of these is a lack of support for security in the products and protocols used to build enterprise storage systems.

Fortunately, there are several strategies that can be used to enhance security for storage systems that do not cost very much to implement. As is always the case with system security, none of these practices can guarantee that an intruder won't damage data in a storage system. These strategies will, however, set obstacles in the path of the malicious and the unwitting.

Separate Networks for Management

One of the best vectors for the malicious or curious is the management interface of a storage system device. Management interfaces must be kept on completely separate networks to ensure that there is no path to the device from anywhere on the main LAN or, especially, the Internet.

It is very convenient for a storage administrator to have access from a standard desktop computer to the devices he manages. Unfortunately, this desktop access provides an opportunity for others to see and perhaps even access the devices' management features. At best, this provides an intruder with valuable intelligence. A more likely scenario is that the network connection is used as the basis for an attack.

The best defense is to have management interfaces on completely separate networks. This network should also be accessible only from a dedicated workstation. A workstation that has access to both the main network and the management network may itself be used as a platform for an attack on the storage system.

IP storage poses a bit of a problem for similar reasons. If the storage devices are accessible from the main network, they may be exposed to attacks from computers on that network. Unlike the management interfaces, though, hosts need to access the IP storage devices. They in turn must be accessible by other hosts, such as desktop computers.

The best solution is to have a separate IP network for the storage system that only the hosts can access. Hosts should be *double homed* (having two Ethernet cards attached to separate networks), and a firewall should be placed between the hosts and the IP storage devices.

Hard Zoning in FC Networks

To begin with, all Fibre Channel SANs should use zoning in some form. It is surprising how often a SAN is put into place without it. That is because there is no default zoning in Fibre Channel. Fibre Channel networks believe all hosts to be trusted and, hence, work under a Default ALLOW posture. Zoning doesn't truly change this, because any host not in a zone has access to any nonzoned resource, but it is better than nothing.

Hard zoning is preferred to soft zoning. Soft zoning is susceptible to WWN spoofing and similar host attacks because it is based on the host bus adapter and not the Fibre Channel switch. With soft zoning, hosts don't "see" the resources outside their zone but could still access them given the proper tools. Thus, the hosts themselves represent a vector that can be used to attack the system.

On the other hand, hard zoning is based on the switch port. This makes it more difficult for the host to be used for an attack by overcoming zoning restrictions. It also is impervious to WWN spoofing.

TIP *All* ports should be zoned, even unused ports. A zone should be established that contains no resources at all, and empty switch ports must be assigned to that zone. This way, even if someone plugs a host into the switch port, it will remain isolated from the other hosts and resources on the SAN.

Virtual Fabrics

So-called intelligent storage switches implement a new feature called virtual fabrics. Virtual fabrics provides a higher degree of isolation than zoning does.

Each host is assigned to a virtual fabric in much the same way that Ethernet hosts can be isolated within a VLAN. What is most important is that each virtual fabric has its own set of fabric services. This differs from zoning, in which major fabric services such as the Simple Name Server and the zoning service itself are shared by all nodes in the entire fabric. If an intruder can find a way to circumvent or disrupt these services, she may cause damage to the entire SAN.

With a virtual fabric, damage would be mitigated only to the virtual fabric that is accessible from the port used for the attack. Even if an attacker can overcome a switch's hard zoning, damage would be isolated to the nodes in the virtual fabric.

Strong Application and Host Security

It's hard for intruders to do damage to the storage system if they can't get to them in the first place. Strong host security is as much a part of storage system security as it is of server security. Specifically:

- Tight access control is a must. Limit user access to the host, especially processes running on their own, such as UNIX daemons.

- Place strict restrictions on which users can run storage utilities. Any storage utility that does not have to be on the host should be removed.

- Restrict the ability for a program to be loaded over the network. This will make it difficult for intruders to place utilities on the host that directly access the storage resources via SCSI commands.

- Use two-factor authentication for all hosts. Although terribly inconvenient, two-factor authentication, especially when one of the factors relies on a physical object such as a swipe card, makes it very difficult for a remote processes to use the host as a vector for an attack on the storage system.

Host security is the "moat" that an attacker needs to cross to get to the storage "keep." It needs to be full of monsters ready to eat intruders.

SAN System Management Software

As discussed previously, rogue computers on the SAN are an excellent way for an insider to make mischief with a SAN. This is especially true for Fibre Channel networks, where it is very difficult to get to the network from outside the SAN.

Proper SAN management helps detect some of the changes that would indicate that an attack has happened; is in progress; or, better yet, is about to happen. Most SAN management software is capable of discovering hosts (via the host bus adapter) and devices as they enter the network. Unexpected hosts may indicate that an attacker has penetrated the system. Good SAN management software can also note changes in device settings and storage provisioning, and even sudden upswings in network usage to a particular port. All of these, if not expected, may indicate an attack in progress or one about to commence.

Finally, SAN management software will usually allow system settings and states to be saved. This feature will allow storage administrators to recover more quickly from attacks if they are successful.

Secure SAN Switch Operating Systems

Some SAN switch vendors offer a version of the switch operating system that includes special security features. Some examples of what a secure switch operating system might include are

- **Virtual fabrics.** Virtual fabrics provide higher levels of isolation, especially of fabric services.

- **Access control for the management port.** Certain secure operating systems allow for access control lists to be set for the management. This limits which hosts can be allowed to manage the switch.

- **Policy-driven management.** Some switches allow for the setting of policies that restrict what switch functions can be used by which users or hosts. This limits the damage that an intruder or poorly skilled technician can do.

- **Port-level access control.** Some secure fabrics implement policy-driven access controls at a port level tied to a WWN. This helps defeat WWN spoofing, because the WWN is bound to a particular port. This is stronger protection than zoning.

Security features can also be found in some storage servers. Although most storage servers focus on basic SAN services, such as virtualization, some have also begun to implement security features lacking in switches. Access controls and inline encryption are two examples of security features included in some storage servers.

When purchasing a SAN switch or storage server, it is important to consider whether the device supports these features. If security is a major concern, the extra money that these options will cost is worth it.

Manage IP Connections

IP SANs—iSCSI in particular—often uses multiple IP connections for the same data stream to get the bandwidth necessary for storage applications. This represents a risk, because it can hide potentially harmful traffic from IDS and firewall devices. In fact, it is better to disallow this capability at the firewall and not rely on it for storage applications.

It is also better not to perform block-level storage over a public network. This represents an opportunity for intruders to get at storage resources that were previously hidden. Using VPN helps, in that the data is encrypted, but even encrypted data can carry a malicious payload. No one can look at the traffic, but it may still be dangerous.

File-level data is different, because many IDS and firewall programs understand CIFS and NFS and are capable of creating the proper security environment for them. In this case, stick to the use of common protocols supported by security devices. It is not safe to use proprietary solutions.

Use LUN Locking in Addition to LUN Masking

LUN masking only hides the storage device from the hosts; it is still accessible. LUN locking, on the other hand, actually disallows hosts from accessing specific

LUNs unless they have permission to do so. LUN locking is a function of the storage device and should be taken into account when purchasing disk arrays and tape libraries.

Having LUN locking in place does not mean that LUN masking should not be used. By masking the LUN, the attacker is initially denied valuable information about the storage system and will have to work for it. Together, LUN masking and LUN locking are much more powerful than each is alone.

Use Encryption

It must be assumed that, despite best efforts, an intruder will penetrate the defense of a storage system. At this point, one might also assume that the intruder will be able to steal lots of important information before doing whatever other mischief she has in mind.

Maybe not. If the data that the attacker gains access to is encrypted, it may not be safe from damage but will not be usable by the attacker. The side benefit of having the data encrypted is that encryption makes it less likely that professional hackers will break in. They won't waste their time stealing data that can't be used or sold. It's like robbing an empty house.

A Storage Security Checklist

When designing storage systems or buying storage products, system security must be part of the equation. Table 6–1 is a checklist of security practices that should be part of your overall storage system planning.

TABLE 6-1 A SAMPLE STORAGE SECURITY CHECKLIST

Best Practice	
Management network separate from LAN and SAN	◯
Hard zoning employed (Fibre Channel)	◯
All ports zoned, even unused ones (Fibre Channel)	◯
Access control in place on hosts	◯
Access control in place on management ports	◯
Access controls in place on SAN switch ports (Fibre Channel)	◯
Restricted use of storage utilities to trusted administrators	◯
Programs cannot be loaded over the network to hosts	◯
Two-factor authentication in place for hosts	◯
Two-factor authentication for management ports	◯
SAN switches have secure operating systems (Fibre Channel)	◯
Switches support virtual fabrics (Fibre Channel)	◯

TABLE 6–1 A SAMPLE STORAGE SECURITY CHECKLIST*(CONTINUED)*

Devices support policy-based management	◯
Single connections for each iSCSI data stream	◯
VPN for iSCSI traffic	◯
Use common protocols for file traffic	◯
LUN locking and LUN masking employed	◯
Data at rest encrypted (disk and tape)	◯
Data in motion encrypted	◯

SECURE FIBRE CHANNEL PROTOCOLS: FC-SP AND FCAP

It is clear that Fibre Channel SAN security suffers from a lack of secure protocols. Initiatives from the ANSI T11 Committee, which sets standards for Fibre Channel, aim to correct this deficit. Several protocols are under consideration, but two plug important holes immediately.

The first is FC-SP, short for *Fibre Channel Security Protocol*. It provides for an encrypted transmission between two Fibre Channel nodes. Similar to IPSec, it protects data in transit. This is especially important in situations in which the Fibre Channel connection can be tapped, such as long-distance FC connections.

The second is FCAP, or *Fibre Channel Authentication Protocol*. Using techniques similar to authentication on IP networks, FCAP allows nodes to be authenticated. It contains provisions for the use of keys and certificates.

Both of these protocols point to an awareness of the need to add security protocols to storage networks.

CASE STUDY: TRANSEND SERVICES

Security is a vital element of the business of Transend Services of Ottawa, Ontario, Canada. Transend provides outsourced financial-settlement services to financial institutions, health-care companies, and manufacturing firms. It handles the financial supply chain for companies in highly regulated businesses. It is crucial that the company be able to provide an environment that is demonstrably secure to help clients meet the demands of their businesses, including regulators. Transend not only has to settle payments between invoices and purchase orders, but also must ensure the presentation of documentation as well.

According to Brent Luckman, CEO of Transend, securing data in transit and at rest was paramount. The company needed to *prove* to clients that data was protected from prying eyes, even when the data was sitting securely on a disk or tape. Clients needed to be assured that the data was safe from external hackers, internal malfeasance, and other clients. Failure to do so could have dire consequences.

The solution was a multilayer security system that set several obstacles in the path of intruders. Because Transend had begun with a NAS environment, IP security techniques were deployed first, including two deep firewalls that deployed different technology; Virtual Private Networks; IDS, virtual LANs; and separate networks for development, testing, preproduction, and production.

As the company began to deploy SANs, it added LUN masking and zoning to the security profile. According to Michael Kapuscinsky, security and storage specialist at Transend, these provided a level of security that fit the perceived risks at a reasonable cost.

To protect data at rest, security appliances by NeoScale Systems were used to encrypt data as it moved to disks and tapes. Through the use of these appliances, Transend was able to use encryption while meeting the performance requirements of its applications. With the NeoScale appliances, only a few Transend and client employees were capable of accessing data on disk or tape even if the data were in some way reachable. The security appliances also provided for firewall-type isolation in the SAN environment.

Using this collection of techniques, Transend was able to assure customers that their data was secure, both at rest and in transit, and that the infrastructure was secure. Clients could outsource important financial processing while maintaining a secure environment that met their internal needs and the requirements of regulators.

KEY POINTS

- Security in a DAS environment is provided by the host to which the storage is attached. Securing the management interface and storage utilities is important to securing the storage.

- Security in a networked storage environment is more complex. NAS and SANs are vulnerable to the same types of attacks as IP networks.

- Fibre Channel SANs lack many basic security features. LUN masking and zoning are used to provide security for a Fibre Channel SAN but are weak. Virtual SANs, LUN locking, and encryption appliances supplement native controls in a SAN.

- NAS and iSCSI SANs take advantage of existing IP security techniques. The dominance of host-level, as opposed to user-level, authentication is still a problem for NAS and iSCSI.

- Isolation of the storage and management interfaces from the LAN and WAN is an important technique, whether it is physical or virtual.

7

POLICY-BASED DATA PROTECTION

In This Chapter:

- Difficulties with Data Protection Strategies
- Data Lifecycle Management (DLM)
- Key Points.

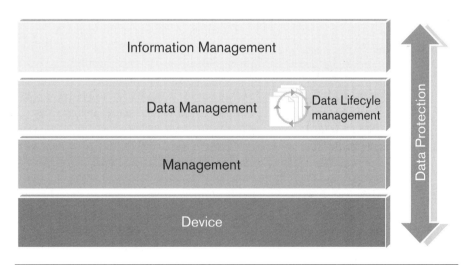

FIGURE 7–0

As more data needs to be protected under more stringent controls, organizations are turning to policy-based data protection. Policy-based data protection helps manage the complexity of enterprise data protection and ensures compliance with data retention and destruction regulations. It also sets the stage for better information management

DIFFICULTIES WITH DATA PROTECTION STRATEGIES

Companies face two important difficulties with data protection: complexity and cost. As the data protection needs of organizations change and grow, the task becomes more complex. With complexity comes the opportunity for mistakes. In regulated environments or public companies, this can be a dangerous problem. Simple errors in judgment or planning can lead to data loss, lawsuits, and fines.

Another problem with many data protection strategies is that all data is assumed to be of equal value. The problems that result from treating all data the same are added expense and wasted time. When unimportant data is dealt with in the same fashion as mission-critical data, valuable resources are assigned to valueless data. Time and effort are also expended on data with little or no value to the organization. This needlessly raises the cost of protecting data. It also increases the odds that important data will not be adequately protected.

What Is Policy-Based Data Protection?

Policy-based data protection is a way of defining data protection methods, tools, and procedures as policies and then deriving rules from those policies. The goal of policy-based data protection is to alleviate some of the difficulties associated with the complexity and cost.

A policy is a set of best practices that the organization *must* follow. These policies are not simply guidelines or suggestions. Policies are a concrete expression of the data protection strategy. If the goal is to protect only valuable e-mail, a policy can be developed that defines what is valuable, what is not valuable, and how to manage it. From policies, a set of rules can be derived that tells the organization exactly what it must do. Policies remove ambiguity from the management of data.

It is important to point out that policies define business processes. They do not mandate that specific technology be used. Technology may be used to automate compliance with policies, but the definition of policies is not dependent on software or hardware.

Policy Development Guidelines

Writing data protection policies is a very difficult task. Despite the fact that it is helpful in the long run, in the short term it is usually an arduous process. Many constituents need to be consulted, and data protection is too critical to leave any of them out. Unfortunately, the initial effort involved inhibits organizations from doing the necessary work of data protection policy development.

Policies are, by nature, hierarchical. Broad policies covering large sections of the data protection strategy are supported by smaller components. These in turn are supported by smaller components. This continues until the desired level of detail is achieved. The level of granularity necessary to create a good policy depends on the organization and on the scope of the data protection strategy.

It is best to start small, choosing either a top-down or a bottom-up approach. In the top-down approach, the first polices developed are broad and cover the overall data protection strategy. The next set of policies drills down and fills in more details. This has the advantage of having all the individual policies governed by a root policy, providing context to the overall hierarchy. The disadvantage is that a lot of work has to go into policy development before it becomes useful to the organization.

The bottom-up approach focuses on one or two small functional areas of the data protection problem and develops detailed policies for them. Other detailed policies are developed over time, which are aggregated into higher-level policies until a full policy set is developed. This type of policy development works best in organizations that already have a clear sense of their overall data protection strategy. Specific, detailed policies can be put into action sooner.

TIP Though the bottom-up approach allows for quick implementation of critical policies, it can create problems later. Individual policies tend not to agree with one another. When the top-level policies are written, they may force changes in the lower-level policies. This creates more work as policies are written and rewritten.

The top-down approach better assures internal consistency among policies and reduces the chance of having to rewrite policies.

Data protection policies have certain characteristics. These *guide* the overall process of developing policies but do not define them. Instead, policies are defined by business needs, company processes, and the data protection strategy.

Characteristics of good data protection policies are that they:

- **Must be written.** All policies must be written down and made available to everyone. If the people who need to follow the policies do not have access to them, they cannot comply with them.

- **Must define a set of processes and rules.** A policy is a failure if it does not clearly tell people what they need to do. It needs to be expressed as a process or procedure that can be easily converted in a set of rules to follow.

- **Must not be vendor- or technology-specific.** Policy is not about technology; it's about business and organizational needs. A good data protection policy should never define specific technology, products, or vendors. *The policy should be valid even if these change.*

- **Must be specific to the organization.** Data protection policies are like a toothbrush—an individual item. Each organization is different and has different needs. Templates and best practices from other organizations are good starting points and guideposts. They are *never* a sufficient substitute for doing the work of policy development.

- **May be hierarchical.** There are advantages to arranging policies in a hierarchical tree. First, it creates clear connections among related policies, making related policies easier to find. Next, it makes it easier to see where subsequent policies have overridden statements in the parent policy. Finally, it provides a structure for future policy development.

- **Must be simple to understand.** Overly complex policies ensure lack of compliance. If the policy is hard to understand, the organization will make mistakes. When the policy is complex and burdensome, it will be subverted.

Many data protection policies are based a need to comply with regulatory and legal requirements. Failure to protect data in a manner that complies with regulations and laws may result in fines and lawsuits. Nonpublic companies in nonregulated industries will not be governed as much by regulations during policy development.

Policy Languages

There is no set language for expressing data protection policies. Using simple statements in a policy that everyone can understand is perfectly fine. For some organizations, a more structured approach is desired. Some popular ways of expressing policies are using the Extensible Markup Language (XML), Unified Markup Language (UML) Use Case diagrams, and flowcharts.

Although all of these approaches have pros and cons, XML has the advantage of being both human readable and machine readable. XML also allows for the use of Schemas, which allow the author first to define the structure of the document. There are hundreds of industry and special-use Schemas for XML. At this time, there is no specific XML Schema for data protection.

A Sample Data Protection Policy

In this example, assume that Widget Corporation (a fictional maker of widgets) has the following requirement regarding corporate e-mail:

All customer and prospect e-mails must be retained.

Widget Corporation defines a customer as anyone who has bought or ordered products in the history of the company. A prospect is defined as anyone who has expressed interest in Widget's products but has not yet purchased anything.

The data protection methods that Widget Corporation are using include continuous replication of e-mails and daily and monthly backups of the e-mail database.

The e-mail retention policies can be described in plain language as:

Name: Customer E-Mail Retention
Policy Type: E-Mail
Data Type: E-Mail
Parent: E-Mail Policy
Description: Policy governing the retention of customer e-mail
Purpose: To support continuing business operations by ensuring that previous e-mail communications with customers are available to Sales, Marketing, and Customer Service.
Creation Date: MAY 4, 2004
Revision Date: FEB 28, 2005
Process:
All e-mails to and from customers and potential customers (also known as prospects) will be copied to a duplicate copy of the e-mail database as they are received. End-users are not allowed to delete customer e-mails in any way, including from their personal mailboxes.
The primary and duplicate e-mail database will be backed up to tape each night; tapes will be rotated according to current IT policy (IT Tape Rotation Policy).
Customer e-mail will never be archived.
Expected Results: All customer e-mail will be available online all the time.
Constraints: There is no automated method of keeping users from deleting e-mails.
Assets: primary_email, secondary_email
Asset Type: Disk array
Asset: backup1
Asset Type: Backup server with attached autoloader

The sample clearly states what the policy is, what is expected from IT and end-users, and how it is to be accomplished. It also recognizes constraints that may affect compliance. By including parent policies, it establishes a hierarchy as well. A typical hierarchy in this case might be as follows:

Data Protection Policy:
E-Mail Policy:
    Customer Retention Policy

      Financial E-Mail Retention Policy
    Database Protection Policy:
      Financial Database Protection Policy
      Manufacturing Database Policy

Each subsequent level of policy adds detail and overrides more general processes in the parent.

In XML, this policy can be written as such:

```xml
<policy policy_type="E-mail" data_type="E-Mail" parent="E-Mail
Policy">
   <name>Customer E-Mail Retention</name>
   <description>
   Policy governing the retention of customer e-mail
   </description>
   <purpose>
   To support continuing business operations by ensuring that
   previous e-mail communications with customers are available
   to Sales, Marketing, and Customer Service.
   </purpose>
   <date>
      <create>MAY 4, 2004</create>
      <revision>FEB 28, 2005</revision>
   </date>
   <process>
   All e-mails to and from customers and potential customers
   (also known as prospects) will be copied to a duplicate copy
   of the e-mail database as they are received. End-users are
   not allowed to delete customer e-mails in any way, including
   from their personal mailboxes.

   The primary and duplicate e-mail database will be backed up
   to tape each night; tapes will be rotated to according to
   current IT policy (IT Tape Rotation Policy).

Customer e-mail will never be archived.
   </process>
   <expected_result>
   All customer e-mail will be available online all the time.
   </expected_result>
   <constraints>
   There is no automated method of keeping users from deleting
   e-mails.
   </constraints>
   <asset asset_types="Disk Array">
```

```
primary_email, secondary_email
</asset>
<asset asset_types="Backup Server">backup1</asset>    </
policy>
```

The XML document can still be read by a nontechnical individual. Unlike the first document, it can also be read by software that might manage or use the policies later. The XML may be extended to include commands for software or devices that tell them to perform specific functions related to implementing the policy. For example, a <command> tag may be added that is read only by software that controls the tape library.

```
<command>
backup -source primary_email -dest backup1 -schedule daily -time
20:00:00
</command>
```

It would be clear, even to a nontechnical person, that this was intended to be a command for a software program that would define a backup process. The plain-language and XML versions could be used together to provide maximum clarity and enhance automation of compliance.

The Reasons Policy-Based Strategies Fail

Developing sound policies is tough. The work can be tedious and tends to uncover all the places where the organization is deficient. There are some common potholes that many organizations step into when developing data protection policies. Some examples are

- **Failure to use logical names for devices.** One of the great strengths of the Internet is that it does not rely on raw device addresses, such as IP addresses. Instead, it uses logical names. Changes in the infrastructure are transparent to users. Designing around physical device names or addresses makes changes difficult. Changes in devices should never force changes in policies.

- **Reliance on human compliance.** Even simple scripts that automate processes help with compliance. Asking end-users to remember to perform tasks, especially when the tasks require multiple steps, assures noncompliance.

- **Expecting users to change their behavior.** The classic problem with document management systems is that they depend on check-in and check-out practices. This is not what people do normally.

WARNING   End-users should never have to change how they work to comply with the data protection policies. Not only is it easy to make a mistake, but forcing changes in human behavior practically invites subversion. Design policies according to accepted and existing *end-user* practices, and people will comply.

- **Focusing on the technology, not the process.** It is natural for IT people to view data protection as a technology problem. Technology then becomes the natural starting point. That is the tail wagging the dog. Policies derive from the process and practices of the organization. The best place to focus attention is on the goals and policies of the organization. Technology exists only to assist compliance with those policies.

- **Having IT do all the work.** Remember to include the other stakeholders in the decision-making process. Even if IT has charge of the data protection policy, many other people in the organization will be affected by it. They need to be part of building and implementing data protection policies.

- **Refusing to fix process problems.** The development of data protection policies undoubtedly will uncover problems with existing processes. Some policies will simply be broken or obsolete; others will conflict with the data protection needs. Refusal to fix process problems first results in data protection policies that users cannot or will not comply with.

The overarching reasons that policies fail, either in development or implementation, are lack of attention to human behavior and too much attention paid to technology. IT professionals especially must focus their attention on the processes and how they affect *people* before considering technology.

DATA LIFECYCLE MANAGEMENT (DLM)

The twin forces of regulation and cost control have changed the way IT managers look at data. The growing awareness that money is being spent on unimportant data has driven changes in how data is managed. At the same time, regulators and lawmakers throughout the world have burdened organizations with data retention requirements. Failure to comply with these requirements can bring about fines, lawsuits, and even prison terms.

There has always been a sense that old data should be archived or removed. Most organizations had procedures, some formal and some ad hoc, for removing old data from online storage. These common practices have been extrapolated into a formal process called *Data Lifecycle Management (DLM)*. Data Lifecycle Management describes how data is treated at different points in time. The policies for data management change as data ages and changes (Figure 7–1). These policies can then be translated into rules or scripts for applications that automate the policy.

As is the case with all policies, each organization must define the lifecycle for its data. There is a general model, however, that most data will follow.

The lifecycle of data is defined by how often the data is accessed. As soon as data is created, it is most useful and used more often. Data created by transaction processing applications and word processors alike has the most value shortly after its creation. At this stage, the data must be kept *online and available all the time.*

As the data gets older, the need to access it immediately diminishes. Data is still kept online, but guaranteed access time is no longer important. Users can wait some time to get it, if necessary. When the data is older still, the need to keep it online at all decreases until it can be removed from online storage altogether. Finally, when the data is no longer useful or when having it represents a liability to the organization, it is destroyed.

Data Lifecycle Management and Data Protection

Data Lifecycle Management is intertwined with the data protection policies of an organization. Data protection policies must take into account the lifecycle of the data to use resources cost effectively. Otherwise, data that is unimportant will be given high levels of protection, resulting in a higher cost than is necessary. Conversely, data that is extremely important may not have adequate levels of protection due to resource constraints.

Data Lifecycle Management policies also have to take into account data protection policies and systems. If the two are not synchronized, it is likely that the policies will be in conflict. It is possible to comply with a Data Lifecycle Management policy that insists that aged data be moved to less expensive storage while violating data protection policies that say all data must be protected to a high standard. Data protection systems by nature copy data to various locations on a

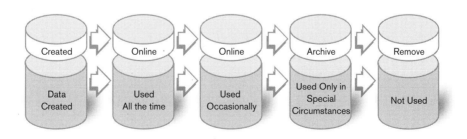

FIGURE 7–1 GENERAL DATA LIFECYCLE MODEL

network or off-site. This may conflict with Data Lifecycle Management policies commanding that data be completely destroyed.

By including Data Lifecycle Management as part of data protection policies, conflicts can be averted, and a more cost-effective data protection system can be implemented.

DLM Policies

Data Lifecycle Management policies are similar to data protection policies. The major difference is that the lifecycle of the data is taken into account when moving, destroying, or copying data.

Data Lifecycle Management alters data protection policies in the following ways:

- **Data retention.** Policies requiring that certain data be preserved will have limits placed on the length of time that data can be kept around.
- **Data destruction.** Data protection policies will be altered to include removing data, which is usually the antithesis of data protection.
- **Different levels of protection.** It will be deemed adequate for some data to have different levels of protection from others, even when it is the same type of data. The age of the data is the deciding factor in the level of protection it gets. Some data will receive no protection.

In the Widget Corporation example, the e-mail retention policy insisted that all customer e-mails be protected and available all the time. In a short time, this would lead to a huge e-mail database. The backup database would grow equally large in the same amount of time. Most of the e-mails, however, would be old and close to useless. Widget Corporation would soon be spending money to buy more storage for e-mails that no one needs anymore.

The company has determined that customer e-mails are hardly ever accessed after two years and have no value after three years. The goals of the data protection policy can be amended to read as follows:

> All customer and prospect e-mails must be retained for two years. After two years, the e-mails are to be archived, and after three years, they are to be destroyed.

The e-mail retention policies can be described in plain language as:

Name: Customer E-Mail Retention and Destruction
Policy Type: E-Mail
Data Type: E-Mail
Parent: E-Mail Policy
Description: Policy governing the retention and destruction of customer e-mail

Purpose: To support continuing business operations by ensuring that previous e-mail communications with customers are available to Sales, Marketing, and Customer Service.

Creation Date: MAY 4, 2004

Revision Date: APR 1, 2005

Process:

All e-mails to and from customers and potential customers (also known as prospects) will be copied to a duplicate copy of the e-mail database as they are received. End-users are not allowed to delete customer e-mails in any way, including from their personal mailboxes.

The primary and duplicate e-mail database will be backed up to tape each night; tapes will be rotated to according to current IT policy (IT Tape Rotation Policy).

Each month, a survey of the e-mail databases and tapes will be done. All customer e-mails two years old or older will be copied to DVD-ROM. They will then be deleted from the primary e-mail database, secondary e-mail database, and backup tapes. All end-users are expected to delete all copies of customer e-mails more than two years old each month.

Each month, DVD-ROMs more than a year old will be sent to a shredding facility and destroyed.

Expected Results: All customer e-mails than older than two years will be available on DVD-ROM. E-mail older than three years will be destroyed. All customer e-mail less than two years old will always be available online all the time.

Constraints: There is no automated end-user e-mail deletion tool. End-users are expected to find and delete e-mails manually each month.

Assets: primary_email, secondary_email

Asset Type: Disk array

Asset: backup1

Asset Type: Backup server with attached autoloader

Asset: dvd_rom_1

Asset: Type: DVD-ROM jukebox

By including Data Lifecycle Management concepts in the e-mail data protection policy, Widget Corporation does not need to increase the size of the e-mail storage as rapidly, saving money. The most valuable e-mails are given the highest degree of protection, less valuable ones are not.

DLM AUTOMATION The Achilles heel of policy-driven strategies is that they often require changes in human processes. System administrators have to perform certain tasks for the policy to be completed. Users have to follow certain procedures, which makes them behave differently in their daily work. Forcing people to change how they perform normal duties leads to errors in judgment, mistakes, and outright subversion of the process. When a process is inconvenient, it is never followed well or at all.

Automation takes the work out of complying with policies. Users and administrators use software to perform the tasks that comprise the policy. When properly configured, the software does not make mistakes or balk at tiresome tasks.

Data Lifecycle Management automation has two components: the *policy engine* and the *data migration software.* The policy engine stores and executes the tasks, references, and constraints that express the DLM policy in terms that computer systems can understand. A policy is translated into a series of commands that other components of a system can then perform. The policy engine may translate a policy that states:

Move all files from Finance to secondary storage after they are one year old.

to a command such as the following:

```
moveOldFiles //Finance //FinanceBackup -365 -day
```

How the policy engine's rules are actually executed, as system tasks, depends on the data migration software. Data migration software may be little more than a group of scripts that execute operating system commands. It may also be very sophisticated software capable of moving data around a SAN, LAN, or WAN.

No matter how the data migration software is constructed, its purpose is to migrate from one data store to another. To support DLM fully, data migration software needs to be able to copy, move, and delete data, based on age and physical location. Data migration software also needs to be able to support a variety of media, especially disk, tape, and optical storage such as CD-RW.

MULTI-TIER STORAGE ARCHITECTURES   To control the costs of policy-based data protection, IT organizations have turned to *multi-tier storage architectures.* Systems based on this architecture organize storage in several tiers or stages, with the most expensive, reliable, and available storage used for the most important data. Progressively less expensive storage is deployed for less important data, with archive systems occupying the lowest tier.

This arrangement, coupled with Data Lifecycle Management software, allows data to be moved from more expensive to less expensive resources as it moves through its lifecycle. The top tier typically is composed of expensive, high-available Fibre Channel disk arrays supported by a full range of data protection systems. The next tier is often disk arrays with SATA drives. These are less expensive yet reliable. SATA systems provide reasonable performance as well. The final tier is filled by archive systems—tape, optical disk (CD and DVD), or both (Figure 7–2).

As data ages, it is moved to the less expensive storage system. This drives down the cost of storing the data. As the data migrates to less expensive systems, the level of protection is reduced as well. At the top tier, extensive and expensive

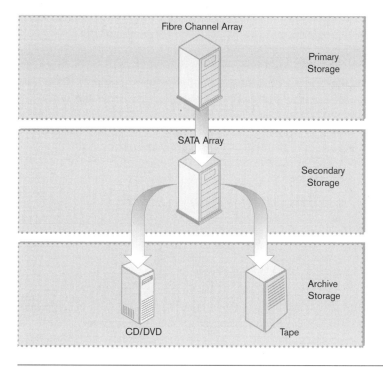

FIGURE 7–2 MULTI-TIER STORAGE ARCHITECTURE

data protection strategies such as remote copy and replication may be used, while at the lowest tier, off-site storage of CDs may be all that is done.

Do not confuse DLM and multi-tier storage. Hardware vendors tend to blur the lines between Data Lifecycle Management and multi-tier storage systems. DLM is a type of policy-based data management. multi-tier storage is hardware architecture. There are many reasons to have multi-tier storage systems that have nothing to do with DLM, and DLM is not dependent on multi-tier storage. They do support each other well, though they are not the same.

Hierarchical Storage Management

Hierarchical Storage Management (HSM) is often used synonymously with both DLM and multi-tier storage. HSM is a data protection strategy for archiving data. As a storage system's *capacity* begins to reach a threshold, the HSM system will move older data out to archive. As the archive system reaches capacity, very old data is moved to less expensive archive data and eventually is deleted.

(continues)

This differs from multi-tier storage systems in that it is archive centric. Its purpose is to *maintain capacity levels* of online storage systems. multi-tier storage systems address online data as well as archives. Data Lifecycle Management is also not centered purely on managing utilization levels. Instead, DLM is used for regulatory reasons and to manage the cost of data protection.

HSM combines aspects of both DLM and multi-tier storage architectures, but is a strategy focused on archive and capacity control.

KEY POINTS

- Policy-based data protection allows for better use of data protection resources. It also helps organizations comply with regulations.

- A policy is a set of best practices that the organization *must* follow. Policies are a concrete expression of the data protection strategy.

- Data Lifecycle Management (DLM) is a policy-based data management methodology. It recognizes that data has a life span based on age. DLM allows for more efficient use of data protection resources as older, less important data is not afforded the most expensive protection.

- An important method of implementing DLM is through multi-tier storage architectures. When multiple levels are used for increasingly less expensive storage, more resources are available for more important data.

8

INFORMATION LIFECYCLE MANAGEMENT

In This Chapter:

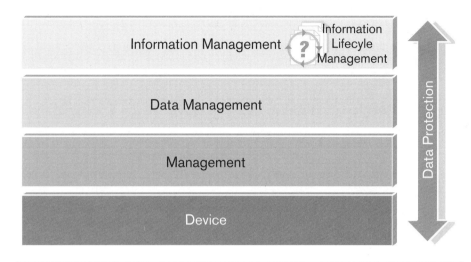

FIGURE 8-0

INFORMATION ASSURANCE AND DATA PROTECTION

Data protection is part of a larger strategy—information assurance. *Information assurance* is the process by which an organization insures, protects, and verifies the integrity of vital information. Without information assurance, it is impossible to know that critical information is what it is assumed to be or where it is supposed to be. Organizations have begun to understand that the information they store as data needs to be managed for information assurance to be realized.

Traditional data protection strategies, such as backup and restore and replication, deal with data, not information. To provide better information assurance, a new type of process is necessary: Information Lifecycle Management (ILM). Without ILM, information is questionable and cannot be used without considerable risk.

WHAT IS INFORMATION LIFECYCLE MANAGEMENT?

Information Lifecycle Management (ILM) is, first and foremost, a strategic process for dealing with information assets. Typically, ILM is expressed as a strategy, which is then used to generate policies. Finally, a set of rules is created and used by the organization or software to comply with the policies. ILM processes take into account what the information is, where it is located, what relationships it has to other information, and the lifecycle of the information.

Initially, ILM appears to be a lot like Data Lifecycle Management (DLM). DLM is also a policy-based process. It has rules and takes into account a lifecycle. The difference is that ILM operates on *information,* not *data.* This is a fundamental distinction that makes ILM a very different process.

Data is raw. It lacks structure that is externally visible. Information, on the other hand, is capable of external validation, even if it requires a human being to do it. Whereas data is completely dependent on applications for meaning, information is independent of applications.

Information is a collection of data within a certain context. When someone receives an e-mail, prints it out and reads it, or imports it into another program, it is still an e-mail. The blocks of data that comprise the e-mail are data. The data becomes an e-mail when the reader (human or computer) recognizes that there are FROM and TO lines and a message body.

Information Has Value

How much is a block of data worth? That's hard to say unless you know what the data is meant to represent. The value of information is easier to understand because *what it is* is known. An order from a customer has a value that can be determined from real costs and loss of revenue. A CFO's presentation to the financial community has a value that can be determined by changes in the stock price of the company. Assigning value to information is based on what is valuable to the organization.

Misconceptions Around ILM

As is the case with DLM, ILM is a strategic process. It is not about technology or products, though these can be used as tools for automating ILM rules. Unfortunately, there is some confusion about how products and existing processes fit into an ILM strategy.

Other technology or processes that are often confused with ILM are

- **Data storage or storage management.** Although storage is often part of the ILM picture, it is not a complete ILM solution. Storage may be considered to be part of the ILM policies, but it is secondary to the process.

- **Content Addressed Storage (CAS).** CAS is a very useful tool for ensuring ILM policy compliance. However, it is not the ILM process or policy in and of itself.

- **Document management and records management.** Document management and records management are considered by some people to be subsets of ILM and can be useful parts of the ILM strategy. Not all information is in document or form, however.

Why Bother with ILM?

There are some clear reasons why organizations bother with ILM. Many are first attracted to ILM because of regulatory compliance. There are, however, many other benefits. Benefits of ILM include:

- **Enables information assurance.** ILM helps organizations verify that data is what and where they think it is.

- **More efficient use of resources.** ILM allows a finer level of resource allocation than DLM does. Less important information can be given less expensive system resources.

- **Data protection in line with information's value.** As with DLM, data protection can be applied to the data that comprises the information. ILM allows decisions about data protection to be made based on the value of the information over its lifetime.

- **Better security.** By using ILM, organizations can better track where information is located. This eliminates duplicate, lost, or misplaced information. Good ILM policies should also help organizations determine when unintentional modification to information occurs. It allows the organization to know when people are looking at, copying, or changing data, with or without authorization.

- **Allows organizations to handle large amounts of ever-changing information.** ILM policies help organizations avoid drowning in useless information. They do this by helping the organization focus on the most important information first.

- **Enhances privacy.** By tracking the copying, destruction, and accessibility of information in an organization, ILM diminishes the likelihood of a privacy breach.

UNSTRUCTURED AND STRUCTURED INFORMATION

Operating systems and file systems know only about blocks and files. They cannot tell what is in those files. They may surmise that a file is a word processor document by its extension or MIME type but cannot be certain. Extensions and MIME types can be changed. Even within applications, information can be recognized only in a gross fashion, as a document or spreadsheet. Applications do not know whether a file is an important document, a financial report, or letter to a friend. Files and similar constructs are considered *unstructured*. Operating systems, file systems, and applications have no external means of understanding the meaning of the data.

The most difficult type of unstructured data to deal with is images. Photographs, x-rays, scanned documents, and other images do not have any internal clues to help determine what the information is. All validation of the object is external and provided by an outside source. This makes management of images through traditional means, such as keyword searching, almost meaningless.

Databases, XML files, and other structured systems are different. They arrange data into information by using a schema. A *schema* is a description of the data that provides context. By applying the schema, order is imposed on the data, and it becomes information. Anyone looking at the schema (at a well-designed schema, at least) and applying it to the data will understand what the data represents.

The advantage of a structured system, as far as ILM is concerned, is that context is already provided. Description of the information is not needed, because the schema provides the necessary context. ILM policies rarely have the luxury of dealing only with structured data.

THE IMPORTANCE OF CONTEXT

Data, by itself, is not very useful. Look at a single number on a page and it tells you very little. Add other numbers and symbols to form an equation, and now there is some meaning, if you know how to read the formula. Combine the formula with text that explains the formula and now there is useful information. The text and the symbols provide meaning to the numbers.

Information differs from data in that it has context. *Context* is other data that imparts meaning and structure to the data. For data to be useful, for it to be information, there needs to be context around it. Context acts as a catalyst, converting raw data to useful information (Figure 8–1).

FIGURE 8–1 CONTEXT TRANSFORMS DATA INTO INFORMATION.

Different Types of Context

There are several forms of context that can be applied to data. *Explicit context* is context that is stated directly. It exists when data has a predetermined and *externally* readable structure. Databases have explicit context. Their schemas are an inherent part of the overall data set, and any application that can read the database tables can also understand the meaning of the data.

Implicit context is the context that is implied by attributes of the data. A file with a .doc extension implies a document. If that file is in a directory or folder titled Marketing Plans, it is implied that the file is part of the organization's marketing planning. Clues in the document also hint at the context of the data. Specific formatting, such as letter format, titles, and formulas, provide evidence as to the meaning of the content.

Finally, there is *rules-based context*. Rules are a way of making implicit context explicit. Rules-based context imposes context on data based on a set of external rules. The following rule illustrates how it is possible to express rules-based context:

> If the file has an extension of .doc, is in the Financials folder, and is dated after the first of the year, it is a year-to-date financial report.

No matter what is actually in the files, no matter what the internal structure of the file, it is now considered to be financial information in report form. Information with explicit context carries the context with it, and implicit context derives only from context based on the data. Information with rules-based context imposes the structure externally without regard to the content of the data.

There are pros and cons to each type of context. Explicit context is easier for software to deal with. Because the context is embedded in the data structures, a computer can read it and know how to process the information. It does not always work well for all types of information. An order can easily be depicted in a database or as a structured object because it has predetermined components, but a letter cannot because it is freeform in nature. Parts of a letter can be given explicit context, such as the address block and signature line, but the body—the most important part of the letter—cannot. There is enough context to know that it is a letter but not enough to know what the letter is about.

Implicit context is difficult to impossible for software to understand. Although research in natural language processing continues, humans are by far the best tool for determining context from content. We can look at unformatted text and tell whether we are looking at a marketing plan or a letter to a friend. Computers cannot do that well.

Rules-based context strikes a middle posture between explicit and implicit context. Almost any type of information can be described by a series of rules.

There will be mistakes, however. If the rules are broad, information will be categorized incorrectly.

Context is what ILM leverages to make better decisions than Data Lifecycle Management. By providing a deeper understanding of what the data represents, context allows policies to be developed that better describe what to do with the data. Context converts the raw data to information, which enables ILM.

Metadata

The context of data is derived from other data. Data that describes other data is called *metadata*. Metadata is used frequently in computing. File systems, for example, use metadata to describe objects and the attributes of those objects. Humans use metadata all the time. We call them clues or hints and process them without even being aware of it.

ILM uses metadata to describe and attribute meaning to data. Rules for interpreting the metadata transform data into information that can then be managed. Data plus metadata plus rules equals information.

Characteristics of Information

Information has several characteristics that are important to ILM. The most important characteristics are as follows:

- **Context.** Context is additional data that provides meaning to the data.

- **Relationships.** Information often includes relationships with other information. Sometimes it's only a casual reference. At other times it's a strong, formal link, such as a hyperlink.

- **Application independence.** Data relies on applications for interpretation; information stands by itself. Different applications using the same data can interpret it in different ways. Information is interpreted the same way, no matter what application is using it. A printed book and an e-book are still the same information.

- **Determinable value.** The value of information can be determined, because it has meaning.

The lifecycle of information is based on context, is affected by the lifecycles of other information, is independent of the applications that use the information, and changes along with the value of the data. Whereas DLM is a function of age, ILM is determined by context and value, of which age is a component.

DETERMINING AND MANAGING INFORMATION CONTEXT

Although any number of attributes can provide context to data, the most important from an ILM perspective are

- Classification
- Content
- Relationships
- State
- Location(s)

Other attributes may also be important, depending on the organization and its information management needs. In many cases, they will be components of the attributes stated here.

The Anatomy of an E-Mail

A good example to consider is an e-mail object. An e-mail has a number of constituent components that make it an e-mail. First, it can be classified as an e-mail. That may be because a person can recognize it as one or because it has a MIME type of `message/rfc822`. It has content that can be examined for e-mail formatting and relationships related to an e-mail, such as an attachment. The object may also reside in a directory that is only for e-mails and may have a file format specific to e-mail systems. Finally, there might be state information, such as the time the object was created, headers, or similar descriptors (Figure 8–2). The object is recognized as an e-mail because it has the context of an e-mail.

Classification

Classification is a quick form of identifying what information is. This is something that humans do quite well but machines do not. For ILM, classification is the most important attribute and will drive most actions within an ILM policy.

Classes may be broad, such as Financial, Marketing, and Personnel. They may also be very specific, such as First Quarter Financial Reports. If classes are too broad, actions will be limited to only those that can take place among many different types of objects. If classes are too specific, the organization will drown in policy documents.

Classifying structured data is easy. The classes are determined by the schema. Unstructured data, on the other hand, can be very difficult to classify. Humans can do this by looking at the data—"Yep, that's our third-quarter financial report"—but computers are terrible at it.

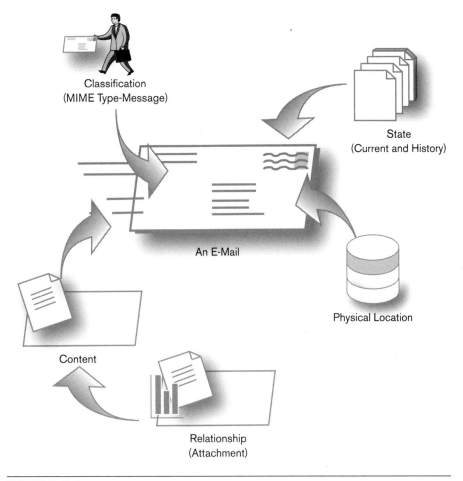

Classification
(MIME Type-Message)

State
(Current and History)

An E-Mail

Physical Location

Content

Relationship
(Attachment)

FIGURE 8–2 ANATOMY OF AN E-MAIL

To classify unstructured data, rules-based context is overlaid on the data and stored as metadata. Various attributes of the *data* are examined to provide a class for the *information*. The existence of an object in a particular directory or folder, along with keywords found in the content of the object, may be used by a rules-based system to determine its class.

Another way to classify unstructured data is through human intervention. When information is created, the person creating the information, or a designated person, can choose a class for it. Even in this case, a set of rules on how to determine a piece of information's class will be needed. Otherwise, classification will be inconsistent and useless.

State

State describes content and metadata—context—at a specific point in time. Changes in some component of the context indicate a change in state. ILM policies may demand that these changes in state trigger actions. The specific metadata that defines state in an ILM system is described by policies. Within ILM policies, state is the catalyst for actions. If a state change occurs, an action, proscribed by policies, must also occur.

Age

Age is a concept central to all lifecycles. To say that something has a lifecycle is to indicate that it is changing over time, or aging.

For ILM, age does not really exist by itself. Time is a component of state, and aging is a function of the differences between two different states. Two different timeframes, such as two different dates, represent two different states. When ILM policies are written, actions should be triggered by changes in state, not just changes in time. Other elements of a piece of information's context may also have changed in that same interval and will affect decisions.

Tracking State and History

Time is a necessary element of state, even if the timeframe is only now. It is possible to only define a current state, although it is more useful to define state in other timeframes. By tracking state over time, it is possible to accumulate a history of the information. The timeframe "now" defines a current snapshot while other timeframes define history.

This is a powerful tool for managing information. By tracking state, it is possible to compare the *current state* against an *expected state*. Changes in state will help determine whether the information:

- Has been copied, deleted, or moved
- Has had a constituent component modified or whether a new version has been created
- Has had related information changed

- Has been transformed into another type of information
- Has aged past a defined point

Information Transformations

Information is frequently transformed from one type into another. The act of copying the contents of an e-mail into a word processor document does not change the content. Instead, it transforms the information from one class of information (e-mail) into another class (document). This represents a change in state. Depending on how ILM policies are designed, the document may now be considered a new document with a relationship to the e-mail or a new version of what the e-mail represents.

In either case, this transformation will be detected if changes in state are tracked. The state of the e-mail will have changed, because either a new relationship will be added to the current state that was not in the previous state or a new branch of the e-mail's state will be created.

Tracking this transformation is important for complying with ILM policies, especially those regarding information retention and destruction. If a policy exists that requires all information of a particular class to be destroyed at some point in time, transformed documents may need to be destroyed as well. The same is true for retaining information.

Content

The important part of any information is its content. Content is the "stuff" of information—the words in the document, the numbers in the spreadsheet, and the picture in the image. In a computer system, content is stored as data.

Much of the context of information can be derived from the content. By examining a document, clues can be found that help discern whether it is a letter to a friend or a technical manual. Humans are very efficient at performing this task, whereas computers are not. Knowledge management systems have developed very sophisticated inference engines to do what we do naturally. Inference engines examine the content of a document to determine its meaning, usually for purposes of classification. Through the use of statistical analysis and rules-based systems, context can be rendered from the document. These systems are rudimentary compared with what human inferences can do. They often miscategorize information and need human editors to make corrections.

Search engines are similar to inference engines in that they scan content for clues as to its meaning. Unlike inference engines, search engines are more of a tool to help humans make content decisions. Often based on keywords, a search engine can provide a list of possible targets. The human then decides whether it meets the criteria for classification.

For ILM purposes, humans can do the job of deriving context from content. A person can make the decision as to what the content means. Unfortunately, this is inefficient. It is not too difficult to ask end-users to make a decision as to what the content means for newly created information. It is a daunting job to have people go through existing information and determine context from content.

> **Hashing Data**
>
> In many cases, examination of the actual content is important only when classifying data. After that, it is necessary to note only when content changes. The size of the data may not change even though the content changes. File system dates are unreliable, because they can be changed even when no content has actually been altered. Instead, a hash of the data may be used and compared with hash values taken at later dates. A *hash* is a set of characters generated by running the content through certain algorithms. It is commonly used to generate security keys and digital signatures. The most common algorithms for producing file hashes are MD-5 and SHA-1. For a demonstration of hashing, look at security programs such as GnuPG (www.gnupg.org) and Pretty Good Privacy (www.pgp.com). They generate hashes based on text in a document. These hashes are then used to ensure that the document has not changed in transmission.

LOCATION AND THE INFORMATION PERIMETER

Location tells where the data that comprises information is. This helps to determine whether information is where it is expected to be or whether there is more than one copy of the data. Many ILM decisions will be based on location of the underlying data. Location helps determine the integrity of information. It is essential for managing multiple copies of the same information across an enterprise.

Information Path

On one hand, location is a concrete element of information. Classification and state can be subjective. Location is, instead, physical and tangible. The problem is that file systems and structured data stores have different ways of expressing location. The manner in which a UNIX operating system describes where data is differs from the way in which the Windows family of operating systems does. Data stored on a network introduces additional ways to depict where data is. This can make location statements in ILM policies very difficult.

Instead, it is more useful to use a virtual location that can be mapped to a real location. Called the *information path,* it is a way of describing where information is without subscribing to specific operating system nomenclature. The information path should include at least the following:

- Network path
- Hostname
- File system or application name
- Local object name
- Component names (if needed)
- Version

The network path should be a virtual path not a physical address. When combined with the hostname, a general data storage location can then be given as a virtual address. The file system name or application name is needed to accommodate structured and unstructured information. An application in this case is likely to be a structured data storage application, such as the name of a database. The local object name provides the unique identifier for the *information,* and the component names provide an additional level of identification if the ILM policy calls for it.

The addition of a version identifier supports the ability to have information paths point to different versions of the same data. The information path could then be the same for multiple versions of the same information except for the version. Differences in these paths would point to different data, but the information would be the same.

Information paths could look something like this:

```
Techalignment.com: Spiderman: Oracle: Order_db: Order:Row 456: 1.02
Hightech_Net1: File_Server1: Window XP 2003:
   Big_company_contract.doc: 2.0
Local: myDesktop: eBooks: Adobe Acrobat: Data Protection Book: first
   edition
```

The same information could have multiple information paths. If that sounds like being in more than one place at the same time, that's because it is. Multiple copies of the information are still the *same* information. This is critical to maintaining the integrity of information. For ILM policies to be carried out correctly, all copies of information must have the same rules applied to them at the same time. A copy is the same information, only in an additional location.

Representations of Information Paths

Information paths are very similar to namespaces. They can be represented in several ways. A good way to denote an information path is by use of a Universal Resource Identifiers (URI). URIs are a standard way of identifying virtual or physical resources. They are found embedded in XML documents to designate namespaces and in programs to provide a virtual address. A Uniform Resource Locator (URL), also known as the ubiquitous web address, is a type of URI. The syntax for URIs can be found in RFC3986 from the Internet Engineering Task Force (www.ietf.org).

Information paths as described by a URI might look like this:

```
Oracle://technologyalignment.com/spiderman/
   order_db/order/row456?Version1.02
File:///Hightech_Net1/File_Server1/WindowXP2003/
   Big_company_contract.doc?Version2.0
```

Another way to represent information paths is with XML. Although more complicated than a URI, XML has the advantage of being easier to read by a human. Both URI and XML information paths could be used by software automation tools more easily than homegrown naming conventions.

Information Perimeter

When information is in certain locations—on a laptop or home computer, for example—the information cannot be verified as to whether changes in state have occurred. It is beyond the control of systems and monitoring. Subsequently, state changes to the information cannot be tracked. The boundary between where an ILM policy can expect to have control and where it cannot is called the *information perimeter* (Figure 8–3). Information stored beyond the information perimeter cannot be verified as to state, context, or even existence.

The information perimeter defines

- Where data is and whether that's where it is expected to be
- Where it has gone to
- Where copies might be

Information Lifecycle Management policies must address what happens when information crosses the information perimeter. Specifically, there need to be procedures for deciding whether information that is outside the information perimeter is considered to be valid.

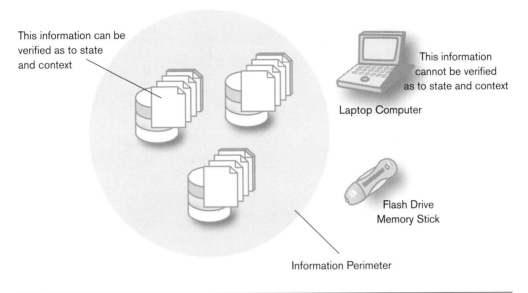

This information can be
verified as to state
and context

This information
cannot be verified
as to state and context

Laptop Computer

Flash Drive
Memory Stick

Information Perimeter

FIGURE 8-3 THE INFORMATION PERIMETER

THE INFORMATION LIFECYCLE

Information has a lifecycle. It is created, changes, and finally is destroyed. ILM manages this lifecycle to optimize the use of resources, meet regulatory requirements, and ensure the integrity of the information. When a lifecycle has been developed for a class of information, it can be expressed as a series of policies.

A General Model

There is no set information lifecycle. Some *products* will impose a particular lifecycle on an organization, but ILM does not dictate this. An information lifecycle is dependent on the needs of an organization and the nature of the information.

All information lifecycles can be derived from a general model (Figure 8–4). The model states that information is created, its state changes in some fashion,

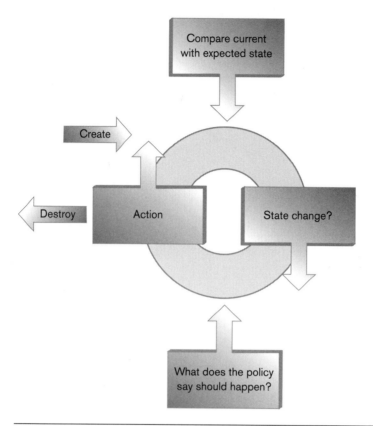

FIGURE 8-4 The general case of the information lifecycle

an action may occur due to that state change, and eventually it is destroyed. Creation is the initial action and destruction the final one

ILM policy must define which state changes trigger actions and what those actions will be. Some changes that may trigger an action are

- **Aging.** The difference between the current state's timeframe and a previous one has exceeded a threshold.
- **Copied.** There is a new, additional information path associated with the information.
- **Moved.** An information path has changed.
- **Transformed.** The information has been changed from one class to another.
- **Relationship.** A relationship with another piece of information has been changed, added, or removed.
- **Content.** Any alteration in the content of the information should trigger an event, even a null event. Comparing the current hash with the previous one shows that content has changed.

Changes in metadata or content represent a change in state. This in turn may trigger actions under ILM policies. This continues with changes in state and new actions until the last action possible is taken: destruction.

A Standard Lifecycle

The difficulty with using a general model for a lifecycle is that it generates a lot of work for the people designing it. Analysis has to be performed to determine the lifecycles for different classes of information. Policies then need to be developed to express these in concrete terms. Developing policies can be tough enough, but having to determine individual lifecycles for many classes of information adds time and complexity to policy development.

Set lifecycles have been proposed, mostly by vendors. These were fairly simple affairs, with set stages and actions for all information. The Storage Networking Industry Association's Information Lifecycle Management Initiative group (www.snia.org/tech_activities/dmf/ilm/ilm) is also working on a definition of ILM and the information lifecycle. This will provide a good starting point but should not be adhered to religiously. Information lifecycles are unique to organizations and classes of information.

Life and Death of Information

What if Widget Corporation, a maker of high-quality widgets, is no longer happy with the results of its Data Lifecycle Management e-mail policy? Too often, e-mails that should be retained are not, and others that were supposed to be destroyed have not been. Now the company has angry customers and upset lawyers. The costs of storage and e-mail management continue to rise, though at a slower rate.

The problem is not that Widget Corporation can't manage e-mails in general. What it cannot control, with the DLM policies in place, is information that doesn't fit the rules the company has set up. Widget Corporation has discovered, for example, that many employees in Sales copy e-mails into documents not covered by the e-mail policy. Conversely, many e-mails are destroyed, but not the original documents attached to the e-mails. The company also realizes that many customer e-mails really aren't important and should not be protected. Attention must be turned to *what the e-mails mean* to lower costs and better protect the company.

Widget Corporation turned to ILM to solve some of these problems. The object "e-mail" is too coarse for Widget's purposes. Instead, e-mails and other documents must be classified, a lifecycle determined, and policies written.

IT and Customer Service have decided that only three categories will be needed initially: Orders, Proposals, and Other. Classification is based on content, especially specific clues inside the e-mail text. Orders can be identified by the order number in the e-mail, for example. Other metadata items that IT and Customer Service feel are important to the ILM process are

- **Location.** Information paths will help identify copies.
- **Type.** Object types will be tracked to look for transformations from e-mail to documents.
- **Relationships.** This is especially important for tracking the source of attachments.
- **State.** Being able to compare changes in content and metadata at different points in time will allow for more directed actions. The company can also guard against changes in Order e-mails after they have arrived.

With this in hand, Widget will be able to apply different levels of protection to different types of e-mails. Rules can be applied to attachments and their source documents (and vice versa). A history of changes in state will show when content and other metadata has changed. Finally, when it is time to make decisions about destroying e-mail, all copies and references to the e-mail can be considered in the decision-making process.

AN ILM SCHEMA

ILM is more involved then DLM. With different metadata, actions, and different types of classes, it helps develop a set schema to use in policy making. Schemas and data dictionaries are popular in vertical applications for managing the semantics and operations of information. There are, for example, a multitude of XML schemas designed for protocol communications and data stores, many designed for specific industries.

As is true of all elements in ILM, there is no set schema for all circumstances. A general schema might start with the following:

```
Information
    Class
        Attributes
            File Type
            Content Clues
    State
        Timestamp (Last Accessed Date)
        Content (Hash)
        Information Paths
            URI
        Relationships
```

```
                Information Paths
                      URI
            Value
        Timestamp (Date Created)
Action
Policy
```

Rendered as XML, the ILM schema would look like this:

```
<ILM>
    <Information ID="">
        <!--Information encompasses all the context that describes
the information-->
        <Class ID="">
            <!--Class drives the policies. Policies will be applied
to different classes of information, resulting in many different
actions-->
            <Attributes File_Type="" Owner="">
                <!--Attributes define the class in terms of metadata-
->
                <Content_Clues>
                    <Content_Rule/>
                </Content_Clues>
            </Attributes>
        </Class>
        <State ID="">
            <!--State carries the changeable metadata that needs to
be tracked-->
            <Information_Paths>
                <URI/>
            </Information_Paths>
            <Last_Access_Time/>
            <Content_Hash/>
            <Relationships>
                <URI/>
            </Relationships>
            <Value/>
        </State>
        <Timestamp/>
        <!--Include an initial creation data to help set a
benchmark-->
        <History>
            <!--History is a collection of previous states-->
            <State/>
        </History>
    </Information>
    <Actions>
```

```
<!--Actions are permissible actions that ILM policy allows-
->
    <Move ID="" Destination_URI=""/>
    <Copy ID="" New_URI=""/>
    <Destroy ID=""/>
    <No_action ID=""><!--It is permissible to do nothing at
all--></No_action>
  </Actions>
  <Policies>
    <!--The lifecycle of the information is expressed by these
policies-->
    <!--ILM is a set of policies that include a trigger and an
action-->
    <Policy Name="" Owner="" Description="">
      <Trigger>
        <State/>
        <Rule/>
      </Trigger>
      <Action/>
    </Policy>
  </Policies>
</ILM>
```

There are other ways than XML to represent the ILM schema, including plain text. No matter which method is used to explain the XML schema, it is an important part of designing consistent ILM policies.

MATCHING INFORMATION VALUE TO PROTECTION OPTIONS

Placing a value on information is difficult. Organizations value information in their own ways. Some organizations may place a high value on certain types of information, such as customer contact information or orders. Others may find practically no value in the same type of information.

A report by the U.S. Department of Transportation[1] notes that decision makers value information based on the ability of information to reduce costs, save time, improve decision making, and improve customer satisfaction. These dimensions make sense but can still be hard to quantify.

A general way to look at the value of information is to consider:

---

1. Value of Information and Information Services, Volpe National Transportation Systems Center, Research and Special Programs Administration, October 1998.

- The replacement value of the information
- The cost to create the information
- Opportunity cost
- Regulatory failure costs

Certain information is necessary if the organization is to operate properly. The costs associated with disruptions caused by loss of the information can be calculated directly. How much more would it cost to process returns, for example, if the customer history information is missing?

Even if the value of information cannot be determined directly, the cost to replace it can be. If the order database was destroyed, what would it cost to have all the orders entered by hand from paper records? By the same token, the cost to create information in the first place also places a value on it. A certain amount of the scientific grant money was absorbed by the cost of gathering cases. How much was that? What were the budget dollars associated with inside sales that can be attributed to order taking?

There are also measurable effects of lost opportunities. The value of the information associated with an order, for example, can be said to be the value of the order. Finally, costs associated with failing to comply with regulations are straightforward. The amount of money that might be spent on lawyers, fines, and judgments can be determined by laws and case history.

ILM uses the value of information to trigger decisions regarding the disposition of information. As value changes, actions may be taken on the data, such as moving the information to less expensive storage. Gross measures of value are useful to ILM in this regard. Even coarse value levels (important, useful, and garbage) will work in some ILM policies; in others, a dollar amount will be necessary.

THE CHANGING VALUE OF INFORMATION

Information becomes more valuable or less valuable over time. Events can alter the value of information as well. Generally, as information gets older, it becomes less applicable to the current situation and less valuable unless updated. Passage of time is a change state, because time is a factor in state. Data protection and storage resources need to change as the value of the information changes over time (Figure 8–5).

Take the case of the customer service e-mail. When an e-mail that contains an order is first received, it is very valuable. It represents potential revenue that must be protected. Loss of that e-mail means a loss of revenue. A second e-mail, which contains a note of thanks, may have some value from a quality-assurance or marketing perspective. It is not, however, nearly as valuable as the order e-mail. As

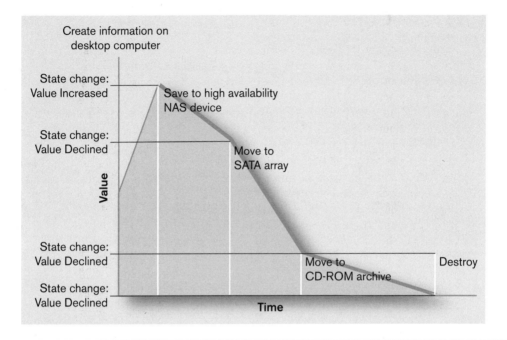

FIGURE 8-5 A LIFECYCLE BASED ON VALUE OVER TIME

time goes on and the order is processed, it is still quite important and valuable. Loss of this information may mean that it will be impossible to complete the order in a timely fashion. When the order is fulfilled, however, the value of the e-mail begins to drop. It may be needed to answer questions of the customer or provide historical reports, but the revenue is already realized.

After a while, if the customer hasn't called to complain, it is unlikely that she will. The source e-mail has already had the important information extracted from it for purposes of business intelligence. The original e-mail has practically no value. As information, it has degraded to the point of being valueless.

Each change in the value of the information, from high to moderate to none, represents a change of state that could trigger actions. It would be reasonable to move the e-mail to less expensive storage at each change in value. Eventually, when the e-mail has no value, it can be destroyed.

REGULATORY CONCERNS

A common reason that many organizations implement ILM is to address regulatory concerns. Throughout the world, new regulations that attempt to safeguard privacy or control the behavior of public organizations are affecting how information is retained and destroyed. In the United States, Sarbanes-Oxley and the Health Insurance Portability and Accountability Act (HIPAA) have caused corporations and other organizations to examine how information is handled and who has access to it. The European Community has established privacy regulations, such as the e-Privacy Directive, which place specific requirements on holders of other people's information. Regulations such as these force organizations to manage information better, monitor how long it exists, ensure that it is destroyed when it is supposed to be, and control who has access to it.

Privacy and corporate regulations that affect information management exist worldwide. The following represent some examples of current trends in regulations as they pertain to Information Lifecycle Management and data protection.

Sarbanes-Oxley

In 2002, the U.S. Congress passed U.S. Public Law Number 107-204, also called the Sarbanes-Oxley Act of 2002. Known colloquially as Sarbanes-Oxley or SOX, the law's passage came during a period of profound distrust of corporate executives, auditors, and directors. It was fueled primarily by corporate scandals culminating in the collapse of two multibillion-dollar companies, Enron and WorldCom. In the wake of the failure of these companies, thousands of people worldwide were left out of work. It was felt by many politicians in the U.S. Congress (and investors throughout the world) that the executives and directors of these companies had benefited at the expense of individual investors, employees, and the common good.

Sarbanes-Oxley, Section 302, places upon executives of public companies the burden of verifying the truthfulness of the information in the companies' financial statements. Furthermore, they are responsible for maintaining internal financial controls. The law outlines criminal and civil penalties for those who do not comply with it and creates an oversight board (the Public Company Accounting Board) to ensure compliance.

IT managers are being called upon to help companies comply with these regulations. With almost all financial information stored electronically, especially in databases and spreadsheet files, IT must provide solutions for assuring the integrity of information that eventually becomes official financial statements. ILM is a tool to help accomplish this. By defining classes of information that relate to the financial statements, ILM allows a lifecycle to be created that is pegged to the requirements of SOX. In addition to the lifecycle, state changes can be monitored so as to allow executives to know when information changes without their knowledge. This tells them whether or not they can certify that the information they present is truthful to the best of their knowledge. *Information that can change without their knowledge cannot be verified as correct.*

Health Insurance Portability and Accountability Act

The Health Insurance Portability and Accountability Act, or HIPAA (U.S. Public Law 104-191), was designed to ensure that health information is available to those who needed it while safeguarding it against unauthorized access. When the law was passed in 1996, it was felt that individuals needed protection against fraud and misuse of medical information, and that regulated access to medical information would enhance delivery of services.

What has caused the biggest angst among health-care providers and insurers are the rather vague provisions calling for health-care information security and privacy. For example, Section 1173 (d) (2) states that

> Each person described in section 1172(a) who maintains or transmits health information shall maintain reasonable and appropriate administrative, technical, and physical safeguards—
> (A) to ensure the integrity and confidentiality of the information;
> (B) to protect against any reasonably anticipated—
> (i) threats or hazards to the security or integrity of the information; and
> (ii) unauthorized uses or disclosures of the information; and
> (C) otherwise to ensure compliance with this part by the officers and employees of such person.

These are not very specific provisions or definitions. Since the bill was passed, the U.S. Department of Health and Human Services has issued several regulations based on the act that help to define what it means. Even though the text is nonspecific, it is clear what the intention is: Care must be taken to protect health information from unauthorized destruction or access.

ILM deals with information and can discern the differences between information that needs to comply with HIPAA and information that does not. Separate policies can be developed that address different classes of information that are covered by HIPAA so that this information can be treated differently. Most of all, ILM policies can help verify that information is handled under the rules of HIPAA. ILM is an important tool in HIPAA compliance.

E-Privacy Directive (Directive 2002/58/EC)

The European Community (EC) and European Union have been on the forefront of information privacy, often well ahead of the United States. In 2002, the European Parliament adopted Directive 2002/58/EC, known as the e-Privacy Directive. It defines an extensive set of rules regarding the protection of electronic information. Much of the directive deals with the protection of information gathered through electronic commerce. In the main, it charges those who gather electronic information for commercial purposes to ensure the privacy of that information. The entire electronic supply chain is involved.

ILM would help organizations comply with these rules by allowing companies to control the information paths associated with the information. Actions would be triggered based on the additions to or changes in the path. Access control could also be enhanced if those who touched the data were tracked as part of the state of the information. Controls could be built around the ILM policies to ensure that information does not go anywhere it is not authorized to go and is not touched by anyone who is not authorized to do so.

Other Regulations and Laws

Many other regulations and laws throughout the world pertain to information, the rights of individuals to control that information, and the requirements that apply to organizations that hold that information. The United Kingdom's Data Protection Act of 1998 is an example.

Many information rules are buried in other legislation or regulations. The U.S. Securities and Exchange Commission and the Comptroller of the Currency have numerous regulations that require financial institutions to manage information so that it is accessible, protected, and secure from invasions of privacy. The international community is also creating rules through agreements such as the Basel II Accords. Designed to regulate banks' credit risk, Basel II has requirements regarding the management of historical financial information.

As is the case with SOX, HIPAA, and the e-Privacy Directive, control of information—where it is, what is happening to it, and who is touching it—is a major element of compliance. This is precisely what ILM is about.

PROTECTING INFORMATION USING ILM POLICIES

Information Lifecycle Management helps with regulatory compliance, security, and most of all, data protection. Policies based on ILM principles allow data protection strategies to become more cost effective and provide insight into how effective data protection methods really are. Data protection *costs* are now associated with the *value* of the information, which allows for a *value-oriented resource assignment.* Resources can now be adjusted as the value changes, ensuring maximum protection for the most valuable information and not as much protection for less valuable information.

ILM policies also draw attention to changes in the environment that impact data protection. It is common to back up all files based on a schedule, for example. With ILM, backups could instead be tuned to happen when certain changes in state occur. Perhaps a file is copied to near-line backup only when it changes and if it is classified as critical. The type of action may change when the information's value drops and, in its place, be backed up infrequently to tape. Only one copy of the information, no matter what its form or location, would be copied, and duplicate information would be ignored. This is more efficient and, ultimately, more effective. Files would be backed up when they need it and to resources that coincide with the value of the information they hold.

CONTROLLING INFORMATION PROTECTION COSTS

One goal of ILM is to control the cost of protecting information while providing maximum protection. Some factors associated with the cost of protecting information are

- **Performance.** Faster access costs more.
- **Availability.** It costs more money to ensure high levels of availability.
- **Scope.** Scope denotes how much information must be protected.
- **Duplication.** Money is wasted when duplicate information is protected.

ILM policies can be used to limit all these factors. By knowing the value of the information, the organization can adjust the performance and availability of the systems used to provide protection. Moving information from a Fibre Channel SAN with Fibre Channel arrays to an iSCSI SAN with SATA arrays may cost less. The performance and availability of the iSCSI SAN/SATA systems are less, but that's fine for less valuable data. Instead of buying more expensive infrastructure, the organization uses less costly infrastructure.

With ILM, the organization makes decisions on what is important information and what is not. Certain classes of information will be deemed unworthy of any protection at all or of only the most rudimentary protection. Solid ILM policies will allow organizations to narrow the scope of what is to be protected and what is not. With less to be protected, not as much money is allocated to new protection and storage resources. This helps control infrastructure costs.

Duplicate data is not the same as duplicate information. The same information may exist in many forms throughout an enterprise. Different data can then hold the same information. ILM policies help decide when information is a duplicate of existing information and which form should be protected. Again, this helps limit the scope of what is protected and what is not.

Most data protection strategies have a one-size-fits-all philosophy. Data Lifecycle Management begins to break out of that paradigm by imposing an age-based model for data protection. ILM takes this a step further and looks at the information for guidance. ILM policies act like medical triage. They determine which information needs what resources and how soon. The organization can then focus its resources on the most valuable information.

AUTOMATING ILM

It is possible to implement ILM without any software or hardware at all. ILM is, first and foremost, a process. It is a very difficult process to implement without tools, however. Tracking information and complying with ILM policies sound good until an organization realizes how tough it is actually to monitor state changes. The classification process can be nearly impossible without some tools to categorize existing information. So what if the policies say that certain actions are supposed to happen when a state change occurs? If the change can't be detected and tracked, it might as well have not happened. If there is no way to audit changes in information, how can the organization know whether it is complying with its ILM policies? ILM is too complex unless there are tools to assist in classifying, auditing, and moving information assets.

Electronic information is stored on data storage systems. No particular storage architecture is required for ILM. Instead, the ILM automation tools need to fit the overall storage architecture. If the predominant storage devices are file servers, automation needs to be designed for a file-based environment. The same is true for networked storage in a SAN or NAS environment. ILM automation is done with software. The hardware matters only in that it supports the needed software.

The areas in which automation can help are

- **Classification.** Determining class from content and metadata, especially for existing, unstructured information.
- **Auditing and tracking.** Ensuring compliance with policies by tracking state changes and saving them as history.
- **Decision making.** Automating decisions such as whether a state change has occurred and what actions to take based on that change.
- **Moving and copying.** Shifting or duplicating information to different information paths based on policy.

■ **Access control.** Ensuring compliance with policies by limiting the ability to change or view information.

ILM automation is still in its infancy, as is ILM. Some areas are well addressed by products; others are just emerging. Purely storage-oriented technologies, such as information movers, content addressable storage, and access control systems, are more developed, often because they were adapted from existing products. Other technologies, such as classification tools and ILM auditing, are still very early in their product lifecycles (Figure 8–6).

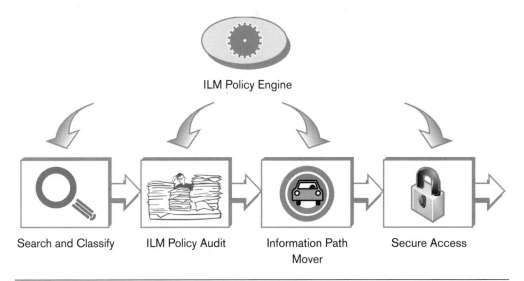

FIGURE 8–6 ILM AUTOMATION TECHNOLOGY

Policy Engines

What makes a software system an ILM tool is a policy engine. As is the case with Data Lifecycle Management, a policy engine is needed to drive the ILM automation process. Considering the fragmented nature of ILM technology today, several policy engines will be needed in a *complete* ILM automated solution. Unfortunately for the IT manager, this means having to manage duplicate ILM policies in different software systems.

The policy engine is designed to make the software behave in accordance with the ILM processes called out by the ILM policies. There are several data movers out there. To be considered an ILM mover, an ILM policy engine has to be directing the moves and updating the state history.

Many vendors have created ILM automation software by grafting policy engines onto their existing software. E-mail archiving products, document management, and records management tools have been converted to ILM automation tools by adding policy engines.

Search and Classification Engines

Search engines have been around the Internet since the early 1990s. Most users of the Internet see the client side of the search engine. Type in some keywords or a phrase, and up pops a list of possible web sites. Hidden from view are the sophisticated processes that search out the Internet, catalog the words in the web pages, and categorize the pages based on rules.

These search tools are now being adapted for desktop and enterprise storage systems. The engine scans a storage unit and catalogs the files on it, as well as gathers metadata. This database is then used to find information based on content and metadata. Major search engine companies, such as Yahoo!, Google, and Microsoft, have all released desktop search engine products. Enterprise-strength search engines from Copernic and X1 (which supplied the desktop product to Yahoo!) are available as well.

Although not an ILM tool per se, this type of software can be adapted to develop a classification engine. A *classification engine* scans information in a system, applies rules, and assigns a class to it. When ILM rules are applied to the metadata, classes of data can be derived from the existing base of metadata. Many commercial search engine products have APIs that expose the gathered metadata and could be developed into a classification engine.

Rudimentary classification engines are also part of other ILM software. Policy engines often include some form of classification scanning to accommodate existing information.

ILM Auditing and Tracking

A large part of the ILM process is designed to ensure that the information in the organization is what it is supposed to be and where it is expected to be. In structured data systems such as databases, auditing the information can be accomplished through the use of transaction logs. File systems, on the other hand, often do not track changes in information. Even in cases in which metadata tracks changes, such as whether an object has been accessed, file systems do not monitor changes in content. Opening and closing a word processor file will change metadata fields. If nothing was done to the file's information, no real change has occurred in the information. Software used to track changes in information, including content and audit reports, based on ILM policies, is an emerging technology.

Content Addressed Storage

Content Addressed Storage, also called Content Aware Storage and CAS, is a specialized storage device that locates and manages information based on its content. As information is stored on a CAS array, a hash of the content is created and stored along with the information object. It then prevents changes to the information's content. Some systems will automatically version information if the content changes.

The advantage of CAS systems is that they prevent undetected changes to content. CAS is mostly used for fixed content, which is content that is not supposed to change. ILM policies stating that information can never be changed until it is destroyed, or insisting on versioning changes to information, benefit from storage on CAS arrays. Digitized images such as check and x-ray images are popular targets for CAS usage. Rapidly changing information like that found in databases is not a good candidate for CAS systems. CAS assumes that the content will not change and wards off any changes.

CAS also fits in well with ILM because the information is accessed based on content, not on filenames or other artificial constructs. Because ILM information paths are not dependent on any file-naming scheme, the CAS namespace assures a unique information path for all information.

Information Movers

One of the most common actions of an ILM policy is to move information. As the value of information declines, less expensive resources are used to house and protect the information. Something needs to move it there. Many system administrators accomplish this through simple scripts. Unfortunately, scripts tend to be static and must be rewritten if policies change. Software that does this automatically, when ILM state changes dictate an action, ensures that moves happen when they should. Some information movers are DLM systems with an ILM policy engine embedded in them.

CASE STUDY: MIDAMERICA BANK

The U.S. banking industry has been on the forefront of Information Lifecycle Management. It is a regulated industry in which the delivery of information about customers' finances is a key component of value. The ability of a bank to handle information well affects customer satisfaction, regulatory compliance, and costs.

MidAmerica Bank is a bank with more than 75 branches and 500 ATMs throughout the upper Midwestern United States. The bank started as a savings and loan but has since transformed itself into a public company with more than $9.5 billion in assets. To comply with data retention regulations and achieve high levels of customer satisfaction, MidAmerica has begun to deploy ILM processes and technology. ILM helps the bank manage its information more efficiently.

The value of information held by the bank is based on how old the data is, as well as the frequency with which it needs to be accessed. Certain information is more valuable than other information, either because regulations demand it or because customers do. Certain types of information, especially statements and check images, start out having high value, which changes over time.

A good example of ILM in action is the handling of check images. MidAmerica has defined a lifecycle for checks that is different from that of other types of information. According to First Vice President and Data Center Manager Paul Stonchus, the check information is created in the form of a TIFF image. At that time, attributes are assigned to the information that set the context for later decisions. For the first 45 days, the ability to access the check is available online from the bank's web site. During this time, access averages three to five times—one reason why it must remain highly available.

After 45 days, the check is no longer available online, which coincides with the release to the customer of his statement. The check image is retained, but for legal and regulatory purposes. Customer access in no longer necessary, and the check is moved to an EMC Centera CAS system. The CAS system ensures that the image does not change. It is essentially archived but can be retrieved quickly if needed. Regulations require that it be kept for seven years after that, at which time it is deleted.

MidAmerica defines the information based on metadata. It then sets a policy for certain classes of information based on the value of the information over time. The bank tracks changes in the state of the information by monitoring certain attributes, such as time and content. Finally, actions are taken when state changes occur. ILM allows the bank to deliver what customers want, regulators demand, and the business requires.

KEY POINTS

- ILM is a process by which information is managed according to a lifecycle. This lifecycle is defined in terms of the value of the information.

- Information differs from data in that it has context. Context is derived from various attributes of the information, including content, class, location, relationships, state, and age.

- ILM enhances data protection by ensuring that more valuable resources are applied to more valuable information and not to less valuable information. This helps control costs and enhances service delivery.

- A general model of an information lifecycle calls for the creation of information, followed by the detection of changes in state that cause actions to occur. This continues until the last action—destruction—happens.

- Changes in state can happen because an attribute of the information changes or its content changes.

- Many ILM initiatives are driven by regulatory concerns. Financial, corporate, and privacy regulations contain requirements for information retention and protection that ILM addresses.

- Automation will make management of and compliance with ILM policies much easier. Tools to classify, audit, secure, and move information are making the task of implementing ILM more palatable to organizations.

APPENDIX A

XML SCHEMAS AND DOCUMENT TYPE DEFINITIONS FOR POLICY STATEMENTS

XML is an excellent method of expressing policies. It has the advantage of being human readable, while software can process it. In its simplest form, XML is text surrounded by tags, in much the same vein as HTML. In fact, as of HTML 4.0, HTML is defined as a specific set of XML tags.

Tags are expressed by a pair of angle brackets (< and >) with text in between. XML tags always come in pairs, with an opening tag containing only the angle brackets and a closing tag using angle brackets and a slash. For example, an ILM field can be described in XML as:

```
<ILM> Some ILM Policy </ILM>
```

XML allows for hierarchical structures through the use of nested tags. This allows for very complex structures to be designed while maintaining the readability of the text. Most XML-based applications and parsers have an inherent backward compatibility. Like web browsers, they ignore tags that they don't understand. That allows standard applications to process the XML document, while specialized applications can take advantage of additional information encoded in it. XML is a naturally extensible language. This makes it a prime candidate for expressing DLM and ILM policies.

Unlike a database, XML does not require an external method of defining the structure of a document. The structure can instead be derived from the tags within the document. It is still good practice to design a schema to ensure consistency among documents, as well as to communicate better the intent of the internal structure. Many standard schemas are designed by vertical industries or support broad applications. Web Services, which implements a standard method of communication among web applications, uses a standard set of XML structures. RDF does the same for documents. As of the writing of this book, no standard ILM or DLM structures exist.

Two common methods of defining XML document structures are XML Schemas and Document Type Definitions (DTDs). The latter is an older way of defining XML documents and is being superseded by XML Schemas. DTDs are easier to design and parse, but XML Schemas provide a richer description of the document's structure.

The XML Schema and DTD for the DLM examples from Chapter 7 would be rendered as follows:

```xml
<?xml version="1.0" encoding="UTF-8" ?>

<xs:schema xmlns:xs="http://www.w3.org/2001/XMLSchema">
  <xs:element name="asset">
    <xs:complexType mixed="true">
      <xs:attribute name="asset_types" type="xs:string"
use="required" />
    </xs:complexType>
  </xs:element>

  <xs:element name="constraints">
    <xs:complexType mixed="true" />
  </xs:element>

  <xs:element name="create">
    <xs:complexType mixed="true" />
  </xs:element>

  <xs:element name="date">
    <xs:complexType>
      <xs:sequence>
        <xs:element ref="create" />
        <xs:element ref="revision" />
      </xs:sequence>
    </xs:complexType>
  </xs:element>

  <xs:element name="description">
    <xs:complexType mixed="true" />
  </xs:element>

  <xs:element name="expected_result">
    <xs:complexType mixed="true" />
  </xs:element>

  <xs:element name="name">
    <xs:complexType mixed="true" />
  </xs:element>
```

```
  <xs:element name="policy">
    <xs:complexType>
      <xs:sequence>
        <xs:element ref="name" />
        <xs:element ref="description" />
        <xs:element ref="purpose" />
        <xs:element ref="date" />
        <xs:element ref="process" />
        <xs:element ref="expected_result" />
        <xs:element ref="constraints" />
        <xs:element ref="asset" maxOccurs="unbounded" />
      </xs:sequence>
      <xs:attribute name="parent" type="xs:string" use="required" />
      <xs:attribute name="policy_type" type="xs:NMTOKEN"
use="required" />
      <xs:attribute name="data_type" type="xs:string" use="required"
/>
    </xs:complexType>
  </xs:element>

  <xs:element name="process">
    <xs:complexType mixed="true" />
  </xs:element>

  <xs:element name="purpose">
    <xs:complexType mixed="true" />
  </xs:element>

  <xs:element name="revision">
    <xs:complexType mixed="true" />
  </xs:element>

</xs:schema>

<!ELEMENT asset ( #PCDATA ) >
<!ATTLIST asset asset_types CDATA #REQUIRED >

<!ELEMENT constraints ( #PCDATA ) >

<!ELEMENT create ( #PCDATA ) >

<!ELEMENT date ( create, revision ) >

<!ELEMENT description ( #PCDATA ) >

<!ELEMENT expected_result ( #PCDATA ) >

<!ELEMENT name ( #PCDATA ) >
```

```
<!ELEMENT policy ( name, description, purpose, date, process,
expected_result, constraints, asset+ ) >
<!ATTLIST policy data_type CDATA #REQUIRED >
<!ATTLIST policy parent CDATA #REQUIRED >
<!ATTLIST policy policy_type NMTOKEN #REQUIRED >

<!ELEMENT process ( #PCDATA ) >

<!ELEMENT purpose ( #PCDATA ) >

<!ELEMENT revision ( #PCDATA ) >
```

The XML Schema more clearly shows the nested structure of the DLM policy. It should be noted that no attempt was made to tweak the constraints or data types. XML Schemas have a rich set of data types.

The ILM policy example in Chapter 8 would have a Schema and DTD such as this:

```
<?xml version="1.0" encoding="UTF-8" ?>

<xs:schema xmlns:xs="http://www.w3.org/2001/XMLSchema">
  <xs:element name="Action" type="xs:string" />

  <xs:element name="Actions">
    <xs:complexType>
      <xs:sequence>
        <xs:element ref="Move" />
        <xs:element ref="Copy" />
        <xs:element ref="Destroy" />
        <xs:element ref="No_action" />
      </xs:sequence>
    </xs:complexType>
  </xs:element>

  <xs:element name="Attributes">
    <xs:complexType>
      <xs:sequence>
        <xs:element ref="Content_Clues" />
      </xs:sequence>
      <xs:attribute name="Owner" type="xs:string" use="required" />
      <xs:attribute name="File_Type" type="xs:string" use="required"
/>
    </xs:complexType>
  </xs:element>

  <xs:element name="Class">
    <xs:complexType>
```

```xml
      <xs:sequence>
        <xs:element ref="Attributes" />
      </xs:sequence>
      <xs:attribute name="ID" type="xs:ID" use="required" />
    </xs:complexType>
</xs:element>

<xs:element name="Content_Clues">
  <xs:complexType>
    <xs:sequence>
      <xs:element ref="Content_Rule" />
    </xs:sequence>
  </xs:complexType>
</xs:element>

<xs:element name="Content_Hash" type="xs:hexBinary" />

<xs:element name="Content_Rule" type="xs:string" />

<xs:element name="Copy">
  <xs:complexType>
    <xs:attribute name="ID" type="xs:ID" use="required" />
    <xs:attribute name="New_URI" type="xs:anyURI" use="required" /
>
  </xs:complexType>
</xs:element>

<xs:element name="Destroy">
  <xs:complexType>
    <xs:attribute name="ID" type="xs:ID" use="required" />
  </xs:complexType>
</xs:element>

<xs:element name="History">
  <xs:complexType>
    <xs:sequence>
      <xs:element ref="State" />
    </xs:sequence>
  </xs:complexType>
</xs:element>

<xs:element name="ILM">
  <xs:complexType>
    <xs:sequence>
      <xs:element ref="Information" />
      <xs:element ref="Actions" />
      <xs:element ref="Policies" />
    </xs:sequence>
  </xs:complexType>
```

```
        </xs:element>

        <xs:element name="Information">
          <xs:complexType>
            <xs:sequence>
              <xs:element ref="Class" />
              <xs:element ref="State" />
              <xs:element ref="Timestamp" />
              <xs:element ref="History" />
            </xs:sequence>
            <xs:attribute name="ID" type="xs:ID" use="required" />
          </xs:complexType>
        </xs:element>

        <xs:element name="Information_Paths">
          <xs:complexType>
            <xs:sequence>
              <xs:element ref="URI" />
            </xs:sequence>
          </xs:complexType>
        </xs:element>

        <xs:element name="Last_Access_Time" type="xs:dateTime" />

        <xs:element name="Move">
          <xs:complexType>
            <xs:attribute name="ID" type="xs:ID" use="required" />
            <xs:attribute name="Destination_URI" type="xs:anyURI"
use="required" />
          </xs:complexType>
        </xs:element>

        <xs:element name="No_action">
          <xs:complexType>
            <xs:attribute name="ID" type="xs:ID" use="required" />
          </xs:complexType>
        </xs:element>

        <xs:element name="Policies">
          <xs:complexType>
            <xs:sequence>
              <xs:element ref="Policy" />
            </xs:sequence>
          </xs:complexType>
        </xs:element>

        <xs:element name="Policy">
          <xs:complexType>
            <xs:sequence>
              <xs:element ref="Trigger" />
```

```
      <xs:element ref="Action" />
    </xs:sequence>
    <xs:attribute name="Name" type="xs:string" use="required" />
    <xs:attribute name="Owner" type="xs:string" use="required" />
    <xs:attribute name="Description" type="xs:string"
use="required" />
  </xs:complexType>
</xs:element>

<xs:element name="Relationships">
  <xs:complexType>
    <xs:sequence>
      <xs:element ref="URI" />
    </xs:sequence>
  </xs:complexType>
</xs:element>

<xs:element name="Rule" type="xs:string" />

<xs:element name="State">
  <xs:complexType>
    <xs:sequence>
      <xs:element ref="Information_Paths" minOccurs="0" />
      <xs:element ref="Last_Access_Time" minOccurs="0" />
      <xs:element ref="Content_Hash" minOccurs="0" />
      <xs:element ref="Relationships" minOccurs="0" />
      <xs:element ref="Value" minOccurs="0" />
    </xs:sequence>
    <xs:attribute name="ID" type="xs:ID" use="optional" />
  </xs:complexType>
</xs:element>

<xs:element name="Timestamp" type="xs:dateTime" />

<xs:element name="Trigger">
  <xs:complexType>
    <xs:sequence>
      <xs:element ref="State" />
      <xs:element ref="Rule" />
    </xs:sequence>
  </xs:complexType>
</xs:element>

<xs:element name="URI" type="xs:anyURI" />

<xs:element name="Value" type="xs:string" />

</xs:schema>


<!ELEMENT Action EMPTY >
```

```
<!ELEMENT Actions ( Move, Copy, Destroy, No_action ) >

<!ELEMENT Attributes ( Content_Clues ) >
<!ATTLIST Attributes File_Type CDATA #REQUIRED >
<!ATTLIST Attributes Owner CDATA #REQUIRED >

<!ELEMENT Class ( Attributes ) >
<!ATTLIST Class ID CDATA #REQUIRED >

<!ELEMENT Content_Clues ( Content_Rule ) >

<!ELEMENT Content_Hash EMPTY >

<!ELEMENT Content_Rule EMPTY >

<!ELEMENT Copy EMPTY >
<!ATTLIST Copy ID CDATA #REQUIRED >
<!ATTLIST Copy New_URI CDATA #REQUIRED >

<!ELEMENT Destroy EMPTY >
<!ATTLIST Destroy ID CDATA #REQUIRED >

<!ELEMENT History ( State ) >

<!ELEMENT ILM ( Information, Actions, Policies ) >

<!ELEMENT Information ( Class, State, Timestamp, History ) >
<!ATTLIST Information ID CDATA #REQUIRED >

<!ELEMENT Information_Paths ( URI ) >

<!ELEMENT Last_Access_Time EMPTY >

<!ELEMENT Move EMPTY >
<!ATTLIST Move Destination_URI CDATA #REQUIRED >
<!ATTLIST Move ID CDATA #REQUIRED >

<!ELEMENT No_action EMPTY >
<!ATTLIST No_action ID CDATA #REQUIRED >

<!ELEMENT Policies ( Policy ) >

<!ELEMENT Policy ( Trigger, Action ) >
<!ATTLIST Policy Description CDATA #REQUIRED >
<!ATTLIST Policy Name CDATA #REQUIRED >
<!ATTLIST Policy Owner CDATA #REQUIRED >

<!ELEMENT Relationships ( URI ) >
```

```
<!ELEMENT Rule EMPTY >

<!ELEMENT State ( Information_Paths?, Last_Access_Time?,
Content_Hash?, Relationships?, Value? ) >
<!ATTLIST State ID CDATA #IMPLIED >

<!ELEMENT Timestamp EMPTY >

<!ELEMENT Trigger ( State, Rule ) >

<!ELEMENT URI EMPTY >

<!ELEMENT Value EMPTY >
```

Once again, the XML Schema is richer. It better expresses the hierarchical structure of the ILM policy and the expected data types.

There are some disadvantages to XML. XML documents can be long and convoluted, making it hard to read them in their raw form. XML files can take considerable application processing time, especially for a very long document. There are also security concerns with XML documents, because they are plain text that is readable by anyone who can access the document.

When using XML documents for policies, it is important to keep these limitations in mind. Documents should be kept as short as possible. The structure should be as simple as the policy goals allow, and encryption should be used whenever the documents are at rest or are being transferred between applications or over a network.

APPENDIX B

RESOURCES

BOOKS WORTH READING

No single book can tell the whole story of anything. This is especially true of a multidisciplinary subject such as data protection. Following is a list of some of the books that I refer to on a regular basis. Some provide more detail on specific subjects; others, simply a different point of view.

Building Storage Networks, by Marc Farley (Osborne/McGraw-Hill). This book is still one of the most comprehensive tomes on storage technology. It is a soup-to-nuts reference book on all things storage, especially storage networks.

Using SANs and NAS, by Curtis Preston (O'Reilly). Short and concise, this book's strength is its excellent explanation of backup and restore.

The Essential Guide to Telecommunications, by Annabel Z. Dodd (Prentice Hall). This is a comprehensive introduction to telecommunications. Although much of the book deals with phone systems, the portions on data communications are excellent, especially for planning remote copy and replication systems.

XML in a Nutshell, by Elliott Rusty Harold and W. Scott Means (O'Reilly). For those who want to use XML to express DLM and ILM policies, this book is a handy reference. It covers all the major topics without verbosity.

Network Security: A Beginner's Guide, by Eric Maiwald (Osborne/McGraw-Hill). A good starter book for those who are interested in security topics. It's an easy read because the author makes complex, security subjects understandable to us mere mortals.

Ancot Corporation publishes two small books that are great primers on storage technology. *Basics of SCSI* and *What Is Fibre Channel?* are available for free on the web site www.ancot.com. The books are very technical in nature and contain ads for Ancot products. They are an excellent reference for those who want to delve deeper into storage protocols without reading reams of standards documents.

Tom Clark has also written several interesting books. Two titles of special interest are *Designing Storage Networks* and *IP SANs: An Introduction to iSCSI, iFCP, and FCIP Protocols for Storage Area Networks,* both published by Addison-Wesley Professional. That latter provides in-depth treatment of SANs running over IP networks. It is one of the few books to focus entirely on IP SANs.

ORGANIZATIONS AND CONFERENCES

The computer industry has so many conferences and organizations that it is hard to choose which ones to be involved in. The premier organization in the storage industry is the **Storage Networking Industry Association** (SNIA). SNIA brings together the vendor community with IT professionals to tackle important problems related to storage. Along with media partner ComputerWorld, SNIA runs a series of conferences under the moniker **Storage Networking World.** Versions of the conference are held throughout the world and are quite worthwhile. More information on SNIA is available at www.snia.org.

For more focused information on SCSI or Fibre Channel, there are the **SCSI Trade Association** (www.scsita.org) and the **Fibre Channel Industry Association** (www.fibrechannel.org). These organizations provide a forum in which vendors work out issues of compatibility and interoperability, as well as map out the future direction of these technologies.

Some other organizations that are worth considering are

- **ILM Summit** (www.ilmsummit.com). The ILM Summit is a conference that is devoted specifically to ILM.

- **Association of Storage Networking Professionals** (ASNP; www.asnp.org). This organization is comprised of IT professionals who are involved in storage networking. Regional chapters meet to further the education of storage networking professionals, as well as to provide networking opportunities.

- **Storage Networking User Groups** (SNUG; www.storagenetworking.org). SNUG is similar to ASNP. The goals of SNUG are education and professional networking. It has a series of chapters in major metropolitan areas. Chapters have formed in cities throughout the world, though most are in the United States.

User groups such as ASNP and SNUG allow IT professionals to learn from one another. They tackle real-life problems in a vendor-neutral environment.

WEB SITES WORTH VISITING

A staggering number of web sites provide information on storage, data protection, and security. Unfortunately, many are vendor sites, where the information must be taken with a grain of salt. They are, after all, trying to sell something. There are several very good reference sites, though.

SearchStorage.Com (www.searchstorage.com) provides news on the storage industry, as well as regular articles by independent analysts and consultants. The online glossary is also very good.

The ANSI **T10** and **T11** committees maintain web sites at www.t10.org and www.t11.org, respectively. There, you will find information regarding the ongoing work in the SCSI and Fibre Channel standards committees, draft documents of new or revised standards, and links to current standards documents.

GOVERNMENT DOCUMENTS AND RESOURCES

Chapter 8 discussed several laws, chief among them HIPAA, Sarbanes-Oxley, and the European Community's e-Privacy acts. All these laws are available online. U.S. Laws such as HIPAA and Sarbanes-Oxley are available at www.thomas.loc.gov. Maintained by the U.S. Library of Congress, this site contains all pending and past U.S. legislation. The site is named for Thomas Jefferson, U.S. patriot, president, and principal author of the Declaration of Independence. Other U.S. regulations and initiatives regarding data protection are available at the web sites of the Federal Emergency Management Agency (www.fema.gov); the Government Accountability Office (www.gao.gov); the Securities and Exchange Commission (www.sec.gov); and the Comptroller of the Currency (www.occ.treas.gov), which is part of the Department of the Treasury.

Laws and regulations of the European Union and European Community are available at the European Union's web site at www.europa.eu.int. Another interesting regulation that pertains to information assurance is "Directive 2000/31/EC: on certain legal aspects of information society services, in particular electronic commerce, in the Internal Market." Individual countries in the EU also have laws pertaining to data protection and information assurance online. The U.K. Data Protection Act of 1998 is available at the United Kingdom's Office of Public Sector Information (http://www.opsi.gov.uk/acts/acts1998/19980029.htm). Other countries also maintain web sites with information about data protection issues. The Canadian government's analysis of the effects of the terrorist attacks of September 11, 2001, on critical infrastructure (Document IA02-001) is a must-read for all those who are involved in data protection and disaster planning.

Finally, information on the Basel Accords and the Basel Accords II is available at the web site of the International Bank of Settlements (www.bis.org). The consultative document titled "The compliance function in banks" provides food for thought for those in the banking industry as they look at how information management and regulatory compliance interact.

APPENDIX C

ACRONYMS

This appendix contains a list of the acronyms found in the book. It is meant as a quick reference to what the letters of the acronyms stand for, not definitions. Definitions may be found in the glossary.

ATA: Advanced Technology Attachment

CAS: Content Addressed Storage

CD: Compact Disc

CIFS: Common Internet File System

DAS: Direct Attach Storage

DASD: Direct Access Storage Device

DLM: Data Lifecycle Management

DNS: Domain Naming Service

DoS: Denial of Service

DTD: Direct Attach Storage

DVD: digital video disk

HA: high availability

HBA: host bus adapter

IDE: Integrated Drive Electronics

IDS: Intrusion Detection System

ILM: Information Lifecycle Management

I/O: Input/Output

IP: Internet Protocol

iSCSI: IP Internet SCSI

IT: information technology

LAN: local-area network

LDAP: Lightweight Directory Access Protocol

LIP: Loop Initialization Primitive

LUN: Logical Unit Number

MAN: metropolitan-area network

MIME: Multipurpose Internet Mail Extensions

MIS: management information systems

NAS: Network Attached Storage

NDMP: Network Data Management Protocol

NFS: Network File System

QoS: Quality of Service

RAID: Redundant Array of Independent Disks

RAM: random access memory

ROM: read-only memory

RPO: Recovery Point Objective

RTO: Recovery Time Objective

RW: read/write

SAN: Storage Area Network

SAS: Serial Attached SCSI

SATA: Serial ATA

SCSI: Small Computer System Interface

TCP: Transmission Control Protocol

UML: Unified Modeling Language

VPN: virtual private network

WAN: wide-area network

WWN: World Wide Name

XML: Extensible Markup Language

GLOSSARY

Access control
Limiting access to resources according to rights granted by the system administrator, application, or policy.

Access time
The amount of time it takes for a controller to find and read data on a media.

Arbitrated loop
A Fibre Channel topology in which all nodes are connected in a loop, with frames passing from one node to the next.

Archive
Copying data, which is only occasionally accessed, to an off-line media.

Array
A device that aggregates large collections of hard drives into a logical whole.

Asynchronous
A process that is not coordinated in time. In data storage processes, asynchronous means that the device or software does not wait for acknowledgement before performing the next I/O.

Authentication
The process by which the identity of a user or process is verified.

Availability
The ability to access data or information on demand.

Backup
Making copies of data to a device other than the original data store.

Backup window
The interval in which backups can be performed without impacting other systems.

Block I/O
The type of I/O where a device or protocol accesses data on a disk as blocks of data without structure. Upper level protocols and applications are then responsible for building higher level constructs from the blocks.

Business continuity
The ability of a business to continue to operate in the face of disaster

Cascade failure
A catastrophic system failure where the failure of one system causes the failure of other systems.

CD-ROM/RW
Compact Disc Read-Only Memory and Compact Disc Read-Write. A mass storage medium that stores data on a small plastic disk. Originally used for music.

CIFS
The Common Internet File System. A protocol for accessing resources such as files and printers on a LAN.

Client
In client-server computing, the process that makes requests for information and then receives them.

Compression
The process of reducing the size of data by use of mathematical algorithms.

Content Addressed Storage (CAS)
A specialized storage device that locates and manages information based on its content.

Content Aware Storage
See Content Addressed Storage.

Context
Other data that imparts meaning and structure to data.

Controller
An interface that allows mass storage devices to connect to a specific type of bus or network.

Data
An atomic element of information. Represented as bits within mass storage devices, memory, and processors.

Data corruption
An event where data is damaged.

Data Lifecycle Management (DLM)
The process by which data is moved to different mass storage devices based on its age.

Data migration
The movement of data from one storage system to another.

Data mover
An appliance that moves data from one storage device to another.

Data protection
The protecting of data from damage, destruction, and unauthorized alteration.

Data retention
Keeping data safe and available for some predetermined amount of time. Often a requirement of government regulations.

Defense in Depth
Having layers of security and detection systems to inhibit an intruder from gaining access to corporate systems and data.

Denial of Service (DoS)
A type of attack on a computer system that ties up critical system resources, making the system temporarily unusable.

Direct Access Storage Device (DASD)
A type of IBM mainframe mass storage device. The precursor to open Direct Attached Storage systems.

Direct Attach Storage (DAS)
A type of mass storage system where storage devices are attached directly to the system peripheral bus.

Director
Large storage networking switches with many ports and high availability features.

Disk-to-disk backup
Backup system based on hard drives rather than tape drives.

Disk-to-disk-to-tape backup
Three-tier backup system that first backs up to a disk, then to a tape.

Diversity of defense
Deploying many different methods of defense, in different layers.

Domain Naming Service (DNS)
A common name resolution system used extensively in internet systems. It associates an IP address with a common name.

Document Type Definitions (DTD)
A method of describing the structure of an XML document.

DVD-ROM/RW
Digital Video Disk, Read-Only Memory and Digital Video Disk Read-Write. A mass storage medium that stores data on a small plastic disk. Originally used for video.

Encryption
The encoding of data so that the plain text is transformed into something unintelligible, called cipher text.

Enterprise
Term used to describe formal organizations such as corporations. Often used to refer to the entire scope of an organization's IT systems.

Extended copy
A set of extensions to the SCSI protocol to control the movement of data between two other devices. Also known as Third-Party Copy, X-Copy, and E-Copy.

Failover
The ability of a secondary device to take the place of a primary device during failure of the primary device.

Fibre Channel
A type of network commonly used for Storage Area Networks. Fibre Channel encompasses hardware specifications and a set of protocols, well suited to performing block I/O in a network environment.

File head
A specialized server that presents mass storage devices as a filesystem on a network.

File I/O
Accessing data through a file system. Applications that do not access data directly as block rely on the file system to provide data in a format with a certain structure, called a file.

File system
A storage system layer that organizes data into general structures such as directories, folders, and files.

Filer
Another term for a NAS array. Originally a product name for NAS devices from Network Appliance.

Firewall
Software or devices that examine network traffic so that it may restrict access to network resources to unauthorized users.

Full backup
A backup of the entire hard drive or array.

Gigabit
1,073,741,824 bits. Used to describe transmission rates in data communications and networking.

Gigabit Ethernet
A networking technology with a transmission rate of one Gigabit or more.

Gigabyte
1024 Megabytes. Used as a unit of computer storage and to describe data transfer rates.

Hard drive

A mass storage device that deploys hard, revolving platters to provide persistent storage of data. Hard drives use magnetism as the method of encoding information on the platters.

Hash

A set of characters generated by running text data through certain algorithms. Often used to create digital signatures and compare changes in content.

High Availability (HA)

The ability of a device to continue operating in the event of component failures.

Host

(1) A computer that contains software or data that is shared through a network.

(2) In the SCSI protocol, the process that receives SCSI commands, processes them, and sends them back to an initiator.

(3) In general usage, a synonym for "client."

Host Bus Adapter (HBA)

A peripheral board or embedded processor used to connect a host's peripheral bus to the SCSI bus or Fibre Channel network.

I/O

Input/Output. The movement of data to or from some device or software element.

IDE/ATA

A mass storage specification and protocol common to desktop computers.

Image copy

A backup of an entire volume. Restoring from an image copy reproduces the entire volume at the point in time that the copy was made.

Incremental backup

Backups that only copy objects that have changed since the last backup.

Information

Information is data with context. It can be externally validated and is independent of applications.

Information assurance

The process by which an organization insures, protects, and verifies the integrity of vital information.

Information Lifecycle Management (ILM)

A strategic process for dealing with information assets. ILM is expressed as a strategy, which is used to generate policies. Finally, a set of rules is created to comply with the policies.

Information mover

A data mover combined with an ILM policy engine. It moves data in response to ILM events.

Information path
A way of describing where information is without subscribing to specific operating system nomenclature.

Information perimeter
The boundary beyond which an ILM policy cannot expect to have control over information.

Intrusion Detection System (IDS)
A device or software system that examines violations of security policy to determine if an attack is in progress or has occurred.

IPSec
An extension to the Internet Protocol that allows for encrypted messaging. Used extensively in secure communications.

iSCSI
A networked version of SCSI that transmits block data over an IP network.

IT
Information technology. A broad term that encompasses a range of technology that is used to manipulate information. Also used to refer to the industry that develops information technology products and the function within organizations that manages information technology assets.

Jukebox
A device that aggregates CD and DVD drives into a larger system.

Latency
The amount of time it takes a system to deliver data in response to a request. For mass storage devices, it is the time it takes to place the read or write heads over the desired spot on the media. In networks, it is a function of the electrical and software properties of the network connection.

Lightweight Directory Access Protocol (LDAP)
A protocol for accessing online directories. LDAP directories may contain all types of directory information, including host addresses.

Least privilege
The maximum amount of access any user, host, or processor should have to system resources.

LIP
Loop Initialization Primitive. A low-level Fibre Channel command that begins the process of loop reconfiguration in Arbitrated Loop topologies.

Load balancing
A method of assuring availability and performance where two devices or components share the processing load. It is also used as a failover technique in which failure of one device simply increases the load of the other devices.

LUN

Logical Unit Number. A SCSI protocol sub-address used to increase the overall number of addressable elements in a SCSI system.

LUN locking

Restricting access to LUNs to specific SCSI initiators. Used to keep unauthorized hosts from accessing storage resources.

LUN masking

The ability to hide SCSI LUNs from unauthorized initiators. The LUNs are still accessible but will not respond to a SCSI Inquiry command.

Magneto-optical disk

A mass storage device, which combines the properties of magnetic and laser-based disks.

Metropolitan Area Network (MAN)

A campus or city-wide network, usually based on optical networks such as SONET.

Media

Objects on which data is stored.

Megabit

Approximately 1024 thousand bits. Used to describe network transmission rates.

Megabyte

1024 thousand bytes. A unit of measure of mass storage used to describe data transfer rates (megabytes per second).

Metadata

Data that describes other data.

MIME type

Multipurpose Internet Mail Extensions. A method of describing the type of a document or object transmitted over Internet systems. Used extensively by e-mail and web applications.

Mirroring

Copying the same data block to different disks in order to have a copy of the block available in the event of a disk failure.

MIS

Management Information Systems. A subset of information technology, MIS is an older term that refers to the IT functions within companies.

MP3

Moving Picture Experts Group Layer-3. A standard format for encoding audio and video. Popular as a way of digitizing music so that it can be played on digital devices such as computers.

NAS head

See File head.

Network Attached Storage (NAS)
A self-contained, highly optimized file server. NAS devices support common network interfaces and file transfer protocols such as NFS and CIFS.

Network Data Management Protocol (NDMP)
A bi-directional communication, based on XDR and a client-server architecture, optimized for performing backup and restore.

Network File System (NFS)
A common networked file system originally from Sun Microsystems. NFS is a common way of sharing data on UNIX and LINUX systems.

Non-disruptive failover
A failover technique that maintains I/Os in progress and completes all transactions, as if the failure had not occurred.

Policy
A set of best practices that the organization must follow. Policies are a concrete expression of a strategy.

Policy engine
A system that stores and executes the tasks, references, and constraints that express a DLM or ILM policy in terms that computer systems can understand.

Quality of Service (QoS)
The guaranteed performance of a network connection.

RAID
Redundant Array of Independent Disks. A schema for using groups of disks to increase performance, protect data, or both.

RAID level
The different types of RAID functions. RAID levels are expressed with a numbering system of 0, 1, 3, 5, 7, and 10.

Read head
The part of a mass storage system that retrieves data off of the media.

Recovery
The process by which data is retrieved from a backup and copied to a primary storage device.

Recovery Point Objective (RPO)
The point in time to which data must be restored.

Recovery Time Objective (RTO)
Following a disaster, the amount of time that a system may be offline before it must be up and running.

Remote copy
The duplication of I/O from one *set* of disks to another similar set, on a block level.

Replication
The duplication of I/O from one set of disks to another similar set, on a file level.

Restore
See Recovery.

Schema
A description of data that provides context and structure. There are many types of schemas, including database schemas and XML schemas.

SCSI
Small Computer Systems Interface. A specification for both hardware and software protocols, used to transfer data between peripheral devices and the peripheral bus in a computer.

SCSI initiator
In SCSI systems, the device that issues commands and requests data block.

SCSI target
In SCSI systems, the device that receives commands and returns requested data blocks.

Security posture
The core philosophy or approach applied to a security plan. The two most common postures are referred to as Default DENY and Default ALLOW.

Serial ATA (SATA)
A serial version of ATA technology.

Serial Attached SCSI (SAS)
A serial version of SCSI technology. Fibre Channel SCSI and iSCSI are also serialized versions of SCSI, but are designed for specific network environments. SAS is designed for its own hardware layer.

Snapshot
A point-in-time virtual copy of the file system.

Solid state storage
A type of mass storage device that uses RAM to store data.

Spoofing
An intrusion technique that replaces a legitimate address with one provided by an attacker.

State
In ILM, this describes content and metadata (context) at a specific point in time.

Stateful failover
See Non-disruptive failover.

Storage Area Network (SAN)
A storage system architecture that defines methods for performing block I/O over a high-speed network.

Storage switch
A switching device designed primarily with storage applications in mind. Fibre Channel switches and iSCSI-optimized Ethernet switches are often referred to as storage switches.

Streaming
To transfer data continuously from a device.

Switched fabric
A Fibre Channel topology that uses a switch to provide full bandwidth connections to all ports.

Synchronous
A process that is coordinated in time. In data storage processes, synchronous means that the device or software waits for acknowledgement before performing the next I/O.

Tape drive
A mass storage device that transfers data to and from magnetic tape.

TCP/IP
Transmission Control Protocol and Internet Protocol. Networking protocols common to most forms of networks. TCP provides for synchronous communications over IP.

Transfer time
The amount of time it takes the disk, tape, or other storage to transfer data from off the media and onto the data bus or network.

Trunking
Aggregating redundant network connections to provide more network bandwidth.

UML
Unified Modeling Language. A language that describes the design, modeling, and deployment of systems. Commonly used in software design, UML also has broader application for describing systems.

Virtual Private Network (VPN)
A connection made over a public or internal network, which uses encryption to provide security. A VPN provides the security of a private connection over an insecure network.

Virtual tape
The emulation of a tape system by a disk-based system. Virtual tape provides backup software with the same interface for a disk system as for a tape system.

Volume
A virtual set of blocks. A volume aggregates blocks from one or many disks into a single logical whole.

Volume manager
Software that creates and manages volumes.

WAN

Wide Area Network. A network topology designed to connect devices over very long distances, typically outside the limits of a single campus or city.

World Wide Name

A unique 64-bit identifier used as an address by Fibre Channel systems.

Write head

The part of a mass storage system that places data on the media.

XML

Extended Markup Language. A markup language that defines the structure of data through the use of paired tags. Commonly used in software protocols and web pages to store moderate amounts of information.

Zoning

A method of limiting access to resources in Fibre Channel networks. Zoning masks resources from hosts not in the same zone.

BIBLIOGRAPHY

Basics of SCSI, Fourth Edition (Ancot Corporation, 1998)

Building Storage Networks, First Edition, by Marc Farley (Osborne/McGraw-Hill, 2000)

The Essential Guide to Telecommunications, Third Edition, by Annabel Z. Dodd (Prentice Hall, 2002)

Network Security: A Beginner's Guide, by Eric Maiwald (Osborne/McGraw-Hill, 2001)

Using SANs and NAS, by Curtis Preston (O'Reilly, 2002)

Web Security, Privacy and Commerce, Second Edition, by Simson Garfinkel and Gene Spafford (O'Reilly, 2002)

XML in a Nutshell, by Elliott Rusty Harold and W. Scott Means (O'Reilly, 2001)

INDEX